SEXUAL INVERSION

SEXUAL INVERSION

THE MULTIPLE ROOTS OF HOMOSEXUALITY

EDITED BY JUDD MARMOR

Basic Books, Inc.
Publishers
NEW YORK, LONDON

THE CONTRIBUTORS

IRVING BIEBER, M.D. Associate Clinical Professor and Training Psychoanalyst, Department of Psychiatry, New York Medical College; Chairman, Research Committee, Society of Medical Psychoanalysts.

ROLLIN H. DENNISTON, II, Ph.D. Senior Professor of Physiology and Director of the NDEA Title IV Program of the Department of Zoology and Physiology, The University of Wyoming.

SAUL H. FISHER, M.D. Associate Professor of Clinical Psychiatry, New York University School of Medicine.

EVELYN HOOKER, Ph.D. Research Associate in Psychology, UCLA.

HAROLD I. LIEF, M.D. Professor of Psychiatry, Tulane University School of Medicine; Director of the Hutchinson Memorial Psychiatric Clinic.

JUDD MARMOR, M.D. Clinical Professor of Psychiatry, UCLA. Training Analyst and past President, Southern California Psychoanalytic Institute and Society; President-Elect, Academy of Psychoanalysis.

PETER MAYERSON, M.D. Senior Resident Physician, Department of Psychiatry, Cincinnati General Hospital.

MARVIN K. OPLER, M.D. Professor of Social Psychiatry, School of Medicine, State University of New York at Buffalo; Professor of Anthropology and Sociology, Graduate School, State University of New York at Buffalo.

LIONEL OVESEY, M.D. Clinical Professor of Psychiatry, College of Physicians and Surgeons, Columbia University.

C. M. B. PARE, M.D., M.R.C.P., D.P.M. Physician, Department of Psychological Medicine, Saint Bartholomew's Hospital, London; Honorary Consultant Psychiatrist, Long Grove Hospital, Epsom.

v

WILLIAM H. PERLOFF, M.D. Chief, Division of Endocrinology and Reproduction, Albert Einstein Medical Center, Philadelphia.

SANDOR RADO, M.D. Professor of Psychiatry; Dean of the New York School of Psychiatry.

MAY E. ROMM, M.D. Training Analyst, Southern California Psychoanalytic Institute; past President, Southern California Psychoanalytic Society.

LEON SALZMAN, M.D. Professor of Clinical Psychiatry, Georgetown University Medical School; Faculty and Member of Board, Washington School of Psychiatry.

ROBERT J. STOLLER, M.D. Associate Professor of Psychiatry, UCLA School of Medicine; President-Elect, Southern California Psychiatric Society; Director, Gender Identity Research Clinic, UCLA Medical Center.

THOMAS S. SZASZ, M.D. Professor of Psychiatry, State University of New York, Upstate Medical Center, Syracuse, New York.

GORDON RATTRAY TAYLOR. Director of The Acton Society Trust, a social research organization.

CORNELIA B. WILBUR, M.D. Associate in Psychiatry, Columbia University, College of Physicians and Surgeons, New York.

CONTENTS

PART III

The View of the Clinician

SEXUAL INVERSION

1 | Introduction

JUDD MARMOR

This volume represents an effort to shed light on one of the most challenging problems in the field of psychiatry—that of homosexuality. My basic orientation in assembling the papers that follow has been that causality in this area—no less than in most other areas of psychopathology—cannot be sought in any single factor but is multifactorial. Accordingly, I have tried to assemble relevant information in every sector of biological and social science that might elucidate the complexity of this problem—history, comparative zoology, genetics, endocrinology, sociology, anthropology, law, psychology, and psychoanalytic psychiatry.

The Problem of Definition

One of the main difficulties underlying any discussion of the problem of homosexuality is that of definition. What, exactly, do we mean when we talk about homosexuality? Is it a state of mind or a form of behavior? Must it be conscious, or can it be unconscious? Is it a universal ontogenetic aspect of all human behavior, or is it a specific form of psychopathology? Is its overt expression the outgrowth of individual familial disturbances or the reflection of broader sociocultural factors?

A search of the literature on homosexuality reveals a wide spectrum of opinion on these and many other questions, with ardent exponents of each point of view. The most influential theory in modern psychiatry has been that of Sigmund Freud, who believed that homosexuality was the expression of a universal trend in all human beings, stemming from a biologically rooted bisexual predisposition. Freud, in line with the strong Darwinian influence on his thinking, believed that all human beings went through an inevitable "homoerotic" phase in the process of achieving heterosexuality. Certain kinds of life experience could arrest the evolutionary process, and the individual would then remain "fixated" at a homosexual level. Furthermore, even if the development were to proceed normally, certain vestiges of homosexuality would remain as permanent aspects of the personality, and these universal "latent homosexual" tendencies would be reflected in "sublimated" expressions of friendship for members of one's own sex and in patterns of behavior or interest more appropriate to the opposite sex—for example, artistic or culinary interests or "passive" attitudes in males and athletic or professional interests or "aggressive" attitudes in females.

Putting aside for the moment the theoretical validity or invalidity of these ideas, it is important to note that the definition of homosexuality in Freud's theoretical system is not linked to overt sexual behavior per se. It is related to a conglomerate system of feelings, attitudes, and reactions that exist in varying degrees in all human beings, although they are most evident in those whose behavior is overtly homosexual.

Although there is nothing inherently illogical in such a definition, it raises a serious practical question. At what point does a person become a homosexual in a clinical sense? Is it a quantitative or a qualitative matter? In terms of Freudian theory, it is clearly an essentially quantitative one; since homosexual patterns are present in the unconscious of all people, the clinical problem becomes one of the *degree* to which they are manifested in thought or behavior. Such a line of demarcation is of necessity vague and indefinite and involves a large borderline area in which the distinction between "normal" and "pathological" is obscure.

It is the conviction of this writer, as well as of most of the authors in this volume, that it is possible to arrive at a more precise *qualitative* definition of homosexuality, although quantitative factors are inevitably involved also. Some authors, such as Bieber (see Chapter 14), attempt to define it very simply, in operational terms: a homosexual is one who engages repeatedly, in adult life, in overt sexual relations with a member or members of the same sex. Such a definition has the advantage of more clearly demarcating the area under discussion and of being more useful operationally. Yet it seems to me that it does not do full justice to some of the complex variables involved, even operationally. A definition based simply on overt behavioral grounds fails to make a distinction between those who indulge in homosexual behavior out of an intense sexual attraction to members of the same sex and those who engage in such behavior for a variety of other reasons. Indulgence in homosexual behavior in contemporary society can be a consequence of prolonged heterosexual deprivation, as among prisoners or sailors, or it may be merely a reflection of weakness of the individual's inner controls—of his "superego." In the absence of such inner controls, an individual may indulge in homosexual behavior for a variety of motives—for money, for adventure, from ennui, from curiosity, from a need to please, or from hostility or rebellion and yet may experience no genuine erotic feelings for his partner.[1] Or such behavior may be the expression of transitory and exploratory sexual interests among adolescents and preadolescents in a society that prohibits them from the heterosexual explorations they would prefer.

A psychodynamic definition of homosexuality, it seems to me, cannot ignore the element of *motivation* and should combine the operational and motivational aspects of homosexual behavior.

---

[1] For example, see Reiss, "The Social Integration of Queers and Peers" (1961), which describes a group of delinquent heterosexual youths who go through a period of allowing themselves to be used, for money, by adult fellators but who neither define themselves as homosexuals nor continue their "homosexual" relationships as they move into adulthood.

Homosexuality, as a psychosexual phenomenon, ought to imply
the same kind of strong and spontaneous capacity to be aroused
by a member of one's own sex as heterosexuality implies in regard
to members of the opposite sex. *I prefer, therefore, to define the
clinical homosexual as one who is motivated, in adult life, by a
definite preferential erotic attraction to members of the same
sex and who usually (but not necessarily) engages in overt sexual relations with them.*[2] Such a definition still encompasses and
retains wide quantitative variations, but it is essentially qualitative in nature. It does not exclude those who are involved in
fantasies of intense sexual longing for members of the same sex
yet are prohibited by fears or moral considerations from actually
indulging in overt homosexual activity. Such individuals are
simply the homosexual analogues to inhibited or repressed heterosexuals. The definition does, however, exclude patterns of homosexual behavior that are not motivated by specific, preferential
desire—the incidental homosexuality of adolescents or the situational homosexuality of prisoners and sailors, for example. Most
members of such groups, who are driven into transitory homosexual patterns of behavior as a consequence of intense heterosexual frustration and who turn, or return, to exclusive heterosexuality as soon as the opportunity arises, are not homosexuals
psychodynamically, and it creates theoretical confusion to place
them in that category. My definition also excludes the transitory, opportunistic homosexual patterns of some delinquents. It
does away too with the ambiguous, essentially meaningless, and
nonoperational concept of "latent homosexuality," with which
Salzman's article (see Chapter 13) effectively deals.

Sexual behavior, no less than other human reactions, is remark-
ably adaptive. In the absence of heterosexual objects, many human beings (as well as lower animals—see Denniston, Chapter
2) will ultimately seek gratification in homosexual objects. Indeed, in the absence of any available human object at all, sexual release may be sought with animals or through the medium
of inanimate objects. Such patterns of behavior, which are dic-

[2] It should be noted that the presence of such a basic homoerotic motivation does not, however, preclude the possibility that other motivations
(power, dependency, hostility, and so forth) may also be involved in homosexual behavior, just as they can be involved in heterosexual behavior.

tated by *situational necessity*, should not be confused with those that grow out of basic personality needs and are *preferentially sought even when alternatives are present*. Only the latter represent genuine homosexuality in motivational terms.

Although innumerable explanations can be found in psychiatric and psychoanalytic literature for the origins of specific cases of homosexuality, there is as yet no single constellation of factors that can adequately explain all homosexual deviations. The simple fact is that dominating and seductive mothers; weak, hostile, or detached fathers; and the multiple variations on these themes that are so often suggested as being etiologically significant in homosexuality abound in the histories of countless heterosexual individuals also and cannot therefore be *in themselves* specific causative factors. In saying this it is not my intention to imply that such family relationships are irrelevant to the etiology of homosexuality. On the contrary, they are highly relevant, as the work of Bieber and his co-workers has convincingly demonstrated. There is little doubt that a boy exposed to the kind of family background Bieber describes (see Chapter 14) has a significantly higher than average possibility of becoming a homosexual. When I say that any particular family constellation is not specifically causative, I am merely indicating that, since cases of homosexuality can and do occur with quite varied family histories, the family background—although an important and relevant factor—is not specifically etiological in the sense that the tubercle bacillus is specific for tuberculosis. We are probably dealing with a condition that is not only multiply determined by psychodynamic, sociocultural, biological, and situational factors but also reflects the significance of subtle temporal, qualitative, and quantitative variables. For a homosexual adaptation to occur, in our time and culture, these factors must combine to (1) create an impaired gender-identity, (2) create a fear of intimate contact with members of the opposite sex, and (3) provide opportunities for sexual release with members of the same sex.

The Question of the Biological Factor

To what extent does the nature of the organism itself—the biological factor—play a role in the genesis of homosexuality? The most potent evidence for a biological predisposition toward homosexuality comes from Kallmann's study (1952) of eighty-five homosexual twin subjects. Forty-five were members of dizygotic pairs, and the concordance rates for overt homosexuality (groups 5 and 6 on the Kinsey scale) were somewhat—but not markedly—higher than those reported by Kinsey for the total male population.

On the other hand, for the forty subjects who were members of monozygotic pairs, Kallmann reports the extraordinary finding of 100 per cent concordance in overt homosexual behavior! This figure indicates a significant and, indeed, decisive genetic "vulnerability," even though Kallmann carefully disclaims any effort to explain the origin of homosexuality on exclusively genetic grounds. He does, however, claim that this finding "plainly diminishes the plausibility of explanations which overstress the importance of such precipitating or perpetuating factors as social ostracism, incompetence of a particular parent, or other potentially traumatizing experiences arising from the effect of uncontrolled imperfections in the structure of modern human societies" (p. 295). Kallmann considers homosexuality analogous to left-handedness, which is "genically [*sic*] controlled" but the manifestations of which can be masked or precluded by conditioning in a predominantly right-handed world.

The scholarly reports of Pare (see Chapter 4) and Perloff (see Chapter 3) clearly indicate that neither chromosomal nor hormonal differences can be demonstrated in homosexuals when compared to heterosexuals. Nevertheless, Pare is sufficiently impressed by Kallmann's "twin studies" to argue that some as yet unidentifiable chromosomal abnormality probably exists. Such an assumption is not unreasonable, provided that Kallmann's findings are reliable.

There is reason, however, to doubt their reliability. First, they have not as yet been duplicated or verified by any independent investigators. Indeed, as Pare indicates, a number of studies of smaller groups of monozygotic twins specifically contradict his findings. Second, Kallmann's scientific objectivity is open to question. He has been an ardent proponent of the basic importance of genetic factors in a wide variety of conditions, and his monozygotic "twin studies" have shown more than 86 per cent concordance in conditions as disparate as schizophrenia and tuberculosis. When an investigator begins with the intention of demonstrating a particular point, unconscious bias may enable him to prove it by subtly influencing his selection of cases as well as his perceptions and judgment. As long ago as 1949, Nicholas Pastore (1949), in a careful review of Kallmann's basic work on the genetics of schizophrenia (1938), pointed out that the study was based on 1,087 *selected* institutionalized patients who had been in the Herzberg Hospital of Berlin from 1893–1902. In selecting these cases, Kallmann made his own diagnoses of schizophrenia, even though some of his diagnoses may have been different from those originally made of the patients. Also, "all cases in which exogenous factors might have played a decisive role in the origin or development of a psychosis which resembled schizophrenia" were ruled out! On the basis of his review, Pastore concludes that "the Kallmann investigation supplies no reliable information for assessing the genetic basis of schizophrenia" (p. 302).

When we consider that all the available evidence from every field of behavioral and biological science points strongly to the relevance of exogenous factors in the determination of sexual object-choice, Kallmann's essentially unsupported evidence cannot and should not be given undue weight unless and until his raw material is carefully reviewed and confirmed by other independent investigators.[3]

This reservation does not mean, however, that biological factors are of no importance at all in the genesis of homosexuality.

---

[3] There are, of course, other possible explanations for the higher incidence of concordant homosexuality among identical twins than the genetic ones. C. W. Wahl of the University of California, Los Angeles, has suggested (1965) that, due to the particularly close identification of identical twins with each other, there may be a lessening of the incest taboo between them; during the period of normal adolescent homosexual explorations, they may be more inclined to participate in such activities with each other, and with less guilt, than are other siblings.

Insofar as a particular kind of bodily appearance, bodily build, or physical incoordination may affect parental or sibling reactions to a child or his ability to participate in peer activities, it may at times play a significant determining part in the gender-role assigned to him by people in his environment or in his inability to identify with his own sexual group. It may thus facilitate an ultimate homosexual object-choice. But even in such instances, the reaction of the milieu is fateful, for, as has often been noted, constitutionally "effeminate" boys or "masculine" girls can develop perfectly normal sexual object-relationships when their family environments and opportunities for appropriate gender-role identification are favorable.

Pare (see Chapter 4) also comments on Slater's finding that the birth order of 401 male homosexuals showed a significant shift to the right—that is, they were born later in the sibship than would be theoretically expected. Pare speculates that the later maternal ages that this shift implies may possibly result in some kind of chromosomal abnormality analogous to that in Mongolism, in which late maternal age seems also to be a factor. This is, of course, theoretically possible, but in the absence of any demonstrable chromosomal abnormality it seems more plausible to assume that mothers are apt to be more deeply involved emotionally with children born late in their lives. There is considerable evidence that homosexuality in Western culture develops more frequently in smaller family units, in which the intensity of intrafamilial relationships is apt to be greater. Furthermore, the younger child in the family is more apt to be "babied" or to develop feelings of inadequacy in relation to older siblings.[4] A younger or youngest child is also more apt to become the prime target of an older mother's affectional needs if the husband's interest in her has begun to diminish. Only if these and similar environmental concomitants of the "shift to the right" were ruled

---

[4] In an unselected review of my own personal case material over the past ten years, eleven of thirty-five homosexuals were only children, and ten others had only one other sibling each (usually a younger one). Of the nine who came from families with four or more children, four were the youngest in their families, one was sixth in a family of nine children, and two were the oldest children.

out would it be justifiable to hypothesize some unknown chromosomal abnormality in the genesis of homosexuality.

The Question of Psychological Bisexuality

But more than any genetic theories of homosexuality, Freud's hypothesis of an innate psychological bisexuality has achieved widespread acceptance among modern psychiatrists. It is a persuasive theory, resting as it does on the apparent early embryological hermaphroditism[5] of the human fetus, and is still tenaciously held despite the absence of any fundamental corroborating evidence for it. Rado's classic article (1940), which is reprinted in this volume (see Chapter 10), was the first significant critique of this theory in the psychoanalytic literature. Since its appearance in 1940, much evidence has been forthcoming in support of Rado's position, most notably the work of the Hampsons and Money. The Hampsons' investigations of the acquisition of gender role in humans point strongly to the presence of psychosexual neutrality in humans at birth—a neutrality that "permits the development and perpetuation of divers patterns of psychosexual orientation and functioning in accordance with the life experiences each individual may encounter and transact" (Hampson & Hampson, 1961, p. 1406). The work of Stoller (see Chapter 11) corroborates these findings. The Hampsons and Money (Money, Hampson, & Hampson, 1957) also suggest that there may be some analogy between the establishment of gender role in early childhood and the phenomenon of imprinting as seen in lower animals.

This is not to deny that, all other things being equal, human beings in any society, in the mass, will develop in a heterosexual direction rather than in a homosexual one. Obviously, any society that fails to do this would be in danger of extinction. The work of Money and the Hampsons, however, corroborates our knowledge of how instincts operate in human beings as compared with

---

[5] A hermaphroditism that does not actually exist, as in almost all human beings biological sex is clearly differentiated at the moment of conception by the XX and XY chromosomal patterns.

lower animals. The lower an animal is on the scale of evolution, the more complex are its inherited instinctual patterns and the less modifiable they are by environmental conditions. As one moves up the evolutionary scale, however, one finds that inherited instinctual patterns become less complex but more subject to modification by learning. This development reaches its apogee in human beings who are born, not with complex instinctual adaptive patterns, but with relatively unfocused basic biological drives. The direction these drives take in human beings and the objects to which they become attached are subject to enormous modifications by learning. It is precisely this fact that gives human beings their remarkable adaptability (Marmor, 1942).

The Etiology of the Homosexual Pattern

The etiology of the homosexual pattern itself is essentially the problem of what determines sexual object-choice. Freud believed that homoerotism was a normal libidinal phase in the life of every child, a stage in the evolution of heterosexuality. In his view, homosexuality as a clinical syndrome represents either an arrest of normal development or a regression to an earlier fixation point as a result of castration-anxiety mobilized, as a rule, by pathogenic familial experiences. The psychoanalysts represented in this volume do not accept the theory of psychological bisexuality or the assumption that homosexuality is a normal phase of libidinal development. Rather, they view it as an ego adaptation to certain environmental vicissitudes, which result in "hidden but incapacitating fears of the opposite sex." There seems little doubt that most modern psychoanalytic evidence supports this thesis. In view of the highly selective nature of the psychoanalysts' clinical material on homosexuality, however (see page 16), it still remains to be demonstrated that such fears are *always* at the bottom of the homosexual symptom. Certainly, in numerous instances of behavioral bisexuality, the evidence of fear of women is less obvious than in cases of exclusive homosexuality. If sexuality operates adaptively, as most of these authors agree it does, then we must concede at least the possibility that a homosexual object-choice can be determined on the basis of early or persistent *positive* conditioning to objects of the same sex, rather than solely by fears of the opposite sex. It has been reported, for example, that some previously heterosexual men who resort to homosexual practices during long periods of imprisonment find it difficult to resume heterosexual relations when released (Karpman, 1948; Wilson & Pescor, 1939). This finding is reminiscent of an interesting experiment reported by Jenkins (1928). He found that, some time after rats had been segregated sexually, homosexual behavior would commence. On being returned to the company of rats of the opposite sex, a number would remain homosexual, depending on the length of time they had been segregated. This behavior is apparently also characteristic of other animals under similar circumstances.

Two arguments can be raised, however, against the significant likelihood of such behavior in humans, at least in modern Western society. The one most frequently heard (that expressed by Bieber and his co-workers, 1962) is that heterosexuality is the "biologic norm" and that homosexuality cannot therefore occur without some anxiety-provoked inhibition of heterosexuality. This argument, it seems to me, does not withstand careful scrutiny. All the evidence from comparative zoology (see Chapter 2) indicates, on the contrary, that bisexuality or "ambisexuality" is the biologic norm and that exclusive heterosexuality is a culturally imposed restriction. Patterns of homosexuality are normally displayed among primates, for example, even, it should be noted, where heterosexual opportunities exist (Marmor, 1942, p. 513). Exclusive homosexuality, however, is also a rarity in the animal world, and its relative frequency in man must therefore also be due to specific features of human life.

There is, however, a more compelling argument against the theory that homosexual object-choices may be the result of positive conditioning. We must examine this theory, not as an abstraction, but within a specific cultural context. Within the matrix of contemporary Western civilization, with its abhorrence of and hostility to homosexual behavior and its powerful pressures toward heterosexual conformity, it does not seem likely that a homosexual object-choice, even if it were initially determined by positive conditioning, could maintain itself in a hostile and punitive environment, *unless there were concomitant anxieties of equal or greater strength blocking the path to heterosexual adaptation.*

For our time and culture, therefore, the psychoanalytic assumption that preferential homosexual behavior is always associated with unconscious fears of heterosexual relationships appears valid.

It must be recognized also that the avoidance of heterosexual relationships may not necessarily always be rooted in physical fear of the sexual act itself. At the basis of such avoidance we often find fear of the responsibilities of marriage and parenthood. Homosexual relationships, by virtue of the fact that they are socially condemned, do not involve the same degree of implied permanence and commitment that heterosexual relationships do. They also attract "people who fear intimacy and yet are equally afraid of loneliness" (Green, 1964, p. 10).

The Question of Social and Cultural Determinants

This discussion highlights the importance of the social and cultural contexts of homosexual behavior in humans. Indeed, as Opler indicates (see Chapter 6), experimental work points to the relevance of social conditions to patterns of sexual behavior even among such lower mammals as rhesus monkeys and Norway rats. Konrad Lorenz's observations (1959) of graylag geese show similar findings; under conditions of crowding analogous to human slum conditions, there was a breakdown of "normal" heterosexual behavior patterns and associated formation of homosexual male pairs.

One of the problems attendant on cross-cultural studies of primitive peoples, as Mead (1961) points out, is that statements on absence of homosexual behavior can be accepted only with great caution, because of such factors as language barriers, unbreakable cultural taboos, needs for personal privacy, distrust of Caucasion investigators, retrospective falsification, and even, in some nonliterate societies, conventions of courtesy that demand telling a questioner what he presumably wants to hear! Opler (see page 112) cautions that there may be widespread variations in investigators' definitions of homosexuality—from the incidental and exploratory same-sex play of adolescents, to highly institutionalized gender-role changes that may be essentially religious in their significance, to genuine adult homoerotic practices. Nevertheless, and bearing all these reservations in mind, there is no doubt that there are widespread cultural variations both in the incidence of homosexuality and in the degree of social sanction it receives.

Gender-role patterns—what is considered "masculine" or "feminine" behavior—also vary markedly among different cultures, despite the common tendency, particularly among classical Freudians, to assume that our Western concepts of masculinity and femininity are rooted in the biological difference between the sexes. Opler (see page 116) points to some striking variations from our own gender-role concepts among the Navajo, the Andaman Islanders, the Cubeo, and the upper-class Tuareg. Mead (1961) calls attention to other significant variations among the Manus, the Iatmul, and others. Constitutional patterns of physique or temperament may also be linked to varying gender-role concepts in different cultures. In some cultures, for example, mesomorphic females are thought masculine and endomorphic or ectomorphic males are considered feminine. Mead (1961) points out that in American culture height is regarded as a factor, small men and tall women being considered respectively somehow less male and less female than their opposites.

These socially determined values may and probably do play a significant part in many cultures in "pushing" people toward inverted gender-roles. Among those American Indian tribes that gave social sanction to the careers of berdaches or transvestite males, male children were observed and tested from an early age to determine whether they were "braves" or "women." Once the elders made the choice, the expected patterns were reinforced by elaborate institutionalized prescriptions. In our society, the unathletic or poorly coordinated boy and the unattractive or "masculine looking" girl are sometimes similarly "pushed" into inverted gender roles, not only by the reactions of people on the outside, but also by distortion of their own self-concepts, which are similarly dependent on the dominant social values of their environments. Even such nonphysiological personality attributes as mathematical ability in a girl or artistic talent in a boy may be endowed by a culture with values that then tend to push such children toward distorted self-concepts and inverted gender roles. It is important to recognize that such value orientations do not necessarily always take place explicitly and overtly. Quite frequently and perhaps even most of the time, they operate through subtle, covert, nonverbal patterns of behavior and interaction—patterns of which the participants themselves may be totally unaware.

Social and cultural factors also have an important bearing on relative attitudes toward homosexuality among males and females in any given culture. In some societies, adoption of cross-gender roles, including transvestism, is open only to one sex or the other (see pages 151 ff.). In modern Western society, male attire on females has a degree of acceptance that is absent for feminine attire on males. As Clara Thompson has pointed out (Green, 1964, pp. 6-7), "Women in general are permitted greater physical intimacy with each other [in our culture] without social disapproval than is the case with men. Kissing and hugging are acceptable forms of friendly expression between women. . . . Two overt homosexual women may live together in complete intimacy in many communities without social disapproval. . . . two men attempting the same thing are likely to encounter marked hostility."

The papers by Romm (Chapter 16) and Wilbur (Chapter 15) in this volume illustrate some of the clinical parallels and some of the differences that exist between female and male homosexuality.

There are probably still other broad social or cultural factors relevant to the genesis of homosexuality. Fisher (see Chapter 9) suggests that, in ancient Greece at least, there was a relationship between the rise of homosexuality and the degraded status of women. Rattray Taylor (see Chapter 8) argues that, in societies that conceive of their deities as mother-figures, incest is the major taboo, while homosexuality is treated as of little importance; and conversely that, in societies that have father-figure deities, homosexuality is regarded as "the overwhelming danger," while incest, although also taboo, "falls far behind homosexuality in importance." Westermarck (1921) related male homosexuality to absence of eligible women (too few or too chaste). Homosexuality as part of the warrior's code among primitive peoples may have been associated with this factor. Westermarck also points out that role-inversion appears to increase at periods of high civilization and particularly with urbanization.

Economic factors probably play a part also, even in relatively simple societies. As Opler (see page 113) points out, the high percentage of male sexual inversion among the Chukchee seems to be related to the difficulties a young man in that highly patriarchal culture has in accumulating enough wealth with which to acquire a wife.

There is reason to think that the growing complexity of our Western civilization renders the achievement of masculine identity increasingly difficult for the adolescent male and enhances the desire to flee the demands and responsibilities of the masculine role. The feminine revolution, the emerging dominant tendencies of many American women, the rise of "momism," and the diminishing importance of the paternal role in the home are other significant sociological factors that reverberate in intrafamily relationships and hinder the development of healthy masculine identifications. The tendency of English upper-class families to send their sons away at an early age to sexually segregated schools is believed to be one of the factors responsible for a relatively high incidence of sexual inversion among them.

Is Homosexuality an Illness?

The problems surrounding the issue of homosexuality are exemplified by still another fundamental question. Is homosexuality an "illness," or is it merely a different "way of life"? Most of the psychoanalysts in this volume (except Szasz) are of the opinion that homosexuality is definitely an illness to be treated and corrected.[6] Bieber's view, for example, is that homosexuality is clearly "pathological" and "incompatible with a reasonably happy life." Hooker (see Chapter 5), on the other hand, argues that, apart from the specific difference in sexual orientation, many of the homosexuals she has studied reveal, on psychological testing, no "demonstrable pathology" that would differenti-

---

[6] Interestingly, Freud himself did not consider it an illness. In his famous "Letter to an American Mother" (April 9, 1935), he wrote, "Homosexuality is assuredly no advantage, but it is nothing to be ashamed of, no vice, no degradation, it cannot be classified as an illness; we consider it to be a variation of the sexual functions produced by a certain arrest of sexual development" (Freud, 1951, p. 787).

ate them in any way from a group of relatively normal heterosexuals.

One possible explanation for these widely varying views comes
immediately to mind. The concepts of psychoanalysts *are all derived from the study of homosexuals who have sought psychoanalytic therapy* or else have been referred because of external difficulties. Hooker's case material, on the other hand, includes many
homosexuals who believe themselves emotionally and interper-
sonally well adjusted and who have no motivation ever to seek
psychotherapy. A strong possibility thus exists that traditional
psychoanalytic concepts about the characterological defects of
homosexuals are based on a skew sampling of homosexuals and
may not accurately represent the spectrum of personalities present
in the total homosexual population.

Hooker's findings justify the conclusion that sexual deviance in
itself does not necessarily mean social maladjustment. Although
exclusively homosexual behavior does—as most psychoanalysts
argue—reflect a functional limitation in the capacity for heterosexuality, the possibility must be granted that under certain circumstances this limitation may not necessarily interfere with
reasonably satisfactory life adjustment. If the judgments of psychoanalysts about heterosexuals were based only on those they
see as patients, would they not have the same skew impression
of heterosexuals as a group?

If we recognize, as the work of Money and the Hampsons
clearly indicates, that the objects of human sexual drives are
experientially determined rather than biologically determined
by the drives themselves, then we must conclude that there is
nothing inherently "unnatural" about life experiences that predispose an individual to a preference for homosexual object-
relations *except insofar as this preference represents a socially
condemned form of behavior in our culture and consequently
carries with it certain sanctions and handicaps.* This fact, it
seems to me, lies at the bottom of both the legal and the clinical
approaches to homosexuality in our time. Both approaches reflect
cultural condemnation of such behavior; the law considers it
antisocial and applies punitive sanctions; the clinical psychiatrist evaluates it as "sick" behavior and seeks to modify it "therapeutically." In other times and in other cultures, however, such

sanctions or modifications have not always been applied (see chapters 6 and 8).

In a very basic sense, therefore, our psychiatric approach to the problem of homosexuality is conditioned by whether we come to it as pure scientists or as practical clinicians. The scientist must approach his data nonevaluatively; homosexual behavior and heterosexual behavior are merely different areas on a broad spectrum of human sexual behavior, the sources of which must be determined and understood, and neither can be assumed to be intrinsically more or less "natural" than the other. The clinical psychiatrist, on the other hand, is, by the very nature of his work, deeply involved in concepts of health and disease, normality and abnormality. These concepts, however, are not absolutes, particularly in the area of social behavior. "What is considered psychologically healthy in one era or culture may not be considered so in another. For example, the normal sexual behavior of an adolescent girl among the Marquesans or Trobrianders would in our society be set down as constituting nymphomania or 'psychopathic personality.' Again, while we label homosexuality as pathological in our Western culture, among the Tanalans and Japanese it [was] accepted as a normal behavior variant and [met] with no opprobrium. . . . Even within the same broad cultural group, there may be significant variations in standards of accepted behavior" (Marmor & Pumpian-Mindlin, 1950, p. 22). It is a logical fallacy, therefore, to try to compare homosexuality in the contemporary Western world with homosexuality in ancient Greece, for example. The psychodynamic patterns were quite different, not only because in ancient Greece the behavior involved was bisexual rather than exclusively homosexual, but also because the cultural attitudes toward homosexual behavior were so different from our own. Homosexual behavior in ancient Greece carried with it neither the derogatory self-image nor the maladaptive social consequences that make such behavior in our culture a "dis-ease" that may cause its possessor to seek "treatment."

The twentieth-century psychiatric clinician in the Western world inevitably reflects the mores of his time and culture when he regards homosexuality as an undesirable modification of or deviation from optimum personality development and adaptation in our society. It is not my intention to denigrate the approach of the clinician. In his efforts to help the homosexual achieve a heterosexual adaptation whenever possible, the clinical psychiatrist—like any other kind of physician—is endeavoring to help his patient achieve an optimum homeostatic relationship with the environment in which he finds himself. This objective is valid and legitimate, particularly, of course, when the homosexual himself comes to the psychiatrist seeking help. I agree with Szasz (see page 132), however, that there is no ethical or scientific justification for forcing such treatment on an unwilling homosexual and that the ordinary adult homosexual who does not wish or seek psychiatric help does not, simply because he is a homosexual, belong within the purview of the psychiatrist. If a homosexual's behavior violates public decency or involves the seduction of minors, it becomes a matter for the application of legal sanctions, just as would corresponding behavior in a heterosexual.[7] When, however, homosexual behavior takes place in private between consenting adults, it should not be even the law's business, as the Wolfenden report so bluntly put it.

On the other hand, we could argue with justification that psychiatric intervention *is* prophylactically indicated for children or adolescents who seem to be failing to make appropriate gender-role identifications. As long as we live in a society that regards homosexuality as an undesirable behavioral deviation, the ultimate adaptations of such children to their inner and outer worlds will be potentially better ones if they can be prevented from developing homoerotic patterns.

The "Homosexual Personality"

The assumption that homosexuals are all alike is a stereotype born of cultural prejudice, the absurdity of which becomes obvious if compared to the corresponding assumption that heterosexuals are all alike. One reflection of this stereotyping is the

---

[7] I disagree with Szasz, however, in his oft-stated argument that *only* legal sanctions should be applied in such instances. The modern tendency among progressive criminologists to advocate therapeutic, rehabilitative measures in addition to legal sanctions is in the best interests of the individual and society, provided that such measures are not forced on an individual against his will.

almost universal belief that homosexuals are not to be trusted with young people of the same sex. The assumption that they are somehow less in control of their impulses than are heterosexuals is the same kind of assumption that underlies white prejudice against Negroes or native-born prejudice against foreigners. In all these instances, the feeling is a reflection of fear based on lack of intimate knowledge of the people involved. A homosexual individual is neither more nor less trustworthy, necessarily, with young people of the same sex than a heterosexual person is trustworthy with young people of the opposite sex. The "dependability" of a homosexual in such a position depends on whether or not he is a responsible human being with an adequate superego, and that factor is the only one to be evaluated; otherwise, his homosexuality is neither more nor less relevant than is the heterosexuality of a male counselor in a girl's camp. What I am saying refers to the individual homosexual, who should be evaluated on his own merits and not on the basis of a stereotyped preconception. I am not denying that the spectrum of personality distribution in homosexuals tends to be more heavily weighted toward neurotic patterns of behavior than is that of heterosexuals. This is inevitable in a society that makes such behavior, *ipso facto,* maladaptive. The inability of most homosexuals to make the transition to heterosexual behavior despite the powerful social sanctions against homosexuality also indicates some defects in ego-adaptive capacity. Therefore, individuals who adopt such deviant behavior in our society are statistically more likely to feel inadequate and to show evidences of less adequate ego formation. Granting all this, there is, nevertheless, as wide a personality variation among homosexuals as among heterosexuals: from extremely passive to extremely aggressive ones; from quiet introverts to loud and raucous extroverts; from hysterics to compulsives; from sexually inhibited and timid types to sexually promiscuous and self-flaunting ones; from irresponsible sociopaths to highly responsible and law-abiding citizens. Their psychiatric diagnoses, apart from the homosexual symptom, run the entire gamut of modern nosology. Their physical appearances are equally varied, of course, and cover a wide spectrum from extreme "femininity" of physique and manner to extreme "masculinity."

The tendency so frequent in the literature to delineate a specific "homosexual personality" will some day, I am convinced, appear as archaic as the old description of the "typical" tuberculous or epileptic personalities now appear. Just as we now recognize that the traditional clinical characteristics of these latter "types" are not intrinsic to the diseases at all but are rather reactions to the prolonged hospitalizations and the social attitudes experienced by these patients, so certain widespread personality characteristics of homosexuals will come to be understood as part of a total fabric that includes a specific kind of social more and value that deprecates and condemns homoerotic behavior and makes life much more difficult and hazardous for homosexuals. We must ask ourselves: Would homosexual persons have the same neurotic characters if they lived in a society (such as that of ancient Greece) that, instead of censuring their behavior, esteemed it highly?

Let us ask the question from still another angle. In 1962, Grinker published a study of a group of young men who, by all current cultural standards, undoubtedly would be regarded as "mentally healthy," well adjusted, and unconflicted. Yet they were all individuals with narrowly limited interests, totally lacking in creative qualities, and strongly conforming to the dominant Protestant ethic and mores of contemporary American society. Would these individuals be equally unneurotic and unconflicted if they were transferred to a society that dismissed them as dull and mediocre people, evaluated them as inadequate men, and treated them as deviants?

The fact is that, apart from certain nonspecific neurotic symptoms that they share with heterosexual patients and certain other difficulties that are uniquely homosexual,[8] homosexuals most often come to treatment precisely because of problems resulting from their interactions with a hostile society—legal, social, or economic threats or inability to accept their homosexuality because of its depreciated image in their own eyes and in those of the world at large.

---

[8] Such forms of inability to function in the heterosexual world as difficulty in attracting partners or, more often, break-ups of important dyadic relationships.

Social Discrimination against Homosexuals

Many authors have remarked that there is a great deal of social discrimination against homosexuals as a group. For example, Cory (1951) noted that, in World War II, homosexuals were subject to compulsory draft into military service, yet when their deviance was discovered they were subject to special discharge barring them from all government benefits under the G.I. Bill of Rights. No other medically discharged men, including psychoneurotics, were barred from such benefits. The Civil Service Commission also bars employment of known homosexuals, placing them in the same category with criminals. Although there is some justification, perhaps, for barring homosexuals from positions involving national security, on the basis that they are subject to blackmail (and that is only because society's condemnation of them makes them vulnerable!), there is no reasonable excuse for denying them ordinary civil service employment. This denial is obviously a reflection of our society's irrational prejudice and hostility toward them. It is noteworthy that the U. S. Supreme Court has scheduled a hearing on a case involving the right of a homosexual to hold a civil service job, and it is possible that eventually the high court will erase this inequity.

Treatment of Homosexuality

The clinicians represented in this volume present convincing evidence that homosexuality is a potentially reversible condition. There is little doubt that much of the recent success in the treatment of homosexuals stems from the growing recognition among psychoanalysts that homosexuality is a disorder of adaptation. The figures cited by Bieber and his co-workers (1962) and by Mayerson and Lief (see Chapter 18) indicate that anywhere from one-fourth to one-half of all homosexuals seeking treatment can successfully achieve reversal of their sexual orientation. Ovesey's excellent discussion (Chapter 8) illustrates the utilization of adaptive psychodynamics in the treatment of homosexuality.

We must recognize, however, that homosexuals seeking psychiatric treatment represent only a small fraction of the total number of homosexuals in our society.[9] The vast majority of homosexuals does not seek or wish such treatment. Clearly, society must ultimately learn to live with them and to accept them as long as they maintain common standards of public decency. Punishment of the homosexual is clearly no solution. Homosexuality is no more common in such countries as France, Sweden, and the Netherlands, where it is not a crime, than it is in Great Britain and America, where it is. Indeed, as we have noted, there is evidence that conditions of imprisonment tend to reinforce homosexual patterns rather than weaken them (Karpman, 1948; Wilson & Pescor, 1939). If society were to undertake to imprison or isolate homosexuals, furthermore, it would lose the services of many of its most talented and creative human beings.

Can the problem of homosexuality ever be totally "solved"? We cannot at this point give a definitive answer to this question, but in all probability there will always be men and women, particularly men, who, when faced with the problems of achieving appropriate gender-identity in our increasingly complex society, will take refuge in homosexuality. As Rattray Taylor puts it, "Homosexuality, like . . . the divorce rate, is no more than a symptom of an underlying state of psychosocial distress. The cure of this state *on a broad scale* [italics mine—J.M.] can be effected only by altering the relevant social conditions" (see page 162). It is to be hoped that the following chapters may contribute to better understanding of some of the complex factors that enter into the development of patterns of homosexual behavior and so enable us ultimately to institute more effective means of prevention than now exist.

---

[9] Estimates vary, but even the most conservative ones calculate that there are 2,000,000–4,000,000 males in America today who are exclusively or predominantly homosexual for most of their adult lives.

REFERENCES

Bieber, I., Dain, H. J., Dince, P. R., Drellich, M. G., Grand, H. G., Gundlach, R. H., Kremer, Malvina W., Rifkin, A. H., Wilbur, Cornelia B., & Bieber, Toby B. *Homosexuality*. New York: Basic Books, 1962.

Cory, D. W. *The homosexual in America*. New York: Greenberg, 1951.

Freud, S. Letter to an American mother. *Amer. J. Psychiat.*, 1951, **107**, 786-787.

Green, M. R. (Ed.) *Interpersonal psychoanalysis, the selected papers of Clara M. Thompson*. New York: Basic Books, 1964.

Grinker, R. R., Sr. A study of mentally healthy young males (homoclites). *Arch. Gen. Psychiat.*, 1962, **6**, 405-453.

Hampson, J. L., & Hampson, Joan G. The ontogenesis of sexual behavior in man. In W. C. Young (Ed.), *Sex and internal secretions*. Vol. 2. (3rd ed.) Baltimore: Williams & Wilkins, 1961. Pp. 1401-1432.

Jenkins, M. The effect of segregation on the sex behavior of the white rat as measured by the obstruction method. *Genet. Psychol. Monogr.*, 1928, **3**, 455-571.

Kallmann, F. J. *The genetics of schizophrenia*. New York: Augustin, 1938.

Kallmann, F. J. A comparative twin study on the genetic aspects of male homosexuality. *J. nerv. ment. Dis.*, 1952, **115**, 283-298.

Karpman, B. Sex life in prison. *J. crim. Law Criminol.*, 1948, **38**, 475-486.

Kinsey, A., Pomeroy, W. B., & Martin, C. E. *Sexual behavior in the human male*. Philadelphia: Saunders, 1948.

Lorenz, K. The role of aggression in group formation. In B. Schaffner (Ed.), *Group processes*. Vol. 4. New York: Macy Foundation, 1959. Pp. 181-251.

Marmor, J. The role of instinct in human behavior. *Psychiat.*, 1942, **5**, 509-516.

Marmor, J., & Pumpian-Mindlin, E. Toward an integrative conception of mental disorder. *J. nerv. ment. Dis.*, 1950, **111**, 19-29.

Mead, Margaret. Cultural determinants of sexual behavior. In W. C. Young (Ed.), *Sex and internal secretions*. Vol. 2. (3rd ed.) Baltimore: Williams & Wilkins, 1961. Pp. 1433-1479.

Money, J., Hampson, Joan G., & Hampson, J. L. Imprinting and the establishment of gender role. *A.M.A. Arch. Neurol. Psychiat.*, 1957, **77**, 333-336.

Pastore, N. The genetics of schizophrenia. *Psychol. Bull.*, 1949, **46**, 285-302.

Rado, S. A critical examination of the concept of bisexuality. *Psychosom. Med.*, 1940, **2**, 459-467.

Reiss, A. J., Jr. The social integration of queers and peers. *Soc. Prob.*, 1961, **9**, 102-120.

Wahl, C. W. Personal communication. 1965.

Westermarck, E. *The history of human marriage.* (5th ed.) London: Macmillan, 1921.

Wilson, J. G., & Pescor, M. J. *Problems in prison psychiatry.* Caldwell, Idaho: Caxton, 1939.

PART I | THE VIEW OF THE BIOLOGICAL SCIENCES

2 | Ambisexuality in Animals

R. H. DENNISTON

The problem of homosexuality—or better, of ambisexuality—in lower animals presents several intriguing theoretical facets that have implications for human beings. The general problem involves the relationship between sex drive and sex behavior. Is the former specific as to sex, that is, are there a male sex drive and a female sex drive, each resulting in its own appropriate behavior? Or is there a general sex drive that expresses itself in behavior appropriate to the anatomy, endocrine balance, conditioning, and present stimulus situation? If the drive is sex limited, is it one drive or, as Beach (1958) and Denniston (1954) have suggested, is there a progressive series of drives for the components of courtship and mating behavior?

There is no question that sex behavior represents a chained response series or that both positive and negative feedbacks play their roles at all levels of its organization. For this response chain to occur, certain prerequisites must be present in the organism and in the environment. The organism must be in a normal nutritional, maturational, and endocrine situation and must have

27

had whatever experience is necessary for the given sex and taxonomic level. The response chain then proceeds somewhat as
follows:

(1) A generalized tendency toward intraspecies gregarious-
ness is aroused by visual, olfactory, auditory, or other distant
cues from a potential partner. The tendency and the stimulus
combine to produce approach behavior toward the source of the
stimuli.

(2) The approach behavior leads to contact or near contact
if the pertinent cues continue to be positive or to afford positive feedback. When contact has been established, the approach
tendency is satisfied temporarily, and an investigatory tendency
takes its place.

(3) If investigatory behavior leads to the appropriate positive
stimulus-producing responses (or possibly simply to absence of
negative ones) from the partner, sexual arousal begins. The rate
of interaction increases with each partner's stimulation of the
other and with positive feedback into the arousal mechanisms.
When arousal is sufficient, appropriate genital contact is established, and a new set of interactions begins. The passive partner
is stimulated to adopt the typical receptive posture. (In many
species, this posture is almost identical to the submissive posture
in an aggressive situation.)

(4) If the stimuli provided by the receptive partner are adequate, seminal emission takes place, and the ejaculatory drive is
reduced for a variable time during the post-ejaculatory period.
Each step in the chain is caused by appropriate stimuli interact-
ing with the psychobiological condition of the organism. The response to each step leads to a change from one set of stimuli to
another: from distant to near contact, then to special receptor
contact, and finally to genital contact. At each step, a tendency is
satisfied, and another is aroused. As is typical of positive feedback situations, the activities accelerate to climax.

Before going further, we might well attempt operative definitions of some terms, from the psychobiological point of view (see
Beach, 1958; Verplanck, 1957): *aggression*—threat and attack behavior; *ambisexuality* (*bisexuality*)—sexual behavior with either
sex; *dominance*—subordination hierarchy, pecking order; *drive*
—an organism's tendency to change the rate and direction of

its behavior in relation to certain categories of stimulus complexes (The general effect of such behavior is return to homeostatic balance. The behavior is referred to as a *response* to the stimuli in question.); *hermaphroditic* (*monoecious*)—referring to an individual organism that contains both male and female reproductive systems; *homosexuality*—sexual behavior with a member of the organism's own sex; *instincts*—sets of responses characteristic of a species, preceded by definite stimuli and drives and demonstrable under conditions calculated to preclude learning; *oestrus*—behavioral female sex receptivity; *reinforcement*—a stimulus previously demonstrated to strengthen the probability of the response which precedes it; *sex receptivity*—behavior of a female animal that permits or encourages copulation.

One of the interesting problems in homosexual behavior is its relationship to the relative dominance positions of the active and passive partners in the social group. Much male courtship behavior is indistinguishable from aggressive dominance behavior per se, and only by considering the environs and consequences of such behavior can it be categorized. *That such socially conditioned homosexual behavior is almost universal among animals is one of our themes.*

Another problem is the evolutionary or phylogenetic progression of sex-specific behavior. Some primitive animals tend to be monoecious or functionally bisexual, producing both eggs and sperm. In the very common cases—as in the earthworm—of mutual cross-fertilization, it would be most interesting to analyze the involved behavior patterns in a careful and systematic way. In those organisms that are protandric (functionally male) when young and functionally female when older, what are the behavior patterns in the male, transitional, and female stages?

According to Coe (1940), in the marine snail (*Crepidula*) all young are functional males and change to functional females as they grow older. There are two types of young male. The one that has more primary ovocytes in the ovotestes shows less masculine behavior and is always more passive (female-like). Association of the young with females prolongs the male phase of life. Coe speculates that this prolongation of maleness is due to stimuli received from the female. Sometimes the transitional phase from male to female is prolonged and accompanied by appearance and behavior of an intergrade type. In other varieties, there seems to be a dedifferentiation toward a neuter type before femaleness starts to develop. Chaetopod annelids of the genus *Ophryotrocha* show a similar protandrous development, except that under certain unfavorable circumstances a re-reversal from female back to male may take place. When two females are confined together, the more vigorous may obtain a mate by biting the other female in two or by eating all the available food. As the female is somewhat exhausted by the egg-laying process, the male may grow once again, change into a female, and bite his "wife" in two, thus reversing the roles.

The influence of deleterious environmental conditions, including crowding and consequential malnutrition and accumulation of waste products, leads to the birth of males from organisms that have been reproducing for generations as parthenogenetic females. The social implications here are worth pondering. Certainly, in many phyla of invertebrates, sexuality is extremely labile, with an individual functioning at times as a male and at other times as a female. (That biological bisexuality extends into the chordate phylum is also well supported by abundant evidence of both an observational and an experimental nature.) Coe concludes that more or less numerous representatives of nearly every phylum of invertebrates and of every phylum of plants are functionally hermaphroditic (1940).

Vertebrates

Ambisexual behavior in the invertebrates almost always seems to have an obvious physiological background. It may be in terms of functional hermaphroditism (so that the term "homosexual" should not be applied) or of transitional stages in species that normally undergo sex reversal. Eleven of the fifteen many-celled invertebrate phyla contain monoecious members. *Among the invertebrates, true homosexuality, in which a functional individual of a given sex has anything approaching sexual relations with a member of the same sex, seems to be unreported in the available literature.* In the vertebrates apparent homosexuality increases as we ascend the taxonomic tree toward the mammal.

A word of caution should be entered here. There are at least two possible reasons why such an apparent increase in homosexuality may not be real. First, there has been far less objective and well controlled study of the behavior of lower vertebrates than of the higher ones; second, investigations have been more difficult to interpret on sex-recognition and empathetic grounds.

Before discussing the data on chordates, it is well to consider possible causal factors in animal homosexual behavior, so that we may apply "Ockham's Razor" to anthropomimetic explanations of such acts.[1]

(1) One such factor could be failure to discriminate the true sex of the partner. In forms that lack distinct sexual dimorphism, such as the common grass frog, indiscriminate sexual approaches may be the rule, with behavioral warning or lack of receptivity the pertinent *discriminandum*.

(2) A second and frequently confusing situation involves dominance–subordination behavior, in either sex, that closely resembles aggression–submission. Domestic chickens illustrate this point beautifully.

(3) Finally, the "play" activities of juvenile organisms may include sex-type mounts and may be quite indiscriminate as to the sex of the participants—as seems to be true of almost all mammals.

•

In fish, sex discrimination may be quite poor in strange situations and may be established only in terms of responses to courtship approaches. This writer has observed male guppies courting each other for weeks while confined in a one-sex group. This behavior included the "S" curve dance, nipping of the genital area, and gonapodial swinging. Areas in which fish have been accustomed to breed or in which there has been chemical conditioning of the water by ripe females are likely sites for the induction of homosexual behavior by the utilization of suitable hormones, either applied directly to the fish or dissolved in the aquarium water.

Desmond Morris (1952) reports a well-controlled series of experiments on male sexual behavior in the ten-spined stickleback

---

[1] Morris (1952) lists the first two of these factors.

in response to crowding. Among these fish, the males make nests of water weeds glued together with their own secretions. Only the dominant males are able to build and maintain such nests under crowded conditions. Such males are black, whereas subordinate males are parti-colored. Having built a nest and established a territory, which implies the repeated vanquishment of subordinate males, a dominant male dances head down before a female, attempting to lead her to the nest and to have her enter it and deposit eggs. Although subordinate males may not establish territories or build nests, they are very highly motivated. They dance for the females, produce "glue," bore into weeds as though they were nests, and seem to try to show females such imaginary nests. Homosexual courting behavior is shown by the dominant male in cases in which females have previously been present. Usually, courted males will not follow the dominant and are therefore bitten and chased by him. Sometimes, however, a subordinate male will push aside a female from the nest entrance and pass through the nest in her stead. We shall refer to such behavior as "feminine male homosexual" (FMH). The dominant male shivers along the pseudo-female's tail once it is in the nest just as if it were a true female, thus showing "masculine male homosexuality" (MMH). Once homosexual behavior has started in the nest, the pseudo-female shows all aspects of normal female behavior except actual egg-laying. Morris indicates some possible ways homosexual behavior functions under such crowded conditions: as an outlet relieving sexual frustration and as a device limiting the production of fertilized eggs, thereby cutting the population density. That endocrine abnormalities are not involved in these fish is demonstrated by the fact that the pseudo-female will behave in a normal manner within seconds after his homosexual behavior if given the opportunity.

Morris' classification of homosexuality (slightly modified by the present writer) is of interest.

    I. Sensory (MMH) Active
        A. Lack of sex discrimination
        B. Sufficiency of suboptimal stimulus; possible adequate identification of sex but overriding stimulated motivation

    C. Preference for own sex as a partner (conditioned and strong habit for A or B)
II. Motor (FMH) Passive
    A. Inversion of behavior pattern in response to patterns listed under I (frustration in subordinate males)
    B. Preference for inversion in spite of available heterosexual outlets (conditioned IIA).

It is interesting that none of these categories involves hormonal abnormality or subnormality.

In a later paper, Morris (1955) performed the reciprocal experiment. Crowded females in the absence of males showed male-type dancing (MFH). Other females sometimes followed such dancing (FFH).

Morris lists four possible general causes of homosexual behavior, although they are not related directly to the data presented in the paper: hormonal or structural abnormality, reversal of male–female dominance–subordination roles, frustrated sexual motivation, and some appropriate female-associated stimuli shown by a male or vice versa.

Another set of initials used by Morris distinguishes the relative strengths of tendencies to flee (F), attack (A), and mate (M); an FMH would show FaM.

Tavolga published data in 1955 showing that castration of gobioid fish did not immediately reduce courtship but rendered it indiscriminate as to object. Such castrates will court equally other males, gravid females, and unripe females.

•

The toads and frogs appear to have almost no sex recognition at a distance. A.P. Blair describes the breeding behavior of the American toad as almost entirely nocturnal, which inhibits utilization of visual cues. Males usually call in chorus; the call of one stimulates others to call. If a male sees another moving toad, he quickly approaches and clasps this toad. If the toad clasped is a male, he at once begins chirping and is usually released forthwith. If the toad clasped is a female, there is no chirping; the male maintains his grip, and oviposition and fertilization follow (Blair, 1942).

In addition to the warning chirp, other contact *discriminanda* are the slenderness of the male or spent female and the vibration of the male body when clasped. That this vibration, rather than the other factors, is of paramount importance in sex discrimination has been demonstrated by well-controlled experiments (Aronson, 1944). Among these animals, then, courtship—if it can be called that—is completely indiscriminate, and the contact cue of the clasped male's warning croak or vibration is the first effective indication to the active male that his behavior has been homosexual rather than heterosexual. Sexually active males attempt to clasp members of a pair in amplexus. As the male of the pair is on top, he is clasped 97 per cent of the time and is often dislodged.

•

The mating behavior of lizards and their methods of sexual recognition are much better understood than seems to be the case with snakes and turtles. An early paper by Noble and Bradley (1933) describes the mating behavior of various genera of lizards. Among the *Teiidae,* the active male masturbates by rubbing the genital area on the substratum and then seeks a mate of either sex. As the active male pokes at the neck of the partner, the latter's cloacal lips erect. He rubs the partner's opposite flank, reaching across to do so, then bites and grasps the rubbed area, swings his tail under the partner's, everts the hemipenes, and inserts the near one into the partner's cloaca. This whole process can be carried out equally well with a passive male or with a female. Homosexual copulation stimulates the passive male, so that he may change roles with the previously active male and complete a copulation in turn. These lizards may pile up three deep in copulation. Among the *Iguanidae,* ten of twenty-one observed copulations were male homosexual. The weaker or smaller males fall automatically into the passive homosexual role, as active males fight or threaten on sexual approach and smaller males and females do not.

In a group of lizards with well-developed male bluffing behavior, much less homosexual activity is seen. In another group, in which the female has a characteristic humpbacked posture, males not showing such a posture may nevertheless be courted.

According to Greenberg and Noble (1944), the American chameleon, *Anolis,* may be one of the few lizards in which female homosexual behavior appears. One of their females showed indiscriminate male-like mounting combined with fairly severe biting, instead of the usual grip used by the male in mounting. Both MFH and FFH behavior were induced in female *Anolis* by implantation of testosterone proprionate. Six of eight females showed both types of homosexual behavior. Certain such treated females tended to be dominant in their cages. They were defeated and then copulated with by aggressive, sexually active males but not by other treated females. These dominant, treated females were the most active in aggression and also in male-like copulatory performance. Testosterone-treated castrate males were more aggressive, courted more, and copulated more than the control castrates. Such treated animals might show either the complete male or female copulatory pattern, depending on relative dominance positions.

Among nocturnal American geckos (Greenberg & Noble, 1944), active males must depend on contact cues for sex recognition. As in nocturnal amphibia, the preliminary stages of courtship are necessarily carried on indiscriminately. Usually a male approached by another male shows fight before much contact is made. The locomotor postures of the sexes are different. Anesthetized males may be courted, and males with female tails attached may have the tails courted.

Collared lizards are diurnal, establish territories, and show well-developed dominance–subordination behavior. Dominant males fight other males that show the conspicuous yellow throat patch. If subordinate males do not show the patch, they may be courted, especially if the dominant male approaches the subordinate from the rear. Since copulation among these lizards, as among the geckos, calls for considerable cooperation by the partner playing the feminine role, homosexual mating seems to be rare.

•

Birds show components of the sex-behavior patterns of reptiles, as might be expected of a class so closely related. The typical locomotion and posture of the courting male, the submissive-receptive crouch of the female, the male's neck grip, and even his treading action have their counterparts in lizards, the most generalized of present-day reptiles. Some pioneers in modern animal-behavior studies have used birds as their principal experimental form. Schjelderup-Ebbe and Allee, who made famous the "peck order" or social hierarchy, and Lorenz and his imprinted geese and ducks are a few who come to mind. The early work of the Chicago group—Koch, Gallagher, Domm, and their associates—is notable (Koch, 1939). They studied the effects of hormonal treatment of chick embryos and newborn chicks on their subsequent sex behavior.

Early in their studies of the pecking order, Allee and his group showed that one social-dominance system held for males and another for females but that any normal mature male was dominant over any female. High social rank among the males carried with it breeding rights (a kind of *droit de seigneur*), whereas high-ranking hens showed rather little breeding activity. Crucial male sex recognition or releaser cues were provided by facing the active rooster and erecting the hackles, whereas a female turned the other way and squatted. If a male happened to be in such a position while taking a dust bath or if he gave a crouching response to the wing-dragging courting waltz of a rooster, he might be mounted by the active male. Males low in the pecking order may be driven and trod upon to such an extent that they are killed or mutilated (Guhl, 1953).

Guhl also reports the conditions under which female homosexuality may appear in a flock of hens (1948). Five of forty-two hens observed took the male role in such behavior with twenty-seven passive hens. The active hens did not crow or waltz. In 173 of 181 homosexual matings, the mounting female was socially dominant to the one mounted. The passive female was either resting on the floor or dusting when the mating transpired. When cocks were present, they trod the active homosexual hens as females. The size of the combs of such active hens was no greater than average, and the hens themselves were in active laying condition at the time the observations were made, which suggests no unusually high androgen titer.

Hale (1955) reports similar findings for sexually aroused turkey hens, which were able to bring passive females to "orgasm" and subsequent temporary reduction in sex motivation. Hale does not indicate whether the sex drive of the active hen was similarly reduced.

Many annually breeding wild birds show rather little homosexual behavior—perhaps because copulation normally occurs only between well-established partners and because establishment of such a pair takes a considerable length of time and a complex interaction of courtship behaviors. An intruding male may show female-submissive behavior in the presence of the holder of a territory. This behavior seemed evident in the finches studied by Hinde (1955).

In the zebra finch, as described by Morris (1954), a frustrated male shows female receptive behavior after thwarted copulation attempts and long, intense courtship. In several pairs, the males were mounted by their mates following such display. This display was not typical of the submissive display when one male is beaten by another, nor was it a typical juvenile pattern. Morris believes that the pseudo-female display may inhibit the female's tendency to flee when she is not ready to respond to courtship, or it may be a result of the male's tendency to flee in such a situation. He says that this pattern differs from that among the stickleback fish, in which pseudo-female behavior is the result of conflict between tendencies to attack and to mate.

Hormonally induced homosexuality in the fowl has been rather thoroughly studied. The normal cock is high in aggressiveness and sex behavior measures compared with the capon. The position in the pecking order and the amount of sexual behavior seem to be positively correlated, although they are probably not independent variables. A classical experiment was performed by Davis and Domm in 1943. They injected androgen into castrated and spayed fowl (capons and poulards) and estrogen into capons, poulards, and cocks. The complete male behavior pattern could be induced in capons by androgen but only with difficulty in poulards, which never reached copulation with the relatively small amounts of hormone used, although they did so in later experiments. Capons receiving estrogen showed the courtship wing flutter and copulated listlessly but did not crow. Poulards receiving estrogen lost aggression and crouched to receive the cock. Precocial development of male sex-behavior components can be induced in chicks by androgen treatment and increases directly in accord with dosage used. Estrogen introduced into four-day eggs led to the development of structural and behavioral

intersex conditions in genetic males. Degree of maleness correlated positively with position in the pecking order. The behavioral
range of the intersexes did not seem to include any part of the
female pattern but extended from neuter to normal male type.

•

Frequent homosexual activity has been described for all species of mammals of which careful observations have been made.
This behavior is so common in domestic stock as to attract little
notice from the husbandman, unless he chooses to use it for
some specific purpose. Cows in heat so frequently mount other
cows that the behavior is considered diagnostic of the oestrous
condition. Young bulls or steers are often used as "teasers" to
arouse mature bulls in preparation for the collection of ejacu-
lates for use in artificial insemination. As a matter of fact, if a
heifer has been used several times as a "teaser" for a bull, the
bull will then react more readily to a "teaser" of his own sex than
to a female.

Young (1961) describes oestrous mounting in twelve species of
animals ranging from the shrew to the chimpanzee. Many workers believe that high levels of estrogen predispose females to
homosexual mounting. Beach (1958) has presented data to show
that such mounting in the rat is more probably influenced by androgen than by estrogen. It is possible that in other species the
excess estrogens present at the time of oestrous mounting are
partly converted into androgenic metabolites. Other workers believe that androgens of adrenal origin are responsible for the
hormonal background of this behavior. Young (p. 1194) indicates
that male-like mounting behavior by oestrous females is only
one of eight possible categories of behavioral effects of gonad
hormones. In each sex there are thus two possible effects of the
two types of sex hormone (or $2^3 = 8$). Those categories pertinent to our present subject include feminine behavior induced in the male under either androgenic or estrogenic hormone influence and the reciprocal situation in the female.

The first such category is Young's Number Three (feminine
behavior shown by a male under androgen influence). The instances of this (FMH) behavior in rodents apparently occur in
the presence of supraphysiological doses of androgen. In other
cases of this behavior, the social conditioning of the dominance

hierarchy seems to be the predominant influence. I have noted occurrences of such behavior involving both the extrinsic androgen treatment and the social-dominance factors in the intact squirrel monkey.

Young's Category Number Four is FMH under estrogen influence. This behavior is notably difficult to obtain and often requires enormous dosages of estrogens in mammals. Some birds show such behavior more readily.

Young's Category Number Seven (MFH), masculine behavior shown by females under the influence of estrogens, has previously been discussed. That similar behavior (Young's Category Number Eight, also MFH) may be elicited under the influence of androgen is perhaps less surprising. It is the easiest of homosexual behavior to obtain under hormonal influences. Female rabbits show this behavior with females but return to the feminine role in the presence of males. Such behavior has been induced in sheep, cattle, and rats. It evidently requires more androgen, however, than the amount needed to restore normal male behavior in male castrates. In addition, this behavior in the female seems to be of lower incidence and strength than in the male.

Young and his co-workers have shown an "organizing" effect of prenatally administered androgens on female guinea pig reproductive structures and subsequent behavior. These pretreated intersexes could be easily induced to assume the male behavior pattern. Evidence from neonatally gonadectomized rodents, however, tends to demonstrate that the homologous hormone is not necessary for such organization. Such early deprived animals are as capable of showing the homologous sex pattern as much later castrates. Furthermore, female guinea pigs of a genetic strain that does not show male-like mounting cannot be induced to show homosexual behavior no matter what the hormone treatment. Relative size, innervation, and sensitivity of the clitoris in androgen-treated females have been too little studied in lower forms.

Most endocrinologists have failed to take into account the factors of both genetic predisposition for tissue reactivity and experiential factors of a psychological nature. Central among reactive structures must be the nervous system. That different centers and circuitry are involved in male and female behavior is in some ways an attractive assumption. Beach's work on the importance of the cerebral cortex for male behavior (1940), its lack of importance for the female (1944), and the reciprocal dependence of female behavior on hormone levels and balance are to the point. It must be kept in mind that both neural mechanisms are present in both sexes. Certain central structures like the hippocampus appear to be involved in both. Those di- and mesencephalic structures and pathways involved in penile erection in the male squirrel monkey (MacLean, Denniston, & Dua, 1961) may well be involved in clitoridean erection in the female.

At the present stage in our knowledge, little consideration has been given to the problems of what, when, and how intermediary structures are affected by gonad hormones and how these structures in turn affect behavior. The intermediary complex is called "soma or substrate" (Young, 1961, p. 1913). It is considered to be organized either innately (male rat—Beach, 1940) or through experience (guinea pig—Young, 1961). Hormones are regarded as nondirective activators of the otherwise organized system. *The difference between the effects of male hormones on female and male reactive somas is simply one of threshold, not of heterologous or homologous directive effects.*

Directive factors seem to include the genetic constitution of the soma and—increasingly as we ascend the taxonomic tree—contact with other animals, including types of early sex experience. Another factor suggested by Ford and Beach (1951, p. 140) is the "degree of need" or "strength of drive." This factor is particularly strong in a male that has been intensely aroused by a female but has not reached orgasm. When mating behavior in rodents is studied with arbitrarily determined observation periods, the male is often returned to a holding cage with other males after a test during which he has failed to reach orgasm. On return to the male cage, he will mount and be mounted by his fellow males. Under similar circumstances, females show similar homosexual activity but with lower incidence and intensity. The receptive females of many species will show male-like mounting of males that are sluggish or partly inadequate in courtship behavior. This behavior is, of course, reversible inversion, not homosexuality.

The dolphin has recently received attention because of its large and highly convoluted cerebral cortex. We might expect this interesting animal to show a corresponding variety of responses, including those of a sexual nature. According to Mc-Bride and Hebb (1948) and other observers, such is indeed the case. The mature male dolphin has perhaps as broad an array of self-stimulating methods as has the mature human male. The males show evidence of sexual excitation throughout the year. Much of this evidence is in the area of homosexual behavior. The male dominance hierarchy is closely related to size. Two sorts of homosexual activity were frequently observed among the larger males. They were apparent attempts at masturbation against the flanks of smaller, less dominant males and incipient intromission with such males. Such activity frequently follows arousal without climax in heterosexual activity.

Animals with highly developed and convoluted cortexes—the porpoises, monkeys, and apes—constitute a separate category in terms of their sex behavior. Homosexual relations are established fairly readily without overwhelming drive either of hormonal or immediate-stimulus source. Both male and female homosexual behavior is shown in the primates, but the former is more obvious and may go to apparent climax *per anum* (evidently rectal smears have not been made under these circumstances). This writer has frequently observed such activity in a colony of squirrel monkeys. The behavior was of two sorts. The commonest was between a mature male and a much smaller but also mature male. Both males were living with a colony of mature females. Often the dominant riding of the smaller male by the larger led to a sexual clasp and pelvic thrusting by the latter. No penetration was observed. Another homosexual situation was sometimes observed between two mature males of nearly equal dominance status after a standard erection presentation situation. In the squirrel monkey, dominance status may be established and maintained when the more dominant male presents his erect penis for inspection by the subordinate male. Ford and Beach (1951) report many instances of male homosexuality among such social primates as the baboons. The relationship is usually established between a mature male and a juvenile, with the latter being protected by the adult. Mutual genital manipulation during the mount is described, as is handling of the submissive male's penis by the dominant or by himself. The adoption of the feminine receptive posture, as in fish and lizards, may be a means of preventing aggression or of obtaining the satisfaction of other biological needs like food.

Female homosexual behavior seems to take the form of mutual grooming, including oral contacts with the external genitalia and occasional mounts. Such activity almost never includes pelvic thrusting.

This survey of homosexual activity among lower animals should serve to explode several widely held misconceptions. First, it certainly is not a uniquely human practice. It occurs in every type of animal that has been carefully studied. Second, it has little relation to hormonal or structural abnormality. Even as lowly an organism as the fish shows homosexuality related to social dominance subordination conditioning rather than to endocrine aberrations. It is behavioral preconditioning that is directive, with hormones playing a permissive or generalized activating role.

REFERENCES

Aronson, L. R. The sexual behavior of *Anura. Amer. Museum of Nat. Hist. Novitiate,* 1944, **6** (1250), 1-15.

Beach, F. A. Effects of cortical lesions upon the copulatory behavior of male rats. *J. compar. Psychol.,* 1940, **29,** 193-244.

Beach, F. A. Effects of injury to the cerebral cortex upon sexual receptive behavior in the female rat. *Psychosom. Med.,* 1944, **6,** 40-55.

Beach, F. A. *Hormones and behavior.* New York: Hoeber, 1958.

Blair, A. P. Isolating mechanisms in a complex of four species of toads. *Biol. Sympos.,* 1942, **6,** 235-249.

Coe, W. R. Divergent pathways in sexual development. *Sci.,* 1940, **91,** 175-182.

Davis, D. E., & Domm, L. V. The influence of hormones on sexual behavior in the domestic fowl. In *Essays in biology in honor of H. E. Evans.* Berkeley: Univer. California Press, 1943. Pp. 171-180.

Denniston, R. H. Quantification and comparison of sex drives in terms of a learned response. *J. comp. physiol. Psychol.,* 1954, **47,** 437-440.

Ford, C. S., & Beach, F. A. *Patterns of sexual behavior.* New York: Harper, 1951.

Greenberg, B., & Noble, G. K. Social behavior of the western banded gecko. *Physiol. Zool.,* 1944, **16,** 110-122.

Guhl, A. M. Unisexual mating in a flock of white Leghorn hens. *Trans. Kans. Acad. Sci.,* 1948, **5,** 107-111.

Guhl, A. M. Social behavior of the domestic fowl. *Tech. Bull. ag. exp. Sta. Kans. St. U.,* 1953, No. 73, 1-48.

Hale, E. B. Defects in sexual behavior as factors affecting fertility in turkeys. *Poultry Sci.,* 1955, **34,** 1059-1067.

Hinde, R. A. A comparative study of the courtship of certain finches. *Ibis,* 1955, **97,** 706-745, and **98,** 1-23.

Koch, F. C. The biochemistry of androgens. In E. Allan (Ed.), *Sex and internal secretions.* (2nd ed.) Baltimore: Williams & Wilkins, 1939. Pp. 807-845.

McBride, A. F., & Hebb, D. O. Behavior of the captive bottle-nose dolphin. *J. comp. physiol. Psychol.,* 1948, **41,** 111-123.

MacLean, P. D., Denniston, R. H., & Dua, S. Di- and mesencephalon loci involved in penile erection and seminal discharge. *Federation Proc.,* 1961, **20,** 331 C. (Abstract.)

Morris, D. Homosexuality in the ten-spined stickleback. *Behav.,* 1952, **4** (4), 233-261.

Morris, D. Reproductive behaviour of the zebra finch with special reference to pseudo-female behaviour and displacement activities. *Behav.,* 1954, **16,** 271-322.

Morris, D. The causation of pseudofemale and pseudomale behaviour: a further comment. *Behaviour,* 1955, **8,** 46-56.

Noble, G. K., & Bradley, H. T. The mating behavior of lizards; its bearing on the theory of sexual selection. *Ann. N.Y. Acad. Sci.,* 1933, **35,** 25-100.

Tavolga, W. N. Effects of gonadectomy and hypophysectomy on pre-spawning behavior in males of the gobioid fish, *Bathygobius soporator. Physiol. Zool.,* 1955, **28,** 218-233.

Verplanck, W. S. A glossary of some terms for use in the objective science of behavior. *Psychol. Rev. Suppl.,* **64,** 1.

Young, W. C. The hormones and mating behavior. In W. C. Young (Ed.), *Sex and internal secretions.* Vol. 2 (3rd ed.). Baltimore: Williams & Wilkins, 1961. Pp. 1173-1239.

3 Hormones and Homosexuality

WILLIAM H. PERLOFF

Homosexuality is defined in *Webster's Third New International Dictionary* as "(1) atypical sexuality characterized by manifestation of sexual desire toward a member of one's own sex. (2) erotic activity with a member of one's own sex—compare Lesbianism. (3a) a stage in normal psychosexual development occurring during prepuberty in the male and during adolescence in the female during which libidinal gratification is sought with members of one's own sex. (3b) the extent to which one's libido is fixated at a homoerotic level." It is interesting that even in this nonmedical dictionary, homosexuality is viewed in three separate and different frames of references. In the first definition, misdirected sexual *desire* is the controlling element. In the second, erotic *activity* with a member of one's own sex is central to the interpretation. In the third, homosexuality is described as a *stage of psychosexual development*. As we are about to consider some interrelationships between hormones and homosexuality, the definition of homosexuality we employ becomes a matter of prime importance.

44

Shall we include in this study only obligatory homosexuals, those who practice homosexuality exclusively and preferentially and refuse or are unable to engage in heterosexual activity? Or shall we also consider those individuals who, for reasons of temporary circumstance, practice homosexuality in passing but prefer heterosexual activity when possible and who return to heterosexual behavior when the environment allows—prisoners, for example? Should we also investigate persons with homosexual desires who, from fear of disapproval or punishment, do not indulge their sexual preferences? It may well be that we must also study subjects with latent homosexual impulses, desires of which they themselves may not be aware, which can often be recognized only after prolonged and intensive psychoanalysis. Kinsey and his collaborators (Kinsey, Pomeroy, Martin, & Gebhard, 1953) argue that we cannot think in terms of "normal" heterosexual and "abnormal" homosexual. They claim that 37 per cent of white males and 13 per cent of white females have had some overt homosexual experience between adolescence and old age. Only 4 per cent of white males and 1 per cent to 3 per cent of white females are exclusively homosexual throughout their lives with a wide range of sexual behavior in between the extremes of exclusive heterosexuality and exclusive homosexuality. There are, of course, many other variations from "normal" or "ideal" sexuality that we have not included in this preliminary discussion. It must be apparent from the beginning, then, that the kind of patient whose hormonal balance or imbalance we mean to investigate may vary from overtly homosexual to "normal," however that word is defined, and we must keep in mind, when reviewing the older literature, that most investigators were aware of, comprehended, and studied only manifest and obvious deviations from what was considered normal in that particular social structure at that particular time.

Another important problem of definition, namely the question of which hormones to study, also arises. Hormones circulate in the bloodstream in extremely small concentrations and, until recently, have not been identifiable quantitatively. Even today, certain hormones can be measured only in relatively gross fashion and sometimes only indirectly. Most studies performed in the past involved urinary excretory products of the basic sex or re-

lated steroids. Interpretation of these results is fraught with difficulty because many metabolic metamorphoses occur between
formation of a hormone within a gland, secretion from the gland,
binding to protein and transportation in the bloodstream, utilization within the body, degradation within the liver, and conversion into a form excretable by the kidney into the urine. So for
example, 17-ketosteroids have been measured widely in the urine
of men, women, and children, for a host of reasons, and these
values have also been used as a measure of androgenic status.
Some members of this group of substances, closely allied chemi-
cally, derive from testosterone, the "male sex hormone," others
from metabolic end-products of cortisone-like substances, and
still others from entirely different steroids like the estrogens, the
"female sex hormones." As a matter of fact, estrone itself is a 17-
ketosteroid. Consequently, urinary 17-ketosteroid levels are not
necessarily indicative of androgenic production in any particular
patient and may actually be misleading. In addition, recent evidence suggests that estrogens and androgens may actually inter-
convert within the body after production or exogenous administration. Studies of plasma testosterone levels versus urinary
17-ketosteroid excretion values in women with hirsutism point up
the absence of correlation between these determinations and emphasize again the dangers involved in ascribing undue importance to urinary hormone values. Nonetheless, most studies performed in the past have used urinary 17-ketosteroid levels as a
base-line measure of androgenicity. In some instances, investigators have painstakingly and laboriously determined the actual
androgen content of urine with bioassay techniques. Laudatory
as it may appear, even this difficult line of endeavor has led to
inaccuracies of interpretation, for at most only 10 per cent to 15
per cent of the androgen produced in the body is excreted via
the kidneys; the amount measured thus represents only a small
and varying moiety of the actually produced, circulating, and
utilized androgen.

There are other areas of confusion resulting from present-day
ignorance of endocrine mechanisms. For example, it has been
postulated that pituitary hormones of the follicle-stimulating
(FSH) type, luteinizing (LH) type, or luteotropic (LTH) type
might influence sexual behavior in important ways. Superficially,

this concept is quite attractive, for LTH is also the lactogenic hormone, considered by some to be the "maternal hormone," a term that is itself prejudicial. Unfortunately, determination of the levels and effects of these hormones involves biological procedures difficult to perform accurately, the end-points of which procedures differ in rats, mice, or pigeons from humans. Because a bioassay depends on the stimulating effect of a hormone on appropriate morphologic sexual characteristics in test animals, it does not follow that a specified biologically active compound will be equally potent in its stimulating effect on *all* secondary sexual characteristics. It must be apparent, then, that direct measurements of hormone levels in blood and urine, including gland secretory rates, present the investigator with a prodigious and, at present, insoluble problem. There are, of course, such indirect methods of measurement as deprivation of hormones by removing the producing gland and restitution of hormonal levels by exogenous administration of pure hormone, which have great clinical value and which we shall discuss later in this chapter.

It must be clear by now that, despite intense and widespread interest in the possible influence of hormones on sexual behavior, this type of research has proved to be extremely frustrating and disappointing, particularly as, after the discovery of the role of gonads as producers of hormones and specifically after the isolation, purification, and synthesis of the steroid hormones, biologists believed that a simple explanation of sexual behavior was at last available.

Many observers have noted that sexual behavior in animals is species specific and that these typical sexual patterns can be eliminated or so altered by castration that copulation is no longer attempted. After purified steroid hormones became available for experimental use, it became apparent that estrogenic materials administered to the castrate female animal are often able to reestablish her sexual pattern and that androgenic materials administered to the castrate male animal are similarly effective. When it became possible to evaluate endogenous production of hormones, it was observed that in lower animals females mate only when estrogen production is at its height. This finding lent further support to the thesis that sexual behavior is under direct and specific hormonal control. Observations of the mating behavior of higher animals revealed some weaknesses in this concept, particularly in regard to the chimpanzee. The subject female chimpanzee would mate at any phase of her cycle and often continued to engage in the sex act even though castrated. The castrate male chimpanzee would seek the female and copulate or attempt to copulate with her. There seemed to be a breaking away from the strict hormonal control of sexual behavior in higher animals. Despite these observations, the hormonal theory of sexual regulation was widely held, perhaps because of its apparent simplicity, as recently as the late 1940's (Perloff, 1949).

To demonstrate the relationship between a biologic process and the activity of a particular hormone, it is necessary that the process be slowed or eliminated following deprivation of the hormone and that it be re-established with exogenous administration of the pure hormone. It is possible, by studying patients with sexual or endocrine disorders, to make a series of such observations. It must be remembered that, in the normal male, androgens are produced by both the testicle and adrenal glands, although in females the ovaries may at times produce variable amounts of androgen, occasionally extremely large amounts.

Case 1. J.L., a thirty-one-year-old white male, was referred to the endocrine clinic because of eunuchism. He appeared younger than his age and had no facial and very little axillary and pubic hair. His span (178.0 cm.) exceeded his height (168.0 cm.), and his pubis-to-floor measurement (91.6 cm.) was greater than his pubis-to-vertex measurement (76.4 cm.). His testicles were pea-sized, and his penis was the size of a preadolescent boy's. Urinary 17-ketosteroids were low, 2.3 mg. per twenty-four hours, and gonadotropins were undetectable. A BMR was minus 23 per cent, and there was roentgenologic evidence of delay in bone age. He presented the typical picture of a pituitary eunuch in whom sexual adolescence had not occurred.

Despite his endocrine immaturity, he was able to have erections and orgasmic experiences but no ejaculations. He was physically attracted to women and desired to have sexual intercourse with them but was unable to complete the sex act satisfactorily because of the small size of his penis. Ashamed of his failures, he had ceased to seek the company of women. The administration of large amounts of androgenic material in the form of testosterone pellets enlarged his penis so that he felt more confidence in his ability to perform sexually. According to the patient, his emotional need for sexual contact did not increase but actually became a less pressing matter from a psychological point of view. He reported an increase in the sensitivity of his penis to stimulation, so that sexual arousal was easier than it had been previous to therapy, and also a feeling of warmth in both the penis and the scrotum. He was able to have ejaculations, and their volume increased gradually—which is not surprising in view of the fact that the production of fluid by the seminal vesicles and prostate depends on androgenic stimulation. In this connection, it is interesting that tumescence of the penis can occur without androgens, although erections may not be complete and long lasting.

This patient, without benefit of gonadal hormones experienced libidinous urges toward members of the opposite sex and was able to achieve erections and orgasms. Treatment with androgens enlarged his penis and increased its sensitivity to stimulation but in no way augmented his libidinous urge. His sexual interest was not homosexual either before or after therapy.

It should be emphasized that pituitary eunuchs are generally impotent and lack libido. This patient is somewhat unusual and is described here because of his relatively normal sexual emotions despite gonadal deficiency. This attitude may have been in part due to the fact that he had had the advantage of therapy with a psychologist and may therefore have learned to accept his physical defect and to adjust to it. In any event, his case helps to illustrate the difference between libido and potency and demonstrates the fact that libido, the psychological urge to have sexual contact with members of the opposite sex, may be present in the absence of gonadal hormone production. Potency, defined as the ability to perform the complete sex act, was, however, impaired to the point of inability to achieve complete ejaculation. The administration of androgen to this patient increased his potency but did not appear to materially affect his libidinous urge.

The second illustrative case involves a similar condition in a female.

•

Case 2. G.N., a twenty-four-year-old Japanese girl, was referred to the endocrine clinic with the chief complaint of primary amenorrhea. Physical examination revealed absence of breast tissue, a hypoplastic vagina and uterus, and a small tuft of pubic hair surrounding the labia. Her height was normal, and she demonstrated no other stigmata of Turner's syndrome. Bioassay of a twenty-four-hour specimen of urine revealed absence of estrogens and more than 250 mouse units of gonadotropins. At laparotomy, a normal but small uterus was found with normal tubes. No ovaries were observed, but in their place bilaterally one could see a 3 cm.-long genital ridge approximately ½ cm. in diameter, confirming the diagnosis of ovarian dysgenesis. Implantation of two pellets of alpha-estradiol, 25 mg. each, subcutaneously, resulted in growth of the breasts, development of the vagina and uterus, increase in the amount of pubic hair, and uterine bleeding, further substantiating the diagnosis.

She readily admitted a strong sexual attraction toward men. Her libidinous urge was, in fact, so strong that it caused her much distress, and she claimed to be in a state of almost continuous sexual arousal. Erotic emotions resulted from the mere proximity of men, and physical contact was not necessary to evoke these reactions. Because of the absence of breasts and menstrual periods and her consequent feelings of shame and inferiority, she had attempted no heterosexual relationships, but masturbation was completely satisfactory and uniformly resulted in orgasm. Therapy with estrogenic pellets in no way influenced her sexual desires but made her feel more normal because of the consequent improvement in her figure.

This patient, who exhibited neither the physical signs resulting from the production of estrogens nor the usual traces of excreted estrogens, nevertheless experienced sexual urges that were at least equal to those of intact adult women and had actually been pathologically intensified. Therapy with estrogenic material succeeded in developing certain secondary sexual characteristics, including breasts and vagina, but had no influence on the sexual urge. It is interesting that her sex object was always masculine. This patient, like the first patient, was atypical, as many women with ovarian agenesis do appear to have diminished or absent libidos. The interest in this case lies primarily in the augmented libidinous drive despite congenitally absent ovaries and estrogen production.

This young woman was studied before the advent of cellular sex-typing, but subsequent patients, similar in every way, have been evaluated in this fashion and have shown forty-five chromosomes (XO) in addition to ovarian dysgenesis, some with typical Turner's stigmata, indicating that, even with an abnormality of nuclear sex, normal libidinous drives may be present.

It may be argued that ovarian remnants in some of these patients produce enough estrogen to influence sexual behavior. It is, however, common experience that menopause, whether spontaneous or surgical, need exert no adverse influence on either libidinous urge or ability to engage in satisfactory sexual relations. It is well known and has been reported frequently that many women enjoy intercourse for the first time after cessation of menses, even after surgical menopause, possibly because they no longer fear pregnancy. Furthermore, human females mate at any phase of the menstrual cycle, regardless of the level of circulating estrogens. Many women report that sexual intercourse is most satisfactory just before the menstrual period when pelvic congestion is at its height and estrogen production at its lowest level. Kinsey, Pomeroy, Martin, and Gebhard (1948, 1953) report orgasms in boys of every age from five months to adolescence and in a female infant of four months, when production of gonadal hormones must certainly be extremely small. It may be reasoned, particularly in the case of mature women with ovarian dysgenesis or menopause, that the adrenal glands are producing high levels of estrogen. Bioassay of the urine of these patients, however, usually reveals no estrogenic activity, in addition to which urinary gonadotropins are markedly elevated, indicating that the level of estrogen circulating in such patients must be low indeed. This finding can often be confirmed by the absence of cornification of the vaginal mucosa.

From these observations, it seems that, in the human being, libido and potency may be present and even normal when gonadal hormones are diminished or absent. This finding implies that such hormones are not essential to the libidinous urge, although, as we shall see, they may indirectly influence libido and *potentia* by affecting the sensitivity of the phallus.

Impotence and Frigidity

During the past fifteen years, certain patients on whom bioassays had been performed were questioned about libido and sexual activity. Some were in psychotherapy or psychoanalysis. Except for some eunuchoid men, in whom the gonadal production of androgens was deficient (as attested by undeveloped secondary sexual characteristics) and in whom levels of urinary 17-ketosteroids were occasionally but by no means universally depressed, there was no correlation between the level of 17-ketosteroids and sexual ability. It is interesting that several patients whose urinary 17-ketosteroids were extremely low were normally active sexually and that some male patients whom we were studying primarily because of impotence demonstrated above-average levels of urinary 17-ketosteroids. It is also noteworthy that males with normal or low 17-ketosteroid output and low libido often demonstrated other psychological manifestations that would have marked them as neurotic and inadequate individuals in any event. The coincidence of low libido and low 17-ketosteroid excretion is not uncommon in a wide variety of chronic debilitating diseases. It should be emphasized once again that excretion of 17-ketosteroids in urine does not necessarily bear any direct relationship to the amount of circulating testosterone, and it is possible and, in fact, even likely that we are not measuring the correct and appropriate substance for our purposes. It is of the greatest importance that circulating plasma testosterone be measured in large groups of normal and impotent males.

Frigidity in females appears to bear even less relationship to the excretion of estrogenic substances in urine. Postmenopausal women whose libidos had previously been adequate and who have suffered declines in sexual urge with the onset of the *climacterium* are often favorably affected by administration of exogenous estrogen. This effect, we believe, is at least partly the result of improvement in the general state of physical and emotional health rather than of any specific sexual change. Nonetheless, the rapid return of normal libido in certain menopausal women under treatment with potent estrogens is occasionally striking. We have no definite information on this phenomenon but suspect that it is related to the increased vascularity and epithelial proliferation of the genital tract, which occur as the result of adequate estrogenic administration rather than to any direct effect on sexuality. In this connection, two other patients are interesting.

Case 3. R.S. had had a panhysterectomy eight years before at the age of forty. Her husband had died shortly after the operation, and the patient reported complete absence of libido since. The subcutaneous implantation of one pellet containing 25 mg. of alpha-estradiol resulted not only in relief of her flushes and other menopausal complaints but also in return of her libidinous urge. At the same time, her breasts became lumpy and painful, and she noted a sense of warmth in the vagina. After two weeks, there was gradual recession in both breast and vaginal symptoms and also in the bothersome sexual desires.

Case 4. P.L. underwent spontaneous menopause at the age of fifty years with amenorrhea, flushes, and loss of libido. The administration of 0.05 mg. of ethinyl estradiol daily relieved her flushes and caused a return of libido. After ten weeks of therapy, she reported a sudden marked increase in her libidinous urge associated with pelvic pain and a sense of pelvic fullness. Three days later she commenced bleeding from the uterus, which lasted eight days. After the third day of bleeding, the patient noted relief from the pelvic pain and a decrease in her sexual desires. A similar episode occurred in the same patient three months later, while under the same therapy.

Estrogens have never been observed by us to increase libido in menopausal women who had been frigid prior to the onset of the *climacterium.* Administration of large amounts of estrogen to young frigid women has also not, in our experience, resulted in any significant improvement in the libidinous urge.

In this connection, experience with administration of large doses of androgen to women is of interest. It has been observed that women who receive large amounts of testosterone in the treatment of metastatic carcinoma of the breast often experience an increase in libido. This change occurs coincidentally with development of acne, hirsutism, and hypertrophy of the clitoris. Such patients report a sense of warmth in the clitoral region similar to that of the penis and scrotum described by men who have received large amounts of androgenic materials. Close questioning reveals that it is not primarily the libido—the psychological sexual urge—that is increased but the sensitivity of the affected erotic area. This increased sensitivity is perhaps not unexpected, in view of the augmented vascularity that develops in both the clitoris and penis as the result of androgenic administration. Androgens appear to act primarily on the somatic and only secondarily on the psychic aspect of this psychosomatic relationship. On the other hand, Waxenberg, Drellich, and Sutherland (1959) have reported that, although there is no effect on sexual drive, activity, and response with oöphorectomy, there is diminished or abolished libido after adrenalectomy, which they ascribe to loss of adrenal androgens. This hypothesis is only inferential, for no one has as yet measured circulating testosterone or androgens in such patients. It must also be remembered that adrenalectomy itself is a major surgical procedure and is usually performed only in patients suffering from metastatic carcinoma of the breast or other serious disease. This disorder can react unfavorably on the libidos of women by virtue, not only of the debilitating process, but also, and perhaps more important, of the psychological implications.

When estrogens are administered in large amounts to men, decreases in penile sensitivity (usually described in the literature as "diminished libido") are reported almost uniformly. Such decreases are coincidental with lowering of urinary 17-ketosteroid excretions, diminution in size of testicles and prostates, and decrease in spermatogenesis.

Case 5. J.L., a fifty-four-year-old white male, volunteered for this study. Except for traumatic arthritis of the hips, he was completely healthy. A pretreatment bioassay yielded thirteen mouse units of estrogen, twenty-eight mouse units of gonadotropins, and 6.9 mg. of 17-ketosteroids per twenty-four-hour specimen of urine. Examination of his seminal fluid revealed 361,000,000 spermatozoa per ml., with 75 per cent motility. His libido and potency were normal.

After administration of 0.7 mg. of estradiol benzoate daily by injection for twenty consecutive days, his breasts became enlarged, nodular, and painful; his testicles became smaller, and his prostate was reduced slightly in size. He was unable to produce a specimen of seminal fluid for comparison and claimed that there was no feeling in his penis and that he could not achieve an erection. At this time urinary estrogens had increased to sixty-seven mouse units, gonadotropins were unchanged, and 17-ketosteroids had fallen to 3.4 mg. per twenty-four hours. He became quite disturbed emotionally because, although he desired sexual intercourse with his wife, he was unable to perform satisfactorily. This situation persisted for six weeks after cessation of therapy, after which there was gradual improvement and return to normality.

He was persuaded to repeat the experiment, but unknown to him 100 mg. of testosterone proprionate was added to the 0.7 mg. of estradiol benzoate which he received daily by injection for twenty consecutive days. This time, it is interesting to note, there was little, if any, effect on penile sensitivity and on his ability to have normal sexual intercourse with his wife, although he did complain of painful breasts. We were unable to obtain a seminal specimen for comparison with the original one.

It seems, therefore, that the simultaneous administration of sufficient testosterone prevents the expected decrease in penile sensitivity. It appears that estrogen, in the male, acts both to depress normal androgenic production and to antagonize the penile-sensitizing effect of androgen.

It is important to keep clearly in mind the difference between libidinous urge, which is largely psychological and is influenced relatively little by hormones, and end-organ sensitivity, which may be directly affected by hormonal substances. This end-organ sensitivity may be increased by exogenous administration of androgens in both sexes and perhaps of estrogens in certain estrogen-deficient females. Except for certain menopausal women, in whom the beneficial effect is both general and to some extent local on the genital tract, not primarily on the psychosexual apparatus, estrogens cannot be expected to exert any favorable effect on frigidity. Testosterone in large, unphysiological amounts occasionally yields good results with frigidity, but undesirable secondary side effects (acne, hirsutism, enlargement of the clitoris) must be expected.

Homosexuality

Estradiol, among its many other metabolic effects, causes growth of the breasts and development of the vagina and uterus. In most animals, it is produced in larger amounts by the female than by the male and has been called the "female sex hormone." Similarly, because of its effects in producing growth of the penis and accessory genital organs and because it is secreted in greater quantities by the male, testosterone has been called the "male sex hormone." This terminology is unfortunate, and to a great extent misleading, because it suggests incorrect concepts and leads to faulty reasoning. As a matter of fact, the stallion produces more estrogenic material than any other animal known, and, had estrogen been isolated first in this animal, it might very well now be called the "male sex hormone."

Homosexuality was, for many years, considered a manifestation of endocrine imbalance, and published reports purported to prove that abnormal ratios of androgen to estrogen might be the basis for homosexual behavior. The following examples illustrate our experience and the opposite point of view.

Case 6. E.S., a twenty-seven-year-old white woman, was referred by a psychiatrist because of homosexual activities. Menses were regular, and she ovulated normally as determined by basal body temperature charts and cervical mucus changes. She had been married five years, was fond of her husband, but was unable to have enjoyable sexual relations with him, although she claimed easy sexual arousal in the presence of attractive women. Physical examination was normal in every respect, and her hormonal pattern was well within the range for women found in our laboratory. Repeated urinary estrogens were actually high normal at times, between sixty-seven and 133 mouse units per twenty-four hours; gonadotropins varied between a trace and thirty-three mouse units; 17-ketosteroids were 11.5 and 12.9 mg.

Case 7. I.H., a twenty-four-year-old white male, was referred by a psychiatrist because of homosexual practices. The patient had long been suspicious of his own masculinity and had attempted heterosexual intercourse several times to test his virility. These experiences were not satisfactory, but numerous homosexual contacts were.

The patient was tall (72¼″) and thin (164 lbs.), intelligent, and with some insight into his own psychological difficulty. He showed arachnodactyly, prominent forehead, laxity of ligaments, congenital subluxation of the lens, and a high arched palate. A diagnosis of Marfan's syndrome was therefore made. His genitalia and hair distribution were normal. A BMR was plus 2 per cent, and blood cholesterol was 185 mg./100 ml. Blood count, urinalysis, and glucose-tolerance test were all normal. Hormone assays of a twenty-four-hour urine specimen showed thirteen mouse units of estrogen, twenty-three mouse units of gonadotropins, and 17.8 mg. of 17-ketosteroids, all perfectly normal levels.

This patient, because of his congenital defects and homosexual interests, considered himself endocrinologically a homosexual. Normal studies proved that such was not the case. Therapy by a competent psychiatrist has helped him to gain further insight into his problem and has resulted in psychosexual improvement.

In our experience, no patient, either male or female, has shown any consistent reversal of endocrine pattern to explain homosexual tendencies. We have never observed any correlation between the choice of sex object and the level of hormonal excretion. Estrogenic substances administered to homosexual females do not alter either the sexual drive or the choice of sex object. Large doses of estrogens administered to male homosexuals occasionally reduce their sexual drives but do not influence the choice of sex object. The mechanism of this decrease in sex urge is, we believe, the repressive effect of estrogen on the patient's own testicular function, with decrease in production of androgen and concurrent lowering of penile sensitivity. Androgenic substances, particularly testosterone, do not change the choice of sex object of either male or female homosexuals. They do, however, when employed in large amounts, tend to increase the sexual activity of females and hypogonadal males.

These observations lead us to believe that steroid hormones of the estrogenic and androgenic types have nothing to do with the choice of sex object and therefore with the determination of homosexuality. Therapy with these substances may occasionally affect the sexual urge but should not be expected to exert beneficial effects on the course of homosexuality.

"Sexual Mannerisms" and Aggressive Behavior

Case 8. S.C., a fourteen-year-old Negro boy, was referred to the endocrine clinic because of "feminine mannerisms and behavior." A right atrophic abdominal testicle had been removed previously. He was an extremely graceful boy with long tapering fingers and delicate facial features. His movements and posture were quite feminine, and his manner of speaking was precise and of the type popularly associated with male homosexuals.

Results of physical examination were normal for a fourteen-year-old male. There was abundant pubic hair and beginning growth of facial hair. The left testicle was normal in size and consistency and in the scrotum, and the penis was well developed. Hormone assays of a twenty-four-hour specimen of urine were well within the normal range for his age group. Urinary estrogens were less than thirteen mouse units, there was a trace of gonadotropins, and 17-ketosteroids were 6.6 mg. He had experienced erections and nocturnal emissions and had, in fact, had satisfactory sexual experiences with several women.

He was deeply religious and had recently determined "to give up the ways of the evil world" and devote himself to the service of the church. He did not hear voices or have visual hallucinations but considered himself "different from other boys." An interview with his father was extremely interesting in that both the physical and emotional similarities were immediately striking.

Case 9. K.R., a fifteen-year-old white female, was referred by a psychiatrist because working papers were required, and her sex was in doubt. She had been considered a girl at birth because on examination neither testicles nor scrotum had been found and a small orifice, where the vagina would ordinarily be, had been present. She had been reared as a girl, and there had been little question of her sex until six months prior to this examination, when, because of some growth of facial hair, enlargement of the clitoris, and slight deepening of the voice, doubts arose in the minds of her teachers and parents. The patient's primary concern was that she had never menstruated.

On physical examination, she appeared to be her stated age. She was feminine in both attitude and mannerisms, was engaged to be married, and considered herself a woman. There was complete absence of breast tissue. A few hairs could be seen on the chin, but only a small amount of axillary hair was present. Pubic hair was abundant, but only a few isolated hairs extended up the middle of the abdomen. The genital organ was either an enlarged clitoris or a very small penis, and a small urethral orifice was present in the perineal region. In each labial or scrotal fold, a small pea-sized nodule was palpable. These felt like small atrophic testicles and proved to be so on histological examination. Bioassay revealed estrogens of thirty mouse units, 17-ketosteroids of 4.8 mg., and more than 125 mouse units of gonadotropins per twenty-four hours (castrate level). A specimen of buccal mucosa was stained for nuclear sexing and was found to be of the male type. Laparotomy revealed no uterus and no adnexae.

This patient was interviewed extensively by a psychiatrist and studied intensively by a psychologist, both of whom agreed that psychological identification was so intensely fixed toward femaleness that it would be a gross error to attempt to change her physical sexual orientation toward maleness. Accordingly, the small testicles were removed from the scrotum; she was treated with estrogen to develop her breasts, and an artificial vagina was constructed. Despite the fact that her genital status was explained to her repeatedly and she was told on many occasions that she could never bear children, she married and became quite concerned when she did not become pregnant after several months. Her recurring dreams at that time involved giving birth to twins, one male and one female. It was the opinion of both the psychiatrist and the psychologist that these dreams referred to the ambiguity of her own sexuality. Because she did not conceive, she divorced her husband and remarried. We lost contact with the patient at that time. In any event, this patient was an interesting combination of the genetic male, the psychological female, and the hormonal castrate. (Perloff & Brody, 1951.)

The opinion has been widely held that a patient's hormonal pattern might be deduced by observation of his behavior. The two patients just described are evidence that such is not the case. Careful psychological and endocrinological evaluation of patients whose mannerisms seem inconsistent with their somatic or nuclear sex patterns has never shown an abnormality of endocrine function. In those patients with whom psychiatric investigation has been possible, the importance of psychological factors has been evident. Except for those with clear hormonal disturbance, it has been impossible for us to prognosticate a patient's hormonal status from physical examination, by observation of his behavior, or by psychological evaluation. Our conclusion, therefore, has been that the so-called "sex hormones" are not important in the determination of "sexual mannerisms" and attitudes.

Many reports have described the "increase in aggression" that occurs in male eunuchs treated with androgenic substances, as well as in some female patients with Cushing's syndrome or the adrenogenital syndrome. We have been unable to reconcile these observations with our own, for some of the most aggressive individuals we have encountered have been untreated eunuchs, and many patients whose psychological aggression is minimal, in terms of social behavior and psychiatric evaluation, show normal or even increased amounts of 17-ketosteroids in their urine. It must be admitted, particularly in the instance of women with the adrenogenital syndrome, that the development of facial and body hair, the reduction of breast size, and the disappearance of menses may confirm the patient's previously existing suspicion that some abnormality of sexuality exists, but, so far as we can determine, there is no direct effect of abnormal hormonal production upon aberrant sexual orientation. This conclusion, we believe, is confirmed by the absence of abnormal sexual orientation in other patients with the adrenogenital syndrome who excrete large amounts of 17-ketosteroids in the urine.

Considerable confusion exists in the literature concerning the difference between lowered aggression and decreased work potential incident to reduction in strength resulting from androgen deficiency. It is certainly true that male patients who have inadequate androgenic production often show decreases in strength and therefore in productive capacity. Administration of testosterone to such patients usually improves their work tolerance, but whether it influences their aggressive drives is a matter of question. It is important in evaluating such factors that the endocrinologist and psychiatrist study the patient together. Otherwise, it is easy to confuse the primary psychological changes with those that are secondary to physical improvement.

Discussion

Money, in his excellent paper entitled "Sex Hormones and Other Variables in Human Eroticism" (1961), describes seven sex variables in hermaphroditic patients: "(1) nuclear sex, i.e., the sex-chromatin pattern of cell nuclei, or the actual chromosome count; (2) gonadal sex; (3) hormonal sex and pubertal feminization or virilization; (4) the internal accessory reproductive structures; (5) external genital morphology; (6) sex of assignment and rearing; (7) gender role and sexual orientation established while growing up." Money concludes that cognitional rehearsals are paramount in determining the direction of erotic inclination in hermaphrodites and that erotic outlook and orientation are psychological phenomena independent of genes or hormones.

The Hampsons (Hampson & Hampson 1961), while elaborating on these variables in their paper entitled "The Ontogenesis of Sexual Behavior in Man," explain,

> By the term, *gender role,* is meant all those things that a person says or does to disclose himself or herself as having the status of a boy or man, girl or woman, respectively. It includes, but is not restricted to sexuality in the sense of eroticism. Gender role is appraised in relation to the following: general mannerisms, deportment and demeanor; play preferences and recreational interests; spontaneous topics of talk in unprompted conversation and casual comment; content of dreams, daydreams, and fantasies; replies to oblique inquiries and projective tests; evidence of erotic practice and finally, the person's own replies to direct inquiry. Lest there be misunderstanding, the term *gender role* is not identical and synonymous with

the term *sex of assignment and rearing.* Sex status can be assigned
to a child by parental, medical, or legal decision. The psychologic
phenomenon which we have termed gender role, or psychosexual
orientation, evolves gradually in the course of growing up and
cannot be assigned or discarded at will. The components of gender
role are neither static nor universal. They change with the times
and are an integral part of each culture and subculture. Thus one
may expect important differences in what is to be considered typical and appropriate masculine or feminine gender role as displayed
by a native of Thailand and a native of Maryland, or as displayed
by the pioneer contemporaries of Peter Stuyvesant and by their de-
scendants in Westchester County suburbia of the 1960's (p. 1406).

For the purposes of this chapter, we have combined, perhaps
somewhat inaccurately, these seven categories into three divi-
sions: genetic, hormonal, and psychological. Our genetic classification includes nuclear sex and, where applicable, gonadal sex,
internal accessory reproductive structure, and external genital morphology. Hormonal sex includes the hormonal secretory pattern,
which may at times influence internal accessory reproductive structure and external genital morphology. Our psychological classification includes sex of assignment and rearing and gender role in
sexual orientation established while growing up.

Margaret Mead (1961) discusses the cultural determinants of
sexual behavior:

All known human societies recognize the anatomic and functional
differences between males and females in intricate and complex
ways; through insistence on small nuances of behavior in posture,
stance, gait, through language, ornamentation and dress, division of
labor, legal, social status, religious role, etc. In all known societies
sexual dimorphism is treated as a major differentiating factor of any
human being, of the same order as difference in age, the other universal of the same kind. However, where in contemporary America
only two approved sex roles are offered to children, in many societies there are more. The commonest sex careers may be classified
as:

1. Married female who will bear children and care for her children.

2. Married male who will beget and provide for his children.

3. Adult male who will not marry or beget children but who

will exercise some prescribed social function, involving various forms of celibacy, sexual abstinence, renunciation of procreation, specialized forms of ceremonial sexual license, or exemption from social restrictions placed on other men.

4. Adult female who will neither marry nor bear children and who will have a recognized status in a religious context or in society (nuns, temple prostitutes, spinsters, etc.).

5. Persons whose special, nonprocreative ceremonial role is important, roles in which various forms of transvestism and adoption of the behavior of the opposite sex are expected, so that the external genital morphology is either ignored or denied, e.g., shamans, etc.

6. Adult males who assume female roles, including transvestism, where this adult sexual career is open only to males.

7. Adult females who assume male roles, including transvestism, where this adult sexual career is open only to females.

8. Sexually mutilated persons, where the mutilation may be congenital or socially produced (e.g. eunuchs) and where the sex behavior includes specific expectations of nonmarriage, nonparenthood, relaxation of taboos on ordinary relationships between the sexes, etc. (eunuchs, choir boys, etc.).

9. Prostitution, in which the adult individual maintains herself (or less frequently himself) economically by the exploitation of sex relationships with extramarital partners.

10. Zoolagnia, a social role combined with a sex preference for an animal (shepherd and sheep).

11. Age-determined sex roles, as where homoerotic behavior is expected of adolescents, or withdrawal from all sex relationships expected from older heads of households, etc., or license is expected before marriage and fidelity afterward, or chastity before marriage and indulgence after marriage, or where widows are expected neither to remarry nor to engage in any further sex relationships.

Any or all of these adult roles may occur in the same society, and the possibility of a child's choosing or being thrust into any of these roles will also be present wherever the role is widely recognized, whether or not the recognition is positively or negatively weighted. Preparation for a life of celibacy and religious devotion begins early in those societies where the monastic life is a common choice; among those American Indians who recognized the *berdache*, or transvestite male, as a likely career, male children were watched and tested from an early age—were they going to be "braves" or "live like women"? Once the choice was made, elaborate prescriptions of correct social behavior were available. But among a people where there is no recognition of any other possibility than 1, 2, and 11, the same sorts of indicators of possible cross sex identification which, among the Plains Indians would assure a boy's being classified and reared as a transvestite, will go unnoticed and uninstitutionalized. The fuller the social repertoire the more possible it is to carry a knowledge of the role in the absence of any person to fill it (pp. 1451-1452).

In his paper entitled "The Hormones and Mating Behavior," Young (1961) concludes:

In the adult, and possibly in the neonatal and sexually immature animal as well, there is no evidence that the hormones have any effect on the organization of the tissues mediating mating behavior. Genetical factors are of obvious importance and account for the differences between species, for the differences between sexes, and, in subhuman species if not in man as well, for many of the differences between individuals. Psychologic or experiential factors are also important, and, as with genetical factors, the extent depends on the species and the sex. But, in contrast to the genetical factors, the influence of psychologic factors is greater in the higher than in the lower mammals (p. 1222).

It is clear from these quotations that many experts in the field of sexuality minimize the importance of hormonal action on human sexuality. Our own conclusions agree with this point of view. The gonadal hormones have a wide range of action. They influence protein metabolism, calcium utilization, and salt retention and have a host of other functions, in addition to their effect on the sexual apparatus. The biological activity of testosterone and estradiol, the so-called "sex hormones," is required for growth and maturation of organs employed in the sex act. These hormones also assist in developing such secondary sexual characteristics as breasts and uterus in the female and facial hair and deepened voice in the male. Testosterone produces, in addition, growth of the prepubertal penis and hypertrophy of the clitoris and an associated augmentation of their sensitivity to mechanical stimulation. Estrogens act upon the vagina and clitoris to cause complete epithelialization and increased vascularization. It is not apparent, from our observations, that these steroid hormones have any other important effect on sexuality.

Their physiological role in the body is predetermined by a specific genetic pattern, and they act only on tissues that are receptive. In the infants reported by Kinsey *et al.*, in whom local stimulation caused erotic arousal to the point of orgasm, there can hardly be any important influence of gonadal hormones, for, as far as we are aware, these substances are not produced in significant amounts during infancy. Despite this fact, the sexual pattern of these infants included the three important components of adult sexual behavior: tumescence of the organ, rhythmic pelvic thrusts, and the intense neuromuscular reaction known as orgasm. It is too early in the life of an infant for this behavior pattern to have been learned, so that we are left with the conclusion that this typical human sexual reaction is dependent on neuromuscular pathways and anatomical structures present in the infant at birth. Proper and suitable stimulation appears to evoke from these infants, as from adults, a series of reactions typical of the human species. An analogous situation is the unlearned sucking and grasping reflexes that can be elicited from infants.

With the growth and social development of the child, another important influence is introduced. This factor is imitative and learned, and the course of its development depends on the society and culture in which the individual lives. This psychological aspect assumes an increasingly important role as the individual progresses chronologically, and the influence of patterns learned in infancy and childhood is felt constantly during adult sexual life.

Children of male sex are soon dressed in accepted male fashion, are given boys' haircuts, are encouraged to play boys' games, and in general are raised very differently from their sisters. Very early they are taught acceptable male behavior and are ridiculed by other children and even by adults if they desire to engage in activities considered suitable only for their sisters. Their experiences, conscious or subconscious, real or fantasied, affect the development of the psychological aspects of sexuality. The effects of these experiences have been shown to have wide and varied expression, and sexual behavior is often markedly influenced by the manner in which the problems resulting from these deep-seated experiences have been resolved.

Despite these arguments, it is inappropriate to leave this subject without first considering the other side of the coin. All evidence furnished to the present time is inferential. No one has actually measured accurately levels of circulating estrogens, androgens, and pituitary hormones in the blood of large numbers of men, women, and children under simultaneous observation by competent psychiatrists and psychologists, interested in their psychosexual status, and it is unlikely that such measurement will be done in the foreseeable future. The reasons for not performing this definitive and important experiment include the present unavailability of satisfactory laboratory techniques, the tremendous expense of salaries for large numbers of professional personnel, the great effort and long time required, and the likelihood that the experiment would conclude with negative results. Finally, even if all known hormones were carefully measured, the argument that some important unknown hormone is related to psychosexuality could not be refuted.

Summary

A reasonable approach to the problem of human sexuality must include careful analysis of the total individual. All three factors that may influence the determination of sexual behavior must be considered. The first is the genetic factor, which predetermines the particular type of sexual pattern and is constant within limits for any one species. This pattern depends on the anatomic configuration of the sexual organs and on the neuromuscular and nervous pathways through which impulses must pass to result in effective utilization of these organs.

The second factor is hormonal; androgenic and estrogenic hormones cause growth and development of the organs needed for the sex act. Androgens, furthermore, increase the sensitivity of these organs to mechanical stimulation so that the genetically determined sexual pattern is elicited more easily. Gonadal hormones potentiate the inherent genetic sexual pattern. Such other endocrine factors as the thyroid hormone influence sexual behavior only secondarily through their general effect on health and strength.

The third important factor is psychological or learned. This mechanism, in the human being, is sufficiently potent so that sexual activity may be greatly repressed or increased, regardless of endocrine status. We have seen that genetic factors exert no influence upon the choice of the sex object. Hormones, similarly, do not influence the choice of the object of affection. The society in which we live teaches heterosexual love, and the choice of sex object is determined by experience. In the usual course of events, the sex object is of the opposite sex. When psychosexual maturity has not occurred, homosexuality may result.

Beginning with the basic genetic pattern with which the infant is born, hormonal psychological influences are gradually added. Early in childhood, the environment is the more important component, but at the time of adolescence, with increased production of steroid hormones, end-organ sensitivity begins to play a significant role. This role, however, is greatly influenced by the individual's earlier emotional experiences. When endocrine maturity is achieved in the late teens or early twenties, the psychological factor becomes once again the predominating influence. In the adult human, abnormalities of sexual behavior may be considered, in the light of our present information, to be results of psychological deviations, with hormones playing at most a secondary role. Endocrine factors can be of importance only when there is other concrete evidence of endocrine disease.

Conclusions

Three elements are involved in the determination of human sexuality. The genetic factor sets the sexual pattern and defines the general limits within which the other factors may operate. The hormonal factor develops the organs needed for the sex act and increases their sensitivity to stimulation. The psychological factor essentially controls the choice of sex object and the intensity of sexual emotions.

Castrated humans may show sexual behavior similar to intact persons, evidence that gonadal hormones are not indispensable to at least partial sexual activity. Studies of the endocrine systems of homosexual subjects demonstrate no constant or significant variation from average for the respective somatic sex. Administration of large amounts of estrogen to normal men decreases their libidos in some cases but does not increase their attraction to other men. Estrogen acts by depressing endogenous production of androgen and by antagonizing androgens directly. The administration of large doses of androgen to normal women may intensify their libidos—possibly by increasing the sensitivity of the clitoris—but does not cause them to assume male sexual roles. Treatment of the homosexual patient with the hormone of his somatic sex will in no way influence his sexual behavior unless this substance be androgen, in which event his sexual activity may increase but always in a direction determined psychologically.

It must be concluded that homosexuality is a purely psychological phenomenon, neither dependent on a hormonal pattern for its production nor amenable to change by endocrine substances.

So-called "sexual mannerisms" and aggressive behavior, as well as impotence and frigidity, cannot ordinarily be related to hormonal patterns. It is usually not possible to prognosticate the type and amount of hormones produced in a patient by observing his behavior, and "sexual mannerisms" cannot be influenced by administration of exogenous hormones.

Investigation of the problems of abnormal sexual behavior must include evaluation of the total individual, and certain disturbances may be ascribed to endocrine factors only when other manifestations of endocrine disease are present. Even in the presence of endocrine disease, libido may be normal; but, when it is not, endocrine therapy may re-establish a previously existing normal sexual state.

REFERENCES

Hampson, J. L., & Hampson, Joan G. The ontogenesis of sexual behavior in man. In W. C. Young (Ed.), *Sex and internal secretions.* Vol. 2. (3rd ed.) Baltimore: Williams & Wilkins, 1961. Pp. 1401-1432.

Kinsey, A. C., Pomeroy, W. B., & Martin, C. E. *Sexual behavior in the human male.* Philadelphia: Saunders, 1948.

Kinsey, A. C., Pomeroy, W. B., Martin, C. E., & Gebhard, P. H. *Sexual behavior in the human female.* Philadelphia: Saunders, 1953.

Mead, Margaret. Cultural determinants of sexual behavior. In W. C. Young (Ed.), *Sex and internal secretions.* Vol. 2. (3rd ed.) Baltimore: Williams & Wilkins, 1961. Pp. 1433-1479.

Money, J. W. Sex hormones and other variables in human eroticism. In W. C. Young (Ed.), *Sex and internal secretions.* Vol. 2. (3rd ed.) Baltimore: Williams & Wilkins, 1961. Pp. 1383-1400.

Perloff, W. H. Role of the hormones in human sexuality. *Psychosom. Med.,* 1949, **11**, 133-139.

Waxenberg, S. E., Drellich, M. G., & Sutherland, A. M. Changes in female sexuality after adrenalectomy. *J. clin. Endocrinol.,* 1959, **19**, 193-202.

Young, W. C. The hormones and mating behavior. In W. C. Young (Ed.), *Sex and internal secretions.* Vol. 2. (3rd ed.) Baltimore: Williams & Wilkins, 1961. Pp. 1173-1239.

Etiology of Homosexuality: Genetic and Chromosomal Aspects

4

C.M.B. PARE

Normal Sexual Development

In the fetus there are two primitive gonads and whether they are activated as male or as female gonads depends on the chromosomes. By inference from the fruit fly (*Drosophila*), it was thought that the X chromosomes were the active sex-determining chromosomes. In *Drosophila*, the autosomes are "male," and two X chromosomes counter them to result in a female, one being insufficient to do so. The Y chromosome is inactive. In man, however, the Y is the sex-determining chromosome. XX is thus female, and XXY or XXXY (types of Klinefelter's syndrome) is male. In the seventh week of fetal life, there is gonad differentiation, and, at that time, sex can also be determined by the presence of chromatin bodies in the cells.

Once having activated the gonads, the chromosomes apparently cease to influence normal sex development, and subsequent sexual differentiation in the fetus seems to be under the control of hormones from the fetal gonads.

In a series of classical experiments, Jost (1953) demonstrated that removal of the testes from a male rabbit fetus in the seventh week resulted in female sexual differentiation. Removal of the testes at later dates caused varying degrees of intersex. If the testis on one side was removed and the other left intact, there was unilateral male development, with female differentiation on the operated side. Testosterone supports Wolffian duct development in a castrated rabbit fetus but does not inhibit Mullerian duct development. Female sex differentiation does not depend on hormones and occurs in both male and female in the absence of gonads. Androgenic hormones can, however, produce intersexual or masculine development of the urogenital sinus and external genitalia in the female fetus, although they do not inhibit development of the Mullerian duct. A clinical example of this pattern is, of course, the adrenogenital syndrome.

For the functioning of normal adult sexuality, a certain hormone level is necessary; libido is diminished in eunuchoidism and can be readily treated by testosterone. In the female, estrogens are responsible for the normal vaginal secretion, but androgens from the adrenal gland are responsible for libido, as can be shown in clinical experiments after oöphorectomy and adrenalectomy for carcinoma and replacement therapy. In addition, sex hormones have what seems to be an independent cerebral influence. The implantation of stilbestrol into the posterior hypothalamus of spayed cats, for instance, resulted in sexual behavior despite a genital tract that remained anestrous (Harris, 1958). There is no relationship between the proportions of androgens and estrogens and the direction of the libido.

The direction of libido seems to be determined by such environmental influences as parental attitudes, although, of course, in the normal course of events those attitudes are dictated by the anatomical sex of the child (Hampson, 1955; Money, 1955; Money, Hampson, & Hampson, 1955a; Money et al., 1955b).

The Etiology of Homosexuality

Although it is probable that in normal sexual development the role of genetic factors is limited to sex determination in the fetus, this limitation does not necessarily mean that genetic factors do not play an etiological role in abnormal sexual development. In fact, very few investigations have been made into the genetic role in the etiology of homosexuality. What investigations have been conducted have been limited to three main fields. First, those relating to Lang's theory that male homosexuals are genetically female; second, "twin" studies; and third, birth order of homosexuals.

Lang (1940, p. 59) suggested that some male homosexuals are ". . . real male sex intergrades which are genetically female but have lost all morphological sex characteristics except their chromosome formula." That is, he suggested that male homosexuals may be genetic females in male bodies. To test this hypothesis, he investigated the sex ratio of the siblings of 1,015 male homosexuals. He found that the sex ratio of the siblings was altered significantly from the normal of 100 females to 105 males to a ratio of 100 females to 121 males and that this trend was even greater in the older and more pronounced homosexuals. This investigation was fully controlled by another large series of 1,296 male probands that showed a normal sex ratio among siblings of 100 females to 107 males. Lang's work was confirmed by Jensch (1941a, 1941b) in 2,072 homosexuals, among whom the sibling sex ratio was 100 females to 115 males. Lang's explanation for these findings was that some of the males in these studies were genotypical females, thus accounting for the high incidence of males among the siblings of homosexuals.

This theory was tested by Pare in 1956; he used the technique of chromosomal sexing. The first satisfactory method of assessing chromosomal sex in man was developed by Barr (Moore, Graham, & Barr, 1953; Moore & Barr, 1955). It was empirically proved that most female cells contained a characteristic spot in the nucleus not present in male animal cells. This finding held true for all tissues and for all species of mammals examined. The method is simple and consists in smearing on a slide, the cells obtained from scraping the inside of the mouth and fixing and staining them with hematoxylin and eosin. When the cells are examined under the high-power lens, a characteristic dense spot of about 1 μ in diameter can be seen on the periphery of the nucleus. This spot is seen in from 40–60 per cent cells in the female and in fewer than 5 per cent in the male. There is no overlap. Sexual dimorphism is also seen in neutrophils (Davidson &

Smith, 1954)—the so-called drum-stick phenomenon. This spot stains as for DNA and is thought to be made of chromatin material, probably part of the two X chromosomes. The actual chromosomes are not seen, however, and the method is called "chromatin sexing" and the spot the "chromatin spot." Using buccal smears, Pare (1956) investigated the chromosomal sex of fifty male homosexuals who had an average Kinsey rating of 4.5 with a standard deviation of 1.49, and these subjects were compared with twenty-five male and twenty-five female controls. *In all cases, the homosexuals were typically male and the incidence of spots similar to those in normal male controls.*

Table 3–1.

The percentage incidence of chromatin spots in cells from mouth scrapings of fifty male homosexuals and twenty-five male and twenty-five female controls.

	Female controls (25)	Male controls (25)	Male homosexuals (50)
Mean	45%	1.52%	1.50%
Range	22–65%	0–6%	0–8%
Standard deviation	11.5	2.0	2.2

This investigation has been confirmed by numerous authorities, and the combined figures from all investigations make a total of 235 male homosexuals studied. In none was the nuclear sex found to be female in type (Bleuler & Wiedemann, 1956; Lüers & Schultz, 1957; Raboch & Nedoma, 1958; Gentele, Lagerholm & Lodin, 1960). These figures are strong evidence against Lang's theory.

A possible explanation of the findings by Lang and Jensch of an abnormal sex ratio among siblings of male homosexuals lies in the manner in which they selected their probands. Both these studies were carried out in Germany, where the police are authorized to keep lists of known homosexuals, and it was from police records that Lang and Jensch obtained their materials. It is obvious that families generally come to the notice of the police only through delinquent or other criminal behavior and that, once a family has been brought to their notice, any homosexuality in the family may then find its way into the police files. As delinquency and criminal behavior are more common among men than among women, the persons through whom the police become acquainted with the family are much more likely to be male than female, and this fact in turn can lead to a higher incidence of males than of females in the families known to the police. It is significant that the control families were not obtained from police records. Other investigations into the sibling ratio of homosexuals, for which subjects have not been obtained from police records, have all involved series of much smaller size, and neither Darke (1948) nor Slater (1958) in series of 100 and 286 male homosexuals, respectively, found any significant difference in the sibling ratio from that obtained for the controls.

Recently, examination of the individual chromosomes has become possible, and much of the credit must go to Tjio and Levan (1956), who first demonstrated convincingly that the normal chromosome number in man is forty-six and not forty-eight. Several techniques are essential to chromosome study: (1) the use of colchicine to inhibit spindle formation so that cells in the metaphase stage of division are spread over the cell and easily seen; (2) the use of hypotonic saline to swell the cell and disperse the chromosomes in the cytoplasm; (3) flattening the cells to spread the chromosomes in the same optical place— either by squashing the cells or allowing them to dry out on the slide. The cells for examination are obtained for cultures of bone marrow (Ford & Hamerton, 1956); solid tissue like skin (Tjio & Levan, 1956; Lejeune & Turpin, 1959); and peripheral blood (Hungerford, Donnelly, Nowell, & Beck, 1959).

Each of these techniques has its own advantages, and, for full investigation, all should be used. There is, however, the danger of changes in genes during culture, and this danger obviously increases with the duration of the culture. Bone marrow is cultured for twenty-four hours, blood for two to three days, and skin (after trypsin digest) for at least a week.

Only one paper has been found in which individual chromosomes have been studied, an investigation by Pritchard (1962). Six male homosexuals of Kinsey grade 6 were studied. In all cases the diploid number was the normal forty-six. That one cell in each of cases 1 and 3 apparently contained only forty-five chromosomes was almost certainly due to the loss of a chromosome during preparation of the slides. In the majority of the cells in each case, it was relatively easy to identify five small acrocentric chromosomes, and, as the individuals were physically normal, it is safe to assume that one of these chromosomes must have been a Y. *In each of the six cases, therefore, the sex-chromosome constitution was that of a normal male.* It was possible to make a more detailed analysis of the karyotype in all but case 6, in which the preparations were not sufficient for this purpose. In no case was there any evidence of autosomal aberration. The six male homosexuals in this study thus had normal male sex-chromosome constitutions.

Table 3–2.

Chromosome number.

Case	Chromosome number 45	Chromosome number 46	Chromosome number 47	Number of cells examined
1	1	29	0	30
2	0	20	0	20
3	1	24	0	25
4	0	20	0	20
5	0	13	0	13
6	0	20	0	20

Cases of Klinefelter's syndrome are somatically male, but examination of cells reveals female sex chromatins. Recently such cells have been shown to have a chromosomal characteristic of XXY or XXXY. A number of these cases has been studied from a psychopathological point of view, and the subjects have been shown to have predominantly heterosexual feelings. Pasqualini, Vidal, and Bur (1957) studied thirty-one cases of Klinefelter's syndrome and found that 70 per cent had had heterosexual relations by the age of twenty and that in only two cases had there been transient homosexual experiences. Raboch and Nedoma (1958) examined thirty-six men with "female chromatin pattern." Thirty-two of these men had distinctly heterosexual trends, and the remaining four were classified as "infantile showing no sexual relations or interest throughout life." Züblin (1957) confirmed male behavior in Klinefelter's syndrome.

It thus appears that gross abnormalities of the sex chromosomes are not necessarily important in the etiology of homosexuality. Nor indeed would such a role be expected from what is thought to be the normal physiological role of the sex chromosomes in sexual development, which seems to be limited to the activation of one or the other of the fetal gonads.

That genetic factors may nevertheless be important in the etiology of homosexuality is strongly suggested by "twin" studies. Kallmann (1952) investigated eighty-five predominantly or exclusively homosexual male twin index cases, the largest series of twins yet studied. All forty monozygotic index pairs were concordant as to overt practice and, even more strikingly, were similar on a quantitative assessment of homosexual behavior, the ratios on the Kinsey scale being 0–6. In the dizygotic group, more than half the co-twins of distinctly homosexual subjects yielded no evidence of overt homosexuality. According to whether or not the dizygotic concordance rates were related to homosexuality rating 5–6 or 1–6, they varied from 11.5 per cent to 42.3 per cent, figures that are only slightly in excess of Kinsey's ratings for the total male population. This difference between uniovular and dizygotic twins is very striking. The 100 per cent concordance ratio in the uniovular twins does not, however, mean that heredity is the only etiological factor of importance but simply that it is important. It does not exclude the significance of other factors. Other series of twin studies are almost nonexistent, apart from a series of eight twins reported by Sanders in 1934. Seven of these twins were monozygotic, and, six had twins concordant for homosexuality. The dizygotic pair was discordant. Other publications have usually involved only single cases, and these reports are suspect, as it is probable that they were published for particular reasons, to demonstrate discordancy, for instance. An example is the study of a pair of discordant monozygotic twins published by Rainer, Mesnikoff, Kolb, and Carr (1960), who set out to find discordant uniovular twins for the particular investigation they had in mind. In fact, they said "a survey of a considerable number of one egg pairs over the past four years yielded only two pairs with overt differentiation in behavior" (p. 253). As Kallmann's work has recently come under considerable criticism, there is a great need for more work on these lines, however difficult it may be. In the meantime, however, it is hard to ignore his findings, with their strong inference that genetic factors do play a part in the etiology of homosexuality.

In a recent study, Slater (1962) investigated the birth orders and maternal ages of homosexuals. He found that the birth orders of 401 male homosexuals showed a significant shift to the right, that they were generally born later in the sibship than would be theoretically expected. Three hundred and thirty-eight epileptic controls did not differ significantly from the expected norm. The maternal ages of these male homosexuals also showed a significant shift to the right, but the variation of maternal age was perhaps even more striking. It was as great as that in the mothers of Mongols and approached the figures obtained with the small numbers of Turner's syndrome and Klinefelter's syndrome that have been reported by other workers. Thirty-two female homosexuals whom Slater also studied confirmed the shift to the right in the birth order. These findings support a hypothesis of heterogeneity in the etiology of homosexuality and suggest that a chromosomal anomaly, such as might be associated with late maternal age, may play a part in causation. If an abnormal gene played a significant etiological role and were inherited in the usual way, we should expect homosexuality to be randomly distributed among the offspring. Slater's work demonstrates that such is not the case. The fact that homosexuals are born later in the sibship is interesting psychodynamically, but, taking into account Kallmann's twin studies, it suggests that a chromosomal abnormality, originating perhaps in the mother's ovary as in Mongolism, may be the mechanism involved in many of the cases. The striking variability of maternal age suggests, however, that there is an etiological heterogeneity.

Discussion

Investigations into the genetic role of homosexuality are few and far between. One thing is definite: homosexuals are not genetically female as Lang originally postulated. Furthermore,

the theory of classical transmission of a mutant gene is also untenable in the majority of cases, in view of Slater's findings that
homosexuals are not randomly distributed among the offspring.
Kallmann's twin studies suggest that genetic factors nevertheless
do play an important etiological role. The mechanism in these
cases may be a chromosomal abnormality arising, perhaps, in
one of the gametes, as is the case in Mongolism. The fact that
Pritchard was unable to find any abnormality in his study of
chromosomes is therefore of little significance. It should be realized that the only chromosomal abnormalities that can be spot-
ted at present are those involving loss or duplication of a whole
chromosome or a large part of it, and it is surprising that life is
possible with such a massive abnormality, particularly when
such a disorder as hemophilia is perhaps caused by a change in
a single base in the side chain of one molecule of DNA. The
crudeness of our techniques is illustrated by the analogue of a
whole symphony played in one second. The detection of a single
false note would be no more difficult than attempting to identify
genes with present techniques. At present, we can only try to
recognize the symphony from its length and the position of its
main interval. Loss of a whole or a large part of one chromosome
is nearly always fatal—because of the recessive lethal genes thus
exposed. But anomalies of sex chromosomes are not so dangerous,
because they contain less genetic material and there is a normal
variation in the number of each kind (Y cannot carry lethal genes,
and X is most unlikely to do so). It is probably for this reason that
monosomy has been found involving only the sex chromosomes.
Until far more refined techniques for the study of chromosomes
become available, further investigations to confirm and elucidate
the genetic factors in homosexuality should therefore follow the
more classical lines of investigation.

The nature of this defect can, at the moment, be only a matter
of guesswork. It should be pointed out, however, that it need not
influence the direction of the libido directly and that its action
can be indirect via general personality characteristics. Environmental factors do, of course, play a part in most genetically determined conditions. That they play such a part in homosexuality
is shown by the occurrence of discordant uniovular twin pairs.
On the evidence to date, it is likely that the etiology of homo-

sexuality is heterogeneous, but the degree to which genetic and environmental factors are important, in homosexuality as a whole and in any individual, remains uncertain.

REFERENCES

Bleuler, M., & Wiedemann, H. R. Chromosomengeschlecht und psychosexualität. *Arch. Psychiat. Nervenkr.*, 1956, **195**, 14-19.

Darke, R. A. Heredity as an etiological factor in homosexuality. *J. nerv. ment. Dis.*, 1948, **107**, 251-268.

Davidson, W. M., & Smith, D. R. A morphological sex difference in the polymorphonuclear neutrophil leucocytes. *Brit. med. J.*, 1954, **2**, 6-7.

Ford, E. C., & Hamerton, J. I. The chromosomes of man. *Nature*, 1956, **178**, 1020-1023.

Gentele, H., Lagerholm, B., & Lodin, A. The chromosomal sex of male homosexuals. *Acta Dermato-vener.*, 1960, **40**, 470-473.

Hampson, Joan G. Hermaphroditic genital appearance, rearing and eroticism in hyperadrenocorticism. *Bull. Johns Hopk. Hosp.*, 1955, **96**, 265-273.

Harris, G. W., Michael, R. P., & Scott, P. P. Neurological site of action of stilbesterol in eliciting sexual behavior. In G. Wolstenholme & C. O'Connor (Eds.), *Ciba Foundation Symposium on the Neurological Basis of Behavior*. London: Churchill, 1958. Pp. 236-254.

Hungerford, D. A., Donnelly, A. J., Nowell, P. C., & Beck, S. The chromosome constitution of a human phenotypic intersex. *Am. J. hum. Genet.*, 1959, **11**, 215-236.

Jensch, K. Zur genealogie der homosexualität. *Arch. Psychiat. Nervenkr.*, 1941, **112**, 527-540. (a)

Jensch, K. Weiterer beitrag zur genealogie der homosexualität, *Arch. Psychiat. Nervenkr.*, 1941, **112**, 679-696. (b)

Jost, A. Problems of fetal endocrinology. *Recent Progr. Hormone Res.*, 1953, **8**, 379-418.

Kallmann, F. J. A comparative twin study on the genetic aspects of male homosexuality. *J. nerv. ment. Dis.*, 1952, **115**, 283-298.

Lang, T. Studies in the genetic determination of homosexuality. *J. nerv. ment. Dis.*, 1940, **92**, 55-64.

Lejeune, J., & Turpin, R. Chromosomal aberrations in man. *Am. J. hum. Genet.*, 1961, **13**, 175-184.

Lüers, T., & Schultz, J. H. Chromosomales geschlecht und sexualpsyche. *Ärtzliche Wochenschrift,* 1957, **12,** 249-254.

Money, J. Hermaphroditism, gender and precocity in hyperadreno-corticism. *Bull. Johns Hopk. Hosp.,* 1955, **96,** 253-264.

Money, J., Hampson, Joan G., & Hampson, J. L. Hermaphroditism: recommendations concerning assignment of sex. *Bull. Johns Hopk. Hosp.,* 1955, **97,** 284-300. (a)

Money, J., Hampson, Joan G., & Hampson, J. L. An examination of some basic sexual concepts. *Bull. Johns Hopk. Hosp.,* 1955, **97,** 301-319. (b)

Moore, K. L., Graham, Margaret A., & Barr, M. L. The detection of chromosomal sex in hermaphrodites from a skin biopsy. *Surg., Gyn. & Obstet.,* **96,** 641-648.

Moore, K. L., & Barr, M. L. Smears from the oral mucosa in the detection of chromosomal sex. *Lancet,* 1955, **2,** 57-58.

Pare, C. M. B. Homosexuality and chromosomal sex. *J. psychosom. Res.,* 1956, **1,** 247-251.

Pasqualini, R. Q., Vidal, G., & Bur, G. E. Psychopathology of Klinefelter's syndrome. *Lancet,* 1957, **2,** 164-167.

Pritchard, M. Homosexuality and genetic sex. *J. ment. Sci.,* 1962, **108,** 616-623.

Raboch, J., & Nedoma, J. Sex chromatin and sexual behavior. *Psychosom. Med.,* 1958, **20,** 55-59.

Rainer, J. D., Mesnikoff, A., Kolb, L. C., & Carr, A. Homosexuality and heterosexuality in identical twins. *Psychosom. Med.,* 1960, **22,** 251-258.

Slater, E. The sex of sibs and children of homosexuals. In D. R. Smith & W. M. Davidson (Eds.), *Symposium on nuclear sex.* London: Heinemann, 1958. Pp. 79-83.

Slater, E. Birth order and maternal age of homosexuals. *Lancet,* 1962, **1,** 69-71.

Tjio, J. H., & Levan, A. The chromosome number of man. *Hereditas,* 1956, **42,** 1-6.

Züblin, W. Geschlechtschromosom, geschlechtshormon, und psychische sexualität. *Schweiz. Z. Psychol.* (Bern), 1957, **16** (2), 118-120.

PART II | THE VIEW OF THE SOCIAL SCIENCES

5

Male Homosexuals and
Their "Worlds"[1]

EVELYN HOOKER

"Knowledge of a society or culture must rest upon knowledge of the individuals who are in that society or share that culture. But the converse is also true. Personal figures get their definition only when seen against the social or cultural background in which they have their being" (Kluckhohn & Murray, 1949, p. xi.). Since Kluckhohn and Murray wrote those words in 1949, our theoretical and empirical knowledge of the complex patterns of relationships between personality variables and cultural, social-system, and structural variables has been greatly enlarged. Such recently published volumes as those edited by Smelser & Smelser (1963) and Cohen (1962) amply demonstrate current theoretical formulations of the central issues, be-

---

[1] There is no completely satisfactory term to describe the collective aspects of homosexuality. The term "world" is being used here, as Shibutani uses it, to refer to groups of persons with shared perspectives—artists or Bohemians, for example. The terms "subculture," "society," and "community" have also been used for this purpose.

side providing empirical research in widely varied substantive areas.

One behavioral area that is mentioned only briefly or is missing altogether in such discussions is homosexuality.[2] It is not difficult to understand why. Traditionally, adult homosexual behavior has been considered as individual psychopathology, the proper domain of the clinician; as social pathology, the province of the sociologist or anthropologist concerned with social deviance; or as biological abnormality, the appropriate concern of the endocrinologist or geneticist. An overwhelming preponderance of the now extensive literature on the topic involves research or speculation by clinicians or personality theorists, on one hand, or by specialists in biological disciplines, on the other. In part, the focus on individual bio- or psychopathology may be a function of the prevailing climate of professional opinion, which tends to determine the major lines of investigation of any problem in a given time period. The fact that in our own society, as well as in many others, such behavior is subject to legal and social taboos (Hooker, 1963) has also contributed in a major way to the relative paucity of research involving groups of subjects who are not to be found through clinics or other therapeutic or correctional agencies. When the taboo exists, access to a population sample that would provide an optimum opportunity for study of the collective subcultural aspects of the phenomenon is difficult.

A brief summary of the major trends in research[3] on the topic, with either a clinical or a social orientation, may help to introduce the focal problem here: the importance of both personality and social or cultural variables in producing and shaping adult patterns of male, overt homosexual behavior. This discussion is restricted to males because (except for Kinsey) there are few re-

---

[2] The term "homosexuality" is admittedly a loose one. It is used here to refer to all manifestations, in either subjective experience or overt behavior, of sexual attraction between persons of the same gender. The term "homosexual," when used as a noun, refers to persons who identify themselves as such and whose patterns of sexual desires and overt behavior are predominantly or exclusively directed to members of their own gender.

[3] References to the research literature are highly selective and presented in the most abbreviated way. The purpose is not to review the literature completely but simply to illustrate major trends.

search studies of females and because my own research has been concerned exclusively with males.

Clinical theories about homosexual behavior are likely to stress personality variables of a largely intrapsychic nature, originating in infancy and early childhood and persisting onto adult life. If cultural or social-system variables are taken into account (as in the research of Bieber, Dain, Dince, Drellich, Grand, Gundlach, Kremer, Rifkin, Wilbur, & Bieber, 1962), they are usually limited to the nuclear family and peer-group relationships, and the critical time of their influence is assumed to be the early years of life. Sullivan (1953), Thompson (1947), and Kardiner (1949) have stressed the theoretical importance of the preadolescent and adolescent periods and the contribution of situational and cultural as well as of intrapsychic factors in determining the final psychosexual object choice. Opler's work (1959) on the contributions of Italian and Irish patients' different cultural backgrounds to their respective homosexual problems and behavior is one of the rare examples of a broader perspective in which cultural and psychodynamic variables are interrelated.

Empirical studies focusing on homosexual behavior in American society from a social rather than from a clinical perspective are not numerous. Kinsey, Pomeroy, & Martin (1948) provided data on the relations of such cultural variables as education, religious affiliation, and urban versus rural background to the incidence of such behavior. Assuming, as did Ford and Beach (1951), that the capacity for homosexual, as well as for heterosexual, response is a basic part of our mammalian heritage, they conclude that cultural pressures and social conditioning determine the final object choice.

Research in such institutional settings as prisons (Clemmer, 1940; Fishman, 1930; Huffman, 1960) has focused on the features of internal organization in such institutions that help to determine the homosexual subculture that develops. Leznoff and Westley (1956) studied the patterning of social-sexual relations within and between "overt" and "concealed" groups of homosexuals in an urban (Canadian) setting and conceptualized the "community" as welded together by the casual and promiscuous contacts between the two groups. Ross (1959) and Reiss (1961) have reported empirical investigations of male "hustling" and some of its relations with other sectors of the homosexual world. Of special importance is Reiss's finding that juvenile delinquents who engage in sexual acts with adult homosexuals, for which they are paid, are prevented by their group norms from defining themselves as homosexual and do not continue homosexual activity as adults. Westwood's (1960) empirical investigation of social aspects of homosexual behavior in England is a contribution to this neglected aspect of research. The literature on social aspects of homosexuality (including fiction works like Rechy [1963]) is, of course, extensive, but most of it does not meet the criteria of empirical research and is simply descriptive or speculative. Cory's account (1951), like Westwood's (1952), is an example of a serious effort to describe and analyze the problem from a social point of view.

Cross-cultural comparisons of societies with respect to the attitude toward and occurrence of homosexual behavior are also limited in number. The most extensive analysis is that of Ford and Beach (1951). Even their very valuable material is limited by the fact that careful and detailed data on homosexual behavior are lacking in many of the ethnographic descriptions in the Human Relations Area Files, on which they relied. Mead's observations (1935) on the character of prescribed sex roles in contrasting cultures and their relation to the occurrence of homosexual behavior, as well as her more recent summary of the cross-cultural material (1961), are important contributions to the clarification of the role of cultural factors in producing sexually deviant patterns.

However limited the data now available from the research studies, they suggest that homosexuality is a many-faceted phenomenon not only in its manifestations in individual and social experience and behavior but also, and correspondingly, in its determination by psychodynamic, biological, cultural, situational, and structural variables. An "either-or" position with respect to any one of these variables simply does not account for the extraordinary diversity of the phenomena to be accounted for. Reductionism, either from the societal level to the individual or vice versa, distorts the picture, as Bendix (1952) and Wrong (1961) have pointed out in discussions of the general issue. What is required is an integration of these complex variables in a more comprehensive framework—but we are far from achieving that goal.

In a discussion of the relations between individual personality patterns and cultural or social variables as they apply to homosexual behavior, it is appropriate to begin with the fact that individual patterns of personality structure and psychodynamics vary greatly among those adult males who engage in overt homosexual behavior. There are no patterns common to all. It was Thompson, I believe, who first drew attention to this fact, in her now classic paper (Green, 1964). Some excerpts from that paper illustrate the point with cogency: "[H]omosexuality is not a clinical entity, but a symptom with different meanings in different personality setups . . . . [O]vert homosexuality may express fear of the opposite sex, fear of adult responsibility, a need to defy authority, or an attempt to cope with hatred of or competitive attitudes to members of one's own sex; it may represent a flight from reality into absorption in body stimulation very similar to the autoerotic activities of the schizophrenic, or it may be a symptom of destructiveness of oneself or others. These do not exhaust the possibilities of its meaning . . ." (p. 8). "There are at least as many different types of homosexual behavior as of heterosexual, and the interpersonal relations of homosexuals present the same problems as are found in heterosexual situations" (p. 11). As Thompson makes clear, these statements are based on her own experiences in analytic work with a variety of patients.

In a research project designed to assess the usefulness of psychological tests in diagnosing overt homosexual behavior and to determine whether or not particular patterns of personality and psychodynamics characterize individuals who engage exclusively in such behavior, this writer also found that wide diversity rather than a specific pattern was characteristic (1957; 1958; 1959). In reviewing the literature in which two projective tests— the Rorschach and the TAT—had been employed in a variety of experimental situations with overt homosexuals and heterosexual controls, it became clear that, although group differences do appear in the test results, the use of these tests for valid and reliable individual diagnosis of overt homosexual behavior is questionable. In commenting on this fact, I wrote,

In the studies cited, two personality pictures of "the" homosexual have been used. To quote Wheeler [1949, p. 123], "If it is possible to accept the rationale . . . for each item in terms of the aforementioned results, a combined picture of the male 'homosexual' would be: A somewhat paranoid individual with derogatory attitudes toward people, especially women, which is accompanied by a feminine identification. There are indications of anal interests and interest in physical relationships between like beings. There is apparently some preoccupation with sex in general and some autoerotic concern." To quote Lindzey [1958, p. 74], "Our tentative findings suggest that the TAT protocols of the individual characterized by strong homosexual tendencies display consistently negative attitudes toward women, a lack of full, rich, and satisfying relations with members of the opposite sex, and occasional reference to manifest homosexuality." A basic assumption which they have in common is that "the" homosexual exists and that he is characterized by attitudes consistent with hatred of, or at least negative attitudes toward, women—a relatively simple construct. I venture to suggest that not only is it too simple but it is not altogether true. Let me hasten to add that many homosexuals can be characterized in this way; but even for them it is a caricature of the complexity of the individuals involved. At the risk of stating a self-evident fact, it is apparent to anyone with knowledge of the wide individual variations in homosexual patterns and life styles, as well as to anyone who has looked at projective test protocols or life histories, that homosexuality is not an entity but is, rather, a multi-manifested phenomenon. We need to get beyond the fact that the individual is homosexual, to the kind of homosexual that he is. We are badly in need of fruitful theory which will take into account the multiplicity of variables which appear to be operating. Projective techniques can be valuable sources of constructs for such theory-building. It is not an easy task; and it is one which, I think, will not be accomplished by the development of "homosexual signs." It seems unlikely that . . . signs will help us to diagnose or understand individuals who are as varied as—to quote judges who have interpreted the projective protocols —"an impoverished, restricted, promiscuous, compulsive homosexual, devoid of the capacity for deep feeling"; "a straight heterosexual—except in the bedroom"; "sensitive, independent, autonomous, with strong control of impulses and with a moral attitude toward sex"; "a positive homosexual who goes through life gently, with lots of strength and no hostility, makes strong relationships, and for whom homosexuality is a way of self-actualization"; "a passive–aggressive iconoclast who has libidinized all of his psychological needs in fellatio"; "a paranoid character who has never made up his mind whether he is a boy or a girl, a tormented, sad homosexual who flees from close relations and is at the mercy of his own intense emotions"; "an individual with lots of strength as a man, who plays the assertive role with men, and with tremendous hostility to women"; and, finally, just to bring this arbitrarily to a close, "a homosexual with pervasive feminine orientation, a very passionate person, an aggressive personality with a paranoid base." The most striking finding of the three judges who examined the projective materials was that many of the homosexuals were very well adjusted. In fact the three judges agreed on two-thirds of the group as being average to superior in adjustment. Not only do all homosexuals not have strong feminine identification, nor are they all "somewhat paranoid," but, according to the judges, some may not be characterized by any demonstrable pathology (1959, p. 279).

Support for the thesis that overt homosexuals exhibit a wide variety of personality patterns is also found in Bieber *et al.* (1962), although the evidence is indirect. The psychiatric diagnosis of the two groups of homosexual and heterosexual patients in psychoanalytic treatment did not show significant differences. Both groups contained individuals diagnosed as schizophrenic, manic depressive, psychoneurotic, and suffering from character disorder—and the differences between groups in each diagnostic category were not significant. In fact, the authors point out that "theories which postulate that homosexuality is a coincidental phenomenon in a more comprehensive psychopathologic process are given minimal support by our data" (p. 309). If "at any age, homosexuality is a symptom of fear and inhibition of heterosexual expression" (p. 309), as the authors claim (a disputable assertion), it is plausible to assume that the particular personality in which such a "symptom" occurs is given very little definition by the description of that "symptom" alone and that, furthermore, persons exhibiting the "symptom" might have little else in common.

To adopt the position that homosexual males cannot be characterized by the same personality patterns or by the same intrapsychic processes is not to deny that there may be clusters of patterns—each cluster exhibiting common features. Many attempts have been made to develop a homosexual typology. Some typologies are dichotomous classifications like active–passive, masculine–feminine, invert–homosexual, true–pseudo, and subject–object. Most of these classifications have been demonstrated to be oversimplifications of more complex patterns of relationship between the hypothesized polar opposites. For example, as Bieber *et al.* (1962), Westwood (1952), Hooker (1962), and others have reported, the classification of roles or types into "active" and "passive" fails to take account of the fact that many persons play an "active" role at one time and a "passive" role at another or simply have no preference and adapt to the demands of the situation. Furthermore, the activity–passivity dimension of experience and behavior is one of many dimensions that require description and analysis if a meaningful personality profile is to be drawn. The need for a meaningful classification or taxonomy of the personality and social patterns of homosexual males is a pressing one.

The developmental routes by which individuals travel to adult status and identity as committed homosexuals are also varied. At critical junctures in individual life histories, the determinants of involvement in patterns of action that will result in final commitment to a homosexual career are not only psychodynamic but also cultural and situational in character. We shall not discuss these variable routes here; a tentative formulation of them has been presented elsewhere.[4] We shall focus on one complex of cultural and situational determinants of the experience and behavior of an individual who has either made or is in the process of making the commitment to the homosexual subculture or "world."

In late adolescence or early adulthood, entry into this world may help to determine whether the person who engages in homosexual acts, as Becker puts it, "makes of deviance a way of life [and] organizes his identity around a pattern of deviant behavior" (1963, p. 30). Leimert's distinction between primary and secondary deviation is highly relevant: whether the behaviors "are merely troublesome adjuncts of normally conceived roles"

---

[4] In my unpublished paper, "Sequences of Homosexual Identification," read at the American Sociological Association Meeting, August 1960.

or "the person begins to employ his deviant behavior or a role based upon it as a means of defense, attack, or adjustment to the overt and covert problems created by the consequent societal re-action to him" (1951, p. 76). For many, the pattern of that "ad-justment" is shaped by the particular homosexual milieu in which they live. For others who may isolate themselves from homo-sexual groups and participate seldom, if at all, in activities in the varied social settings in which homosexuals congregate, knowl-edge about that world may nevertheless serve as a negative ref-erence point and may thus help to shape behavioral patterns. We therefore postulate that, despite individual variability in per-sonality structure and psychodynamics, regularities of behavior appear in social settings that must in part be functions of cul-tural, structural, social-system, or situational variables.

There are many homosexual subcultures or worlds in any large urban center and in other settings like prisons. In this ex-position,[5] some aspects of these subcultures in the city of Los Angeles are described. There are no unique features of this city that serve as necessary conditions for the development of many forms of homosexual "society," and other such "societies" are found in all major cities in the United States, as well as in other parts of the world.

Some comments about my methods of studying these phe-nomena and my access to them may be useful to the reader.

My methods are essentially those of an ethnographer: inter-viewing persons about their activities and participating in those activities whenever possible, with subsequent recording of my observations. Full participation is impossible, for two reasons: my gender—I am studying a male "community"—and my re-search role. My objective is to look at the homosexual world through the eyes of my research subjects, in the belief that it is the only way in which to know what is really going on, to look with the subject at his world as he knows it. Only if I can achieve and maintain an attitude such that nonevaluation is constant and that whatever I hear or see is simply a matter of interest am I able

---

[5] Some of the material that follows is a revision of another paper (Hooker, 1962). The author wishes to thank the Munksgaard Press for permission to use this material.

to establish the conditions of trust for complete frankness. The homosexual mask in the presence of a representative of the dominant culture is so firmly set, the expectation of moral disapproval so constant, and the distrust and suspicion of motives so ready-to-be-alerted that the researcher must prove his trustworthiness again and again. Only if the genuineness of the researcher's interest in simply understanding what he sees and hears is conveyed by his total attitudes is it possible to enlist the full cooperation of the subjects. They must become, in effect, research assistants in the enterprise, seeking to learn as much for themselves about the community in which they live as for the researcher and to enlist others as well.

My original access to research subjects was not deliberately sought but developed quite accidentally in the course of normal processes of social interaction with a group of friends to whom I had been introduced by a former student—a highly successful businessman. After a period of testing my capacity to accept their behavior in a nonjudgmental way while they divested themselves of their protective masks, they made an urgent request that I conduct a scientific investigation of "people like them." By "people like them," they meant homosexuals who do not seek psychiatric help and who lead relatively stable, occupationally successful lives. They had read the clinical literature on homosexuality and felt that much of it was irrelevant to an understanding of their condition. With their offer to supply unlimited numbers of research subjects and to provide entree into homosexual circles and public gathering places, I accepted the research opportunity. The original relationship was thus not that of researcher to research subject but of friend to friend. With the expansion of contacts through networks of mutual friends, the research role became more clearly defined and separated from its social origin. Independent contacts with official homosexual organizations led to other social strata in the community. Participation in the "community" and deliberate efforts to locate such representative members of its varying sectors as male prostitutes, bisexuals, bartenders and bar owners, adolescents, and the aged ultimately produced a wide cross-section.

For some people, the seeking of sexual contacts with other males is an activity isolated from all other aspects of their lives.

For others, the search is a two-fold one, not only for sexual partners, but also for other persons who share their particular form of sexual preference and with whom the effects of the social stigma can be reduced and the pleasures of the in-group enjoyed. The search is soon rewarded by the discovery that the number of those engaged in similar activity is very large. The Kinsey estimates, for example, support the inference that, in Los Angeles, on the basis of the 1960 census data, there are 26,631 white male exclusively homosexual persons aged twenty or over. Exclusive homosexuals, however, account for a small proportion of the total. If we accept the Kinsey estimates, the incidence of those having had some overt homosexual experience between adolescence and old age reaches 37 per cent. The largest proportion has had heterosexual experience as well. The 26,631 figure does not even begin to encompass the total white male homosexual population—to say nothing of non-Caucasians, of whom there are many.

Distributed over a wide terrain, although not at random, and using a particular set of institutions, facilities, or areas, this large population has developed an extended and loosely related contact network. In some parts of the network, "near-communities" have developed, especially in residential areas of the city with heavy concentrations of homosexuals. These areas are described by homosexuals as "the swish Alps" or "boys' town." In these sections, apartment houses on particular streets may be owned by, and rented exclusively to, homosexuals. For the most part, however, the network clusters are those of friends and acquaintances who may be widely scattered in residential location. The forms of these network clusters vary greatly. The three most common are tightly knit clique structures formed from pairs of homosexually "married" persons or singles, many of whom are heterosexually married; larger groups with one or more loose clique structures as sociometrically central and a number of peripheral members; and loose networks of friends and acquaintances who may meet only at private parties or in the public-service or recreational institutions adapted to the purposes of a homosexual clientele. Clique structures and pairs, as well as loose networks of friends, cut across occupational and socioeconomic levels, although particular professions or occupations, such as teaching, medicine, interior decoration, and antique dealing, may form association ingroups that have social gatherings. Police exposés of homosexual circles or rings frequently reveal the widespread occupational and age ramifications of such groups. Although the networks are overlapping, the population is so large that most individuals know only small sectors. For example, in comparing two lists of friends, one of 250 names made by a man of forty and the other of thirty-five names made by a man of twenty-three, I found only one name common to both lists, although the modal ages and ranges and the occupations were strikingly similar.

Because most homosexuals make every effort to conceal their homosexuality from heterosexuals, especially at work, they live in two worlds. In the work world, they share the cultural values and norms of whatever sector in which they participate. Their homosexual world, therefore, is largely one of leisure time or recreational activities. For most, these worlds are clearly compartmentalized. One consequence of this compartmentalization and of the attitudes toward homosexuality in the dominant culture that help to produce it is that the majority of homosexuals do not participate in the activities that go on in "public" institutions, facilities, or areas. A commonplace, but relevant, analogy is the iceberg, in which only the top of a very large mass is visible. The private cliques and friendship groups provide the setting in which the man who is "straight" at work can be "gay" in his social life. The analogy of the iceberg, however, is of limited usefulness because the "private" and the "public" overlap, as we shall see.

The most important of the public gathering places used by homosexuals and adapted by them and the management to their purposes is the "gay" bar. There are also steam baths catering almost exclusively to this specialized clientele, as well as streets, parks, public toilets, beaches, gyms, coffeehouses, and restaurants. Newsstands, bookstores, record shops, clothing stores, barber shops, grocery stores, and launderettes may become preferred establishments for service or for rendezvous, but they are secondary in importance.

In the Los Angeles area there are, at present count, sixty "gay" bars. As their continued operation is subject to surveillance by police and alcoholic beverage-control authorities, it is difficult to keep the list current. They are not randomly distributed over the city, even in areas that permit the licensing of establishments for the dispensing of liquor. A map of the city on which the locations of "gay" bars are plotted shows that, as in residential areas, there is a clustering effect. Bars tend to be grouped in given areas, in part because of the bar-going habits of their clientele. An individual seldom spends an entire evening in a particular bar but usually makes the rounds of bars in a particular area, seeking sexual contacts or social partners. There is, therefore, a large turnover of personnel in a given evening. Bars nearby can capitalize on this fact. The areas in which the clusters of bars occur in Los Angeles are characterized by proximity to one or more of the following areas: residential sections with heavy concentrations of homosexuals; beaches or other places of homosexual group recreation or leisure-time activity; public entertainment districts—theaters and so forth; and areas of high tolerance and relative permissiveness toward other forms of deviant behavior. In Los Angeles there are five regions in which "gay" bars are located. The location of any given bar within a general region, however, depends on multiple factors too complex for elaboration here.

In these bars one finds the largest and widest representation of types, socioeconomic levels, and social strata in the homosexual world—if one goes from bar to bar as the homosexual does. It is estimated that on a Saturday night, between 10 P.M. and 2 A.M., a thousand men will pass through the doors of one of the largest and most successful bars. One may also observe in these bars one of the most standardized and characteristic patterns of social interaction in the "gay" world: the meeting of strangers for the essential purpose of making an agreement to engage in sexual activity, known as the "one-night stand." For many, these bars are social institutions where friends can be met, the news of the homosexual world heard, gossip exchanged, invitations to parties issued, and warnings about current danger spots and attitudes of the police given.

I conceive of homosexual bars as free markets that could arise only under a market economy in which buyers' rights to enter are determined solely by whether or not they have the wherewithal. The term "market," as applied to bars, has two meanings:

a business enterprise in which "leisure" is retailed in the form of
liquor and legitimate entertainment; and a metaphor for transactions between homosexuals, a set of terms relating to the negotia-
tion of exchange of sexual services.

While individual bars are relatively unstable and may be short-
lived, the bar system itself is relatively stable, although subject
to the constant surveillance of appropriate authorities. Its stability may be explained by several factors: bars are highly lucra-
tive for the owners, and, despite harassment and closing of individual bars, licenses are constantly being sought to reopen
them under new ownership or to establish bars in new locations;
they meet the expectations and needs and are geared in an
integral way to the behavior patterns of a large homosexual population; some authorities unofficially believe that elimination of
the system is both undesirable and impossible—"that kind of
person has to have some place to go, and at least they are with
their own kind, and you don't lose them; you just move them
around a little."

The successful operation of a "gay" bar is a highly skilled performance. It requires a knowledge of the tastes and behavior of
homosexual clientele and the ability to create the kind of atmos-
sphere that will attract them in large numbers, as well as the
ability to control behavior within limits to which law-enforce-
ment officers, passing as ordinary clientele, cannot legally object.

Let us turn now to the second meaning of the term "market,"
a place where agreements are made for the potential exchange of
sexual services, for sex without obligation or commitment—the
"one-night stand." If one watches very carefully and knows what
to watch for in a "gay" bar, one observes that some individuals
are apparently communicating with each other without exchanging words, simply by exchanging glances—but not the kind of
quick glance that ordinarily passes between men. Homosexuals
say that, if another man catches and holds the glance, one knows
immediately that he is one of them. The psychological structure
of that meeting of glances is a complex one, involving mutual
recognition of social but not personal identity, sexual intent,
and agreement; but we are far from being able to analyze that
structure. Many men in the bar, then, are not engaged in conver-

sation but are standing along a wall or by themselves at vantage points in the room, so that they may be seen as well as see, and are scanning faces and bodies. Occasionally, one may see a glance catch and hold another glance. Later, as if in an accidental meeting, the two holders-of-a-glance may be seen in brief conversation followed by their leaving together—or the conversation may be omitted. Casually and unobtrusively, they may arrive at the door at the same time and leave. If one were to follow them, one would discover that they were strangers, who had agreed by their exchange of glances to a sexual exchange. The terms of the exchange remaining to be settled will be the place and nature of the sexual act. A few minutes or a few hours later, one or both men may reappear in another bar to begin the same procedure all over again; or they may stay together for the night, seeking new partners the next night. What I have described is one form of "cruising." While the agreements resulting in "one-night stands" occur in many settings—the bath, the street, the public toilet— and may vary greatly in the elaborateness or simplicity of the interaction preceding culmination in the sexual act, their essential feature is the expectation that sex can be had without obligation or commitment. Regardless of person, time, place, or city, in the United States, at least, wherever homosexuals meet, this expectation is a stable, reproducible, standard feature of their interaction.

What stabilizes this pattern of expectation and regularized course of conduct? I do not believe that the answer to this question is to be found only in psychodynamic explanations but requires that system effects also be taken into account.

That system, as a sexual market, grows out of the "market mentality." Riesman comments, "In a market situation pervaded by what Karl Polanyi has termed the 'market mentality' . . . control of the economy will carry with it, to an unusual degree, control of the ethical regime" (1954, p. 60). He suggests that all values are subject to the market and are transformed by it and that, furthermore, "it is not the genuine self that is put on the market . . . but the 'cosmetic' self . . ." (pp. 59-60). Nothing is more conspicuous in the "gay" bar-market than the emphasis on appearance: on dress, manner, and body build. To furnish a genuine self in the exchange of partners, biography and prospects would be essential. In this meeting of strangers, activities disengaged from any ascriptive characteristics are promoted. The pressures toward maintaining secrecy about work and personal biography in homosexual encounters are derived in part from the functional consequences of their being revealed. The legal, occupational, and personal hazards of identification as a homosexual in our society are amply documented. The risk of information leakage from the "gay" world to the work world is high.

But if the market mentality pervades society and if it is the cosmetic self that is put on the market, why should sexual exchange in the relations of male to female be exempt from the characteristics of the "one-night stand"—sex without obligation or commitment? The heterosexual world is *not* exempt, but anything other than monogamous, legally sanctioned, obligated relations is a departure from strongly sanctioned norms, whatever the actual practice may be. That these norms are so strongly sanctioned in the heterosexual world may be in part a function of the fact that sexuality means more to the female than to the male.[6] Women have more to lose by divesting sexuality of rights, obligations, and commitment because their value in the competitive marriage market partly depends on its bargaining power and because their role as child-rearers requires psychological and economic support. The absence of women in the homosexual world, the sanctions of society against homosexual relationships, the pressures toward secrecy, the risks of revealing one's own homosexuality, and the market character of the bar setting in which meetings occur combine to produce the kind of sexual exchange that I have described as a stable feature of the "gay" world.

"Gay" bars also serve other important functions. It is estimated by bartenders that 50 per cent of the patrons on any given evening will be habitués who come at least once a week and, frequently, three or four evenings a week. Every bar has its clusters of friends who gather to exchange gossip, to look over the new faces, and to spend social evenings in an atmosphere congenial to them, where the protective mask of the day may be dropped. Bars are, therefore, communication centers for the ex-

---

[6] Suggested by Erving Goffman, in conversation.

change of news and gossip and for the discussion of problems and hard-luck stories. Practical problems, such as finding jobs, places to live, or lawyers, may be solved with the help of friends or new acquaintances. The opening of the newest bar in town, or a place that has recently become "hot," or that there is a party going to which one might be invited, and similar things provide topics of conversation. They are also, paradoxically enough, security operations. Although arrests are made in bars and the presence of vice-squad officers or alcoholic beverage-control authorities in plain clothes is an ever-present possibility, the bartender or bar owner will warn the patrons of their presence if their identities are known—and they frequently are. Warnings are also passed about particular patrons who are known to be "dirt," that is, who are likely to rob or demand money or possessions or to beat up sexual partners after consummation of the sexual act. News of harassment by the authorities travels quickly from bar to bar. The channels through which it passes are the associations of "gay" bar owners, most of whom are homosexual, and "bar-hopping" homosexual patrons who carry the news from one bar to another.

Bars also serve as induction, training and integration centers. These functions are difficult to separate. The young man who may have had a few isolated homosexual experiences in adolescence or indeed none at all and who is taken to a "gay" bar by a group of friends whose homosexuality is only vaguely suspected or unknown to him may find the excitement and opportunities for sexual gratification appealing and may thus begin active participation in the community life. Very often, the debut, referred to by homosexuals as the "coming out," of a person who believes himself to be homosexual but who has struggled against it will occur when he identifies himself publicly for the first time as a homosexual in the presence of other homosexuals by his appearance in the bar. If he has thought himself unique or has thought of homosexuals as a strange and unusual lot, he may be agreeably astonished to discover large numbers of men who are physically attractive, personable, and "masculine" in appearance, and his hesitancy in identifying himself as a homosexual may be greatly reduced. As he meets a complete cross-section of occupational and socioeconomic levels in the bar, he may become con-

vinced that, far from being a small minority, the "gay" population is very extensive indeed. Once he has "come out," that is,
identified himself as a homosexual to himself and to others, the
process of education proceeds apace. Eager and willing tutors—
especially if he is young and attractive—teach him the special
language, ways of recognizing vice-squad officers, varieties of
sexual acts, and social types. They also assist him in providing
justifications for his homosexual way of life and help to reduce
his feeling of guilt by providing him with new norms of sexual
behavior in which monogamous fidelity to the sexual partner is
rare.

In the bar world, the initiate soon acquires a body of knowledge that includes a set of "common understandings." [7] "Everybody knows" that sex can be had without obligation or commitment; that it is a meeting of strangers and that the too familiar
face does not "make out" in the sexual market; that one cannot
afford to be seen too frequently or one is counted out of the
cruising competition—after the initial newcomer phase; that
preferences for sexual acts may be specialized and congruence of
sexual interests between partners is frequently problematic;
that discrepancy between expected sexual behavior and appearance is not a surprise; that success in the sexual market is increased by "masculine" appearance and the appearance of youth;
that life in the bars, for sexual purposes, is "time limited," that is,
that men of thirty-five or more may not "make out" unless they
pay for partners; that, although the potential supply of partners is large, "making out" is difficult because many in the "gay"
world are afraid of rejection and the criteria of selection may
be highly specific.

I have described the homosexual "community" as analogous
to an iceberg, in which the visible part of the "community"—
visible to those who seek it—is to be found in a round of activities in public institutions, facilities, and areas. I believe, as do
homosexuals whom I have interviewed, that this visible community is a very small part of the whole and that understanding
of the submerged or hidden part—the secret and private activi-

---

[7] The term "common understandings" is borrowed from Harold Garfinkel
(1964).

ties of the world of friendship cliques—is fundamental to an understanding of the whole. In this world are to be found men who have established long-term living relationships with other homosexuals and who rarely, if ever, go to bars or other public establishments because of their sexually predatory and competitive character. They may have had periods of bar-going but have come either to dislike the bar activities or to fear them because of their threat to the stability of established relationships. Others, especially those of high occupational or socioeconomic status, may restrict their community life to private social cliques out of fear of exposure or arrest. Others may not enjoy drinking or may find sufficient sexual and social companionship in homosexual groups, whether they are living alone or with other homosexuals. There are, of course, many homosexuals who are isolates.

In the cliques, groups, and networks of friends, social occasions like evening, dinner, and cocktail parties are frequent, ranging from the simplest to the most elaborate and from the most intimate to the large spur-of-the-moment affairs. "Wedding" anniversaries, birthdays, and other special occasions call for celebrations, much as in the heterosexual world. Some groups make special efforts to maintain social relations with heterosexual couples, usually ones who are "wise," that is, are aware of and at least partially accept their homosexuality. These couples, in my experience, are rare, except in literary, other artistic, and highly sophisticated circles. In the main, members feel uncomfortable in the social presence of heterosexuals and prefer social occasions in which the guest list is made up of homosexuals, so that they can, in their phrase, "let down their hair"—that is, take off their protective masks. Some homosexual cliques or groups make every effort to behave in such a way as to minimize any indication of characteristics that would identify them as homosexual.

In contrast to the "one-night stand" of the "gay" bar world, there is constant seeking for more permanent relationships in the social world outside the bars. Indeed, the hope of many who engage in the "one-night stand" round of activities is that a particular encounter may lead to a more permanent arrangement. Some long-lasting relationships do begin in the bars, but the total system operates against them, as we have seen. In these relationships, sometimes called "marriages," complex problems of role management and practical problems of domestic establishments must be solved, as they are subject to the strains of a hostile heterosexual society as well as to those of the homosexual world. That many do survive these pressures is well established by my data. Accurate estimates of proportions are impossible because I am not engaged in a survey. I have now studied thirty such pairs with some thoroughness and many more in lesser detail. I want to comment only on one characteristic feature of sex and gender role in relationships in the homosexual world as I have observed them. Contrary to widespread belief, these roles are not clearly dichotomized between masculine and feminine. One does observe pairs with well-defined differentiation, but they are in the minority. The terms "active or passive partner" and "masculine or feminine role," to distinguish members of a pair, are inapplicable to the greater number of these pairs. Instead, the variety and form of the sexual acts between pair members, the distribution of tasks performed, and the character of their performance do not permit us to make such a differentiation. New solutions appear for which the old terms are inapplicable. In part, we may attribute the emergence of new solutions to the changing culture of the homosexual world. In what appear to be large sectors of that world, the stereotype of the effeminate is fought. In some, the result is a caricature of masculinity. The motorcycle crowd or the "leather set," with its affectation of tough masculinity, is one form of caricature. In others, the insistence on "being men" despite homosexuality results in a deliberate effort to develop patterns of behavior that are indistinguishable from those of heterosexuals, except, of course, in the sexual sphere, and here the dominant–submissive pattern is consciously resisted.

One of the important features of homosexual subcultures is the pattern of beliefs or the justification system. Central to it is the explanation of why they are homosexuals, involving the question of choice. The majority believe either that they were born as homosexuals or that familial factors operating very early in their lives determined the outcome. In any case, homosexuality is believed to be a fate over which they have no control and in which they have no choice. It follows that the possibility of changing to a heterosexual pattern is thought to be extremely limited. Current pessimism in psychiatric circles about the results of psychotherapy for homosexuals has been assimilated.[8] To fight against homosexuality is to fight against the inevitable, they believe, for they would be fighting against their own "nature" in its essential form as they experience it. They believe that homosexuality is as "natural" for them as heterosexuality is for others. Such belief patterns are widely shared by those who identify themselves as homosexuals and who participate in the rounds of activities I have described. I must reiterate that not all who engage in homosexual practices have accepted this identification and share these beliefs.

I have tried to characterize some features of homosexual worlds, or subcultures, in a large urban setting: the public community of the "gay" bar, which we have conceptualized as a market setting for the exchange of sexual services and as an induction, training, and integration center; the more private community of friendship cliques and group structures, in which more stable patterns are likely to develop and which also serves as an induction, training, and integration center; the common understandings and shared beliefs. Once the individual enters these worlds and becomes involved in their rounds of activities, he is subject to their beliefs, understandings, role prescriptions, and norms.

If "personal figures get their definition only when seen against the social or cultural background in which they have their being," it is necessary to view the homosexual not only against the background of the particular part of the subculture in which he participates but also against the background of the larger society.[9] Many homosexuals are beginning to think of themselves as a minority group, sharing many of the problems of other minority groups and having to struggle for their "rights" against the prejudices of a dominant heterosexual majority. Allport (1954) writes of traits of minority-group members who have been victimized:

---

[8] They have not read Bieber's book!

[9] The material that follows is, with modifications, taken from an early paper (Hooker, 1956).

A child who finds himself rejected and attacked on all sides is not likely to develop dignity and poise as his outstanding traits. On the contrary, he develops defenses. Like a dwarf in a world of menacing giants, he cannot fight on equal terms. He is forced to listen to their derision and laughter and submit to their abuse.

There are a great many things such a dwarf-child may do, all of them serving as his ego defenses (p. 142).

Once an individual identifies himself as a homosexual, he encounters the societal judgments of which Allport speaks. There are, to be sure, wide variations in the responses of an individual to the discovery of his homosexuality, just as there are, in any minority group, wide variations in methods of handling minority-group membership.

It has seemed to the author that there is a striking parallel between the ego-defensive traits, "traits due to victimization" of which Allport speaks, and the traits that characterize many homosexuals. It may be instructive to examine some of them.

"Obsessive concern," for example, is cited as one trait many minority-group members exhibit. Allport suggests that the "racial frame of thought" is inescapable for the Negro, so that there is a haunting anxiety that he cannot escape. He must be constantly on his guard. There can be no doubt, from interview data gathered from homosexuals, that this attitude characterizes a large number of them. The homosexual is often labeled as an obsessive-compulsive personality, and the obsession with his homosexuality is often described as a defense against heterosexuality. In instances, however, in which psychological test materials obtained from homosexuals do not allow this clinical label, the obsessive concern with homosexuality as a target of possible attack is nevertheless conspicuous. The tangle of obsessive features of the defense derived from personality structure and from the social situation needs to be carefully studied.

"Withdrawal and passivity" is another example of ego defense against victimization. Many writers on homosexuality assume that passivity and dependency are among the most characteristic attitudes of a large group of homosexuals. Again a question arises about the role of social factors in producing these attitudes. Are they inherent in the personality structure of homosexuals, or are they in part the result of attempting to cope with a hostile world in a manner that may, in the mind of the victim, produce the least damage to himself?

Many of the other traits of which Allport speaks, like the strengthening of in-group ties, protective clowning, or identification with the dominant group and hatred of himself and his own group, are found in homosexual groups as well as in other minorities. It would be strange indeed if all the traits caused by victimization in minority groups were, in the homosexual, produced by inner dynamics of the personality, for he too is a member of an out-group subject to extreme penalties, involving, according to Kinsey, "cruelties [which] have not often been matched, except in religious and racial persecutions" (Kinsey *et al.*, 1948, p. 17).

REFERENCES

Allport, G. W. *The nature of prejudice.* Cambridge, Mass.: Addison-Wesley, 1954.

Becker, H. S. *Outsiders: studies in the sociology of deviance.* London: Collier-Macmillan, 1963.

Bendix, R. Compliant behavior and individual personality. *Amer. J. Sociol.,* 1952, **58**, 292-303.

Bieber, I., Dain, H. J., Dince, P. R., Drellich, M. G., Grand, H. G., Gundlach, R. H., Kremer, Malvina W., Rifkin, A. H., Wilbur, Cornelia B., & Bieber, Toby B. *Homosexuality.* New York: Basic Books, 1962.

Clemmer, D. *The prison community.* Boston: Christopher, 1940.

Cohen, Y. A. (Ed.) *Social structure and personality.* New York: Holt, Rinehart & Winston, 1962.

Cory, D. W. *The homosexual in America.* New York: Greenberg, 1951.

Fishman, J. E. *Sex in prison.* New York: Commonwealth Fund, 1930.

Ford, C. S., & Beach, F. A. *Patterns of sexual behavior.* New York: Harpers, 1951.

Garfinkel, H. Studies of the routine grounds of everyday activities. *Soc. Prob.,* 1964, **2**, 225-250.

Green, Maurice R. (Ed.) *Interpersonal psychoanalysis, the selected papers of Clara M. Thompson.* New York: Basic Books, 1964.

Hooker, Evelyn. A preliminary analysis of group behavior of homosexuals. *J. Psychol.,* 1956, **42**, 217-225.

Hooker, Evelyn. Male homosexuality in the Rorschach. *J. proj. Tech.*, 1958, **22**, 33-54.

Hooker, Evelyn. The adjustment of the male overt homosexual. *J. proj. Tech.*, 1957, **21**, 18-31.

Hooker, Evelyn. What is a criterion? *J. proj. Tech.*, 1959, **23**, 278-281.

Hooker, Evelyn. The homosexual community. In *Proc. XIVth int. Congr. appl. Psychol., Personality Research.* Vol. 2. Copenhagen: Munksgaard, 1962. Pp. 40-59.

Hooker, Evelyn. Male homosexuality. In N. L. Farberow (Ed.), *Taboo topics.* New York: Atherton, 1963. Pp. 44-55.

Huffman, A. V. Sex deviation in a prison community. *J. soc. Ther.*, 1960, **6**, 170-181.

Kardiner, A. Discussion. In P. H. Hoch & J. Zubin (Eds.), *Psychosexual development in health and disease.* New York: Grune & Stratton, 1949. Pp. 85-88.

Kinsey, A. C., Pomeroy, W. B., & Martin, C. E. *Sexual behavior in the human male.* Philadelphia: Saunders, 1948.

Kluckhohn, C., & Murray, H. A. (Eds.). *Personality in nature, society and culture.* New York: Knopf, 1949.

Leimert, E. W. *Social pathology.* New York: McGraw-Hill, 1951.

Leznoff, M., & Westley, W. A. The homosexual community. *Soc. Prob.*, 1956, **3**, 257-263.

Lindzey, G., Tejessy, C., & Zamansky, H. S. Thematic Apperception Test: an empirical examination of some indices of homosexuality. *J. abnorm. soc. Psychol.*, 1958, **57**, 67-75.

Mead, Margaret. *Sex and temperament.* New York: Morrow, 1935.

Mead, Margaret. Cultural determinants of sexual behavior. In W. C. Young (Ed.), *Sex and internal secretions,* Vol. 2. (3rd ed.) Baltimore: Williams & Wilkins, 1961. Pp. 1433-1481.

Opler, M. K. Cultural perspectives in research on schizophrenias: a history with examples. *Psychiat. Quart.*, 1959, **33** (No. 3), 506-524.

Rechy, J. *City of night.* New York: Grove, 1963.

Reiss, A. J., Jr. The social integration of queers and peers. *Soc. Prob.*, 1961, **9**, 102-120.

Riesman, D. *Individualism reconsidered.* New York: Free Press, 1954.

Ross, H. L. The "hustler" in Chicago. *J. stud. Res.*, 1959, **1**, 13-19.

Smelser, N. J., & Smelser, W. T. (Eds.) *Personality and social systems.* New York: Wiley, 1963.

Sullivan, H. S. In H. S. Perry & M. L. Garvel (Eds.), *The interpersonal theory of psychiatry*. New York: Norton, 1953.

Westwood, G. *A minority—a report on the life of the male homosexual in Great Britain*. London: Longmans, Green, 1960.

Westwood, G. *Society and the homosexual*. London: Gollancz, 1952.

Wheeler, W. M. An analysis of Rorschach indices of male homosexuality. *J. proj. Tech.*, 1949, **13**, 97-126.

Wrong, D. H. The oversocialized conception of man in modern sociology. *Amer. sociol. Rev.*, 1961, **26**, 183-193.

This investigation was supported by Research Grants M-839 and MH-0645 from the National Institute of Mental Health, National Institute of Health, Public Health Service.

6 Anthropological and Cross-Cultural Aspects of Homosexuality

This discussion of homosexuality pivots upon a combined behavioral and social-science view of man's fate. This combination of sciences, however, provides no ready-made answers about the fate of sexual impulses. The anthropological view does not ignore biological and physiological factors and is particularly receptive to psychological ones. At the same time, however, it insists that social and cultural forces not be neglected and that cross-cultural differences be given recognition in any analysis of human behavior (Opler, 1959a). This interdisciplinary view is the minimal requirement of an anthropological approach. But how the biological, psychological, social, and cultural factors are presumed to mesh and operate depends on the scientific synthesis. I shall attempt such a synthesis with regard to the problem of homosexuality.

Let me begin with a psychological point of view, the Freudian. In his analysis of the Schreber case (1911), Freud's insights into Schreber's Oedipal struggles led to the formulation that homosexual trends are a defense against immature infantile desires of males for mothers and females for fathers. Homosexuality was seen as a defensive structuring of unresolved conflicts in this realm. The infantile urges might first be denied with compulsive thought or conduct. But if compulsive, hysterical, displacing, and repressive defenses wore thin, wish projections and distortions might be tried in the Oedipal struggle. The problem of homosexual trends was thus seen as a root problem in paranoid schizophrenia.

The key to this approach is, of course, the theory that psychosexual development is the prime behavioral unfolding that determines all else. As Charles Brenner (1955) and other accurate commentators have pointed out, the point of view is one of psychic determinism with a psychosexual emphasis. But the biologist or physiologist asks, "What of biological and hormonal sexual variations?" The sociologist notes that the Daughters of Bilitis have their own organized press. The epidemiologist points to quantitative variations in the appearance of overt homosexual behavior by class, culture, nation, and perhaps historical epoch. The anthropologist points out that there are cultures in which homosexuality exists and others in which it does not, occasions on which it has behavioral organization and sanction and others on which it exists surreptitiously, and societies in which the raw stuff of Oedipal striving, castration fears, or the Greek or Nazi versions of male solidarity hardly can exist. The suggestion is that what Freud perceptively observed was one set of psychological hazards, behavioral evolution, and conditions of existence (middle-class Viennese society).

What Freud discovered, using one set of factors in one general type of culture in one historical period, hardly could be used in the framework of cultural relativity for different cultures. Yet the matter can be put more fairly to give credit to the factors he did discover. Perhaps most of all, in emphasizing the psychological factors, Freud located one paramount sequence of causality. We shall claim that it is only one part of the causal change or nexus, but this claim does not diminish the importance of the discovery. The principle he established was that biological functioning in humans is subject to profound social and cultural inhibitions and that, in this sense, psychological factors have primacy and control over organic ones. This emphasis, of course, had a tremendous impact on the organicist tradition of German medicine, and Freud was attacked and berated as a sexmonger and sensualist, almost the opposite, of course, of what he really was. A doctrine that stresses the necessity of ego controls and the formative dominant position of the superego in all development is a form of psychic determinism, to be sure, but hardly argues for unilinear and one-sided sexual determinism. In *The Ego and the Id* (1927), Freud called "culture" the "heir of the Oedipus complex"—in just so many words—and, though he lacked the anthropological training and data to know what to do with culture as a prime factor in establishing "ego" and "superego" supremacy over the id, nevertheless he proclaimed it the principle by which individuals are normatively controlled.

In *Totem and Taboo* (1913), however, Freud's lack of anthropological training and data led him to create a fantasy about the nature of primitive societies and cultural evolution, using the aboriginal tribes of Australia as his prime example. Let us consider the Australian tribe that practices subincision of the male penis in coming-of-age ceremonies used as the *rite de passage* for adolescent boys. The casual reader who learns about incisions with stone knives up to the urethra, the laying flat of the whole cylindrical organ, and the binding with leaves for a painful healing after a painful operation without anesthesia and then discovers that the older men (fathers, grandfathers, and paternal uncles) are the mutilators might presume that this operation climaxes or arouses extremely severe castration anxieties in a society in which males and females live nude. Does this ceremony then lead, as it is claimed in Freud's *Totem and Taboo*, to castration anxieties, the primal parricidal myth, and the symbolic injunction against eating the ancestral totem animal (pseudo-"anticannibalism," in the tortured explanation)? Nothing could be further from the truth! The pain is suffered willingly, even proudly, by lads learning tribal lore and religion from patrilineal elder kinsmen. The latter are models of concern and sympathy and, more than that, are sharing precious rites and tribal lore with the novices. Indeed, these boys have seen male and female nudity, know animal anatomy in addition, and are well versed in sexual and reproductive functions far beyond the children and adolescents of our "modern" cultures. Any vestige of castration anxieties—could they even exist—are nullified by the ceremonial ritual in which the penis mutilation occurs, a ritual imbued with the religious sanctity of becoming an adult in the society and coming into the possession of sacred lore, adult prerogatives, and adult fellowship.

The point about these societies and other nonliterate hunting and gathering societies is that homosexuality is generally rare and, in some instances, virtually nonexistent. In the first tribes this author ever studied under field conditions, the Mescalero and Chiricahua Apache, this rarity stands in marked contrast to modern urban American or English culture. The standard work on Chiricahua, *An Apache Life-Way,* by Morris E. Opler (1941), notes that homosexuality is forbidden among them and considered to be a form of witchcraft. Informants had heard about boys, but not adult men, experimenting homosexually. One berdache, or transvestite, who engaged in women's pursuits (but apparently not in homosexuality) was reported to have died before 1880. A few Lesbians dated back to days of detention at Fort Sill in Oklahoma. Some women had masculine interests. But other than these scattered and historical instances, in which, incidentally, no organic findings were available, homosexuality was notable for its rarity. Later, in fieldwork among Ute Indians of Colorado (1955), this author's check on such topics yielded amusement, disbelief, and counterquestioning on American urban culture.

The reactions of nonliterate peoples, on the simplistic hunting and gathering levels of economic development, help to answer the question whether rates of homosexual behavior vary among different societies. Driver, in *Indians of North America* (1961), discusses typical examples of Plains Indian berdaches, or male transvestites. He notes that relations with women were symbols of male prestige in these cultures and that the general social dominance of men over women was probably stronger here than in any area north of Mexico, except the Northwest Coast. In this setting, some men with strong aversions to the ultramasculine role donned women's clothing, did women's work, and sometimes (apparently a minority) lived homosexually in actual fact.

Writers on South American Indians offer equally sparse examples. Steward and Faron, in *Native Peoples of South America*

(1959), mention examples only for the Calamari, among whom there was a special class of male inverts, as well as one of women prostitutes, who went from village to village selling sexual services, and for the Nata townsmen, among whom there was a class of homosexual male slaves who did women's work.

Margaret Mead, in various writings but notably in her book *Male and Female* (1949), goes beyond the bare bones of such reporting to suggest that human societies evince two polarities in regard to sexual arousal. One is a tendency toward erotic specificity, so that sexual arousal depends upon particular conditions. The nape of the female neck in Japanese lore of the past century is one instance of cultural specificity, whereas intersexual bathing and nudity are alleged to have had no such connotations. Among the Ute Indians whom this author has studied, it is claimed that female breasts are devoid of sexual meaning. On the other hand, positive sexual arousal, including homosexual arousal, has been described as being stimulated by a wide and diverse range of nonspecific sources. It is possible, however, that such description derives from generalizations from cross-cultural data such as those of Ford and Beach in their *Patterns of Sexual Behavior* (1951), which stress complex patterns of cultural learning. The Ford and Beach survey lists cultures in which virtually all males engage in homosexual practices at times and other cultures in which such practices are interdicted and relatively rare. Unfortunately, most studies of the survey sort tear information out of context, so that one is quite uncertain whether the investigator is concerned with the normative sexual experiments of preadolescents or with adult homosexuality. By contrast, Rado, in his *Psychoanalysis of Behavior* (1956), distinguishes the "situational homosexuality" of prisoners and sailors isolated from opposite sex mates; the "incidental homosexuality" of some adolescents and preadolescents or of sociopaths; the "chaotic sexuality" of certain impulse-ridden schizophrenics; and the "reparative homosexuality" of some neurotics traumatized from heterosexual contacts.

In my book, *Culture and Mental Health* (1959b), I have reported briefly on Bogoras' fascinating work, *The Chukchee* (1904–1909), which deals with a well-studied tribe of Northeastern Siberia. The developmental course of Chukchee transvestitism practices is carefully described. Bogoras relates the Chukchee practice of insisting on a bride price, or *kalym*, which often takes a man seven years to amass, to high rates of aberrancy. Bogoras also describes the floating population of perennially unmarried laborers. The problems of building the nucleus of one's own reindeer herd or of a son's protracted adolescent status in relation to a long-lived property-owning father indicate two ways in which rigid patriarchal controls over property inheritance may operate. Bogoras describes the frustrations of delayed marriages, the development of fantasy outlets, and the social sanctions for transvestite shamans to practice as a kind of escapism. The pathology he describes, such as notions of wandering out over the tundra, are direct expressions of the escapist theme. That members of the floating populations of laborers, youths, or sons-in-law "serving time" may receive this "call" to respectable livelihoods as shamans is entirely expected, and the relatives are enjoined to be duly respectful of the sanctity of this profession and watchful of the developing shamans' safety. Not all shamans take the route of transvestitism, however. Apparently only a few do go to such lengths, but the cultural sanctions accord the transformed shaman particular compensations in *religious* potency.

Animal studies are not in the least analogous to such rich cultural accounts, but they do give some notion of how extreme discomforts can lead to chaotic sexuality. Harlow's well-known studies (1959) of rhesus monkeys deprived of mothering and further isolated from reparative peer-group contacts show breakdowns of normative heterosexual behavior in both males and females. Calhoun's studies of Norway rats (1962) showed that those subjected to adverse environmental conditions in the crowded settings he calls "behavioral sinks" developed failures in nest building, interruptions in normal transport of young, and both homosexual and infant-rat sexual approaches. In the "pansexuality" that developed, both male and female rats were increasingly bitten on the scruff of the neck during mounting, although female rats sustained these aggressive attacks in greater number. Carefully developed mammalian studies have demonstrated that disturbances in sexual behavior are accompanied by concomitant disturbances in social behavior and other functions.

Indeed, Harlow's study appears to demonstrate that proper peer-group contacts can help to heal wounds occasioned by faulty mothering.

As most persons familiar with anthropological literature know, heterosexual experimentation often has greater social sanction in primitive societies than in Western or European cultures. The Andamanese, described by Radcliffe-Brown in *The Andaman Islanders* (1948), practiced strict monogamy, prohibited and punished adultery, but allowed both boys and girls to participate freely before marriage in sexual experimentation that frequently led to "trial marriages." The Ute Indians of Colorado are in no sense connected historically to the Andamanese, but they practiced precisely the same sexual customs. The Tahitians of Polynesia furnish a third example of a people among whom the years between puberty and marriage are expected to constitute a period for experimental love affairs. Yet these societies, which are permissive in their heterosexual customs, accord homosexuality a most aberrant status. Actually, no society, save perhaps ancient Greece, pre-Meiji Japan, certain top echelons in Nazi Germany, and the scattered examples of such special status groups as the berdaches, Nata slaves, and one category of Chukchee shamans, has lent sanction in any real sense to homosexuality. Regardless of what may be said concerning all the factors—social, legal, and psychodynamic—entering into homosexual behavior, one thing is clear: In the absence of an organic or hormonal basis, homosexuality in practically all cultures is regarded as a deviation from the majority values and norms of conduct.

On the other hand, while most cultures recognize the normative character of heterosexual bonds of one type or another, most also place enormous psychological emphasis on such matters as the social control of sexual behavior. Even the Andaman, Ute, and Tahitian peoples limit heterosexual experimentation to a particular life period. While all three are fairly egalitarian and permissive about divorce, the fact remains that cultural norms and rules still function as social definitions of sexual conduct. The heterosexual norm and its social control in all cultures suggest that the problem of relative incidence of homosexuality is not a function of organic and hormonal variations in humans but of differences in the cultures themselves.

As we have seen, the psychosexual developmental theme of Freudian psychology has extended the causal nexus of experiences influencing organic functioning to include culture, which in turn influences experience. For this reason, mammalian animal studies, while instructive, cannot reach the level of Rado's classification of "incidental, situational or reparative homosexuality" in humans. If we ask whether there may be homosexual subcultural groups, particularly in modern urban and industrial societies, as there are in the scattered primitive instances, the answer is, of course, yes. These subcultural groups are also special responses to strains in the normatively heterosexual cultures and not simply individual psychodynamic phenomena.

As culture is a prime means of human adaptation and in this sense aids individuals in adapting to the world of nature and of social relationships, cultures define norms of sexual conduct in the same settings or patterns that they define social, educational economic, and political relationships. A cultural point of view on any aspect of human behavior therefore stresses *social* identification, as well as *sexual-* and *self*-identification. There are, in all cultures, *social* definitions of conduct linked with *sexual* definitions and with notions of proper *personal* behavior. In fact, such linking is how cultures aid man in adaptations to the world of nature, to the "cosmos," and to others, male and female, in the society. The norms that define sexual conduct are of the same substance as those defining social and personal conduct. Freud discovered parts of these connections in the causal nexus, in particular the connections between sexual and personal functioning. Social functioning was subsumed under such concepts as "sublimation of libidinal energies" or "specific consciences" or "superego" to invoke the notion of human striving beyond the pleasure principle. Because, cross-culturally and biologically, the weight is thrown on the side of heterosexual standards of conduct, it is tempting to assume a fixed biological proclivity in this direction. Yet a biological deviance in hormones and sexual structures such as occasionally occurs in sexual maturation does not always produce so flagrant or florid a form of homosexuality in humans as does mere confusion in social, sexual, and self-identification. Indeed, this point is foreshadowed on the animal level in studies of the Norway rat and rhesus monkey, among which behavior is a function of social, group, and interanimal contacts rather than of biological endowment. In the same sense, biological deviance is only one factor among many in human *gender-role* definition. Indeed, social expectations and self-conceptions may transform the biological deviant into a model male or female from the cultural point of view. Studies of hermaphrodites have indicated that social and familial expectations can shape the outcome toward male or female gender roles, regardless of the actual genetic sex involved.

Not that culture does not ideally stress the existence of usual, normative, and common standards of a male or a female type. The point is simply that this highlighting is done culturally. A Navajo Indian may be a he-man, a gambler, and a philanderer while dressing in bright blouses adorned with jeweled belts, necklaces, and bracelets. French courtiers in the retinues of effete monarchs were equally philanderers, though rouged, powdered, and bedecked with fine lace. The Andaman Islanders like to have the man sit on his wife's lap in fond greetings, and friends and relatives, of the same or opposite sex, greet one another in the same manner after absences, crying in the affected manner of the mid-Victorian woman. Like the Ute, they value premarital sexual experimentation and sexual prowess and technique in any later life period. Obviously, the style of social and sexual behavior is something of an amalgam and is culturally influenced.

The formula of social, sexual, and self-identification combinations, in addition, is useful in defining homosexuality. In our culture, with its tendency toward sex segregation in the latency period, preadolescent and adolescent sexual experimentation is often labeled "homosexual" no matter how rare, intermittent, or experimental the behavior actually is. Such rules of thumb, deriving from the theory of psychosexual dominance, often do considerable harm to an individual's later self-evaluations or are viewed with undue apprehension by physicians. Goldman, in his monograph on *The Cubeo, Indians of the Northwest Amazon* (1963), labels as "homosexual," for lack of a clearer or better term, what appears to me to be limited sexual experimentation on essentially the maturing adolescent masturbation level. Among the Cubeo, in a rare instance of rigid sexual controls that contrast with Ute, Andamanese, and similar customs, adolescents may reach the age of marriage without having had sexual relations with an eligible marriage partner. Instead, young people are limited to semipublic "homosexual" play, in which girls may stroke one another's nipples to produce erection or boys may indulge in mutual masturbation. The alternative to this activity is clandestine incestuous (between sib, not familial, brother and sister) experimentation in which actual intromission is regarded as *really* constituting incest and is avoided, so that the act consists only of external genital rubbing. True coitus or intromission would be punishable by death and, as true incest, would be followed by the offenders' souls becoming animal souls unfit for human association. As Goldman recognizes, *true* homosexuality among the Cubeo is rare if not absent, for he learned of no cases of persistent male homosexuality and of only one organically abnormal "woman" who developed strong male characteristics including, eventually, a penis. The Cubeo premarital limits are balanced by later widespread adultery and by female aggressiveness in enticing sexual intercourse—which continues even after menopause. Cultures in which female sexual aggressiveness exceeds that of the male, such as those of the Cubeo and upper-class Tuareg female courtiers and troubadours, are often those in which males are the social custodians of morality to such an extent that our Western European notions of biological, male-linked, sexual aggressiveness have to be modified. This difference is present not only in sexual but in social and ego-adaptive areas as well.

For those who give psychosexual development primacy, it is well to remember that among the Cubeo it is a common male complaint that wives are too ardent, whereas among the upper-class Tuareg the male would blush furiously in the love court of female troubadours if his veil were to slip (the men rather than the women are veiled). These cultural conditions are by no means common, nor do they negate other normal biological proclivities. Goldman notes, for example, that Cubeo women, no matter how sexually forward, prefer to be vigorously subdued in actual sexual intercourse. The Imashek of the Tuareg, like women in most Sahara cultures, are likewise interested in strong male sexual prowess. What we are describing are profound cultural *modifications* of biological sex but not its obliteration.

In most anthropological theory, the notion that biological needs or drives are modifiable by cultural necessity holds sway. If we were to discuss the matter more philosophically, there might be a tendency to claim that moral or legal sanctions mold behavior in some direction. This formulation, indeed, is one way in which concepts of superego, or conscience, have been used. In Freudian formulations, however, moral or legal sanctions are viewed as part of cultural constriction and as inhibitory rather than formative. Idealistic positions in philosophy might hold, by contrast, that ideas rather than environmental experiences determine conduct. We hold with the Freudian position that moral and legal sanctions are part of the culture pattern, but we should add to Freud's inhibitory notions that cultural patterns of sexual or other biological behavior may be not only restrictive and prohibiting but also prescriptive and positively determining. For example, Cubeo adolescent experimentations are publicly displayed as sexual modalities for children and youth, and masturbation is conducted without shame. Similar prescriptive patterns are observable (in balance with proscriptive ones) in such cultures as those of the Ute, the Andamanese, or the Tahitians, which we have used as examples of predominantly permissive systems. Homosexuality is rare in such permissive but organized and directive systems. Such societies are, of course, culturally homogeneous, well understood by their members, and in aboriginal times so socially and economically integrated that little cognitive mapping was required to give moral and legal sanctions to kinds of sexual behavior. Far from agreeing with Benedict's *Patterns of Culture* (1934) that a process of "psychological selectivity" is at work deriving ethos and outlook from an endless arc of possibilities, we believe the *conditions of existence* in a culture (economic and social, primarily) are determinative of the themes that may be selected. Sexual and self-identification themes are only a part of such an ethos. There is a vast difference between the view that "anything can happen" in a culture and the position that parts of the pattern are more determinative of its details than are other parts. Our concept of pattern excludes the former brand of psychic determinism but includes the latter form of psychosocial determinism, according to the *conditions of cultural existence*.

Although culture is, by and large, a generalized and extrasomatic agency for serving all manner of human needs, it does not follow that the needs themselves are entirely supra-individual or non-somatic. Economics, for example, may aid in the organized procurement and even development of "needs"—some of which may be somatic and some not. It is conceivable that Navajo practices of male adornment may be distantly related to primate tendencies to bedeck and adorn, such as those observable among monkeys and apes, which are not culturally determined. Economics touches, however, upon basic conditions of existence in a culture, and, because of human appetites, economics is enormously and repetitively concerned with daily somatic needs. The Kinsey reports on male and female sexual behavior in American society, even if we disregard the improper and sometimes even curious modes of sampling that they employed, clearly bring out essential class differences in sexual conduct (although the unit of analysis is not conduct but biological orgasm). Similarly, even a psychoanalytic popularizer like Edmund Bergler cannot fail to note in his writings that homosexual symptoms are part of wider personality disorders, are susceptible to educational campaigns and organized medical countermeasures, and have social as well as individual contexts, creeds, and organizations. Few writers on the problem of homosexuality in modern society have failed to notice profound differences in social-class patterns of homosexual behavior analogous to the widely known social-class differences in normative heterosexual behavior. Besides sexual needs, other forces—"needs" for prestige, social desires, and even factors bolstering self-esteem become important. The chief's yam-houses with their rotting yams among the Trobriand Islanders and the burning candlefish oil and broken copper plates of a potlatch, or give-away ceremony, among the Kwakiutl Indians of British Columbia are two well-worn examples of elaborations on simple economic patterns (Benedict, 1934, Ch. 6). Sexual customs are similarly elaborated, as in the Trobriander's myth of no physical paternity or the Cubeo's claim of female sexuality increasing to the menopausal years. At the same time, the Trobrianders, even those from the rich garden districts of Kiriwina, do not omit garden magic; the Kwakiutl do not neglect the basic subsistence economy contained in fishing and timber; and the

Cubeo formulate sexual restrictions until marriage—all for good reasons. To presume that an economic system can be based on prestige ideology alone, that sexuality does not have social definition and regulation, or that the cultural ethos does not attach to elements important in the daily round of the culture is poor anthropology indeed.

We begin with economics and the cultural pattern as examples because, in most discussions of the psychic economy, it has so often been assumed that the sexual factor is not only preeminent but that it operates alone. To our way of thinking, these conceptions of a psychic (and organic) *primum mobile* acting alone are inadequate in explaining the amazing adjustments sometimes achieved by the organically inadequate and the variations in both type and quantity of abnormal conduct in cultures in which the physical human organisms are essentially normal in biological endowment. Similarly, zonal theories of development, such as that of Erikson in *Childhood and Society*[1] (1950), are negated as *primum mobile* theories when we contrast his warlike Sioux Indians with the peaceful Ute of Colorado. The Sioux roamed the plains and showed cruelty to women occasionally, not because of cradleboard inhibitions to movement or nursing past the stage of tooth eruption, but because Sioux culture is esssentially patrilineal and nomadic in its hunting of buffalo. The Ute, who did not roam the plains and were egalitarian in sexual codes, used a similar cradleboard and nursed infants and children even longer, but Ute culture was organized differently in its social and economic aspects. Neither do purely individual sexual ideologies determine sexual conduct and proclivities. We have never encountered a purely individual ideology about sex. Although the psychosexual factor has tremendous importance in the total development of individual behavior, it is doubtful that we can abstract sexual development from concomitant social and self-identification processes. The basic error of the *primum mobile* theory of psychosexual development is that it tears sexual development from its meaningful context and ceases to weigh it together with other connected developments in human growth.

In nonliterate societies, social groupings by kinship, age group,

---

[1] *Cf.* Erikson's later position (1956).

clans, sibs, and associates in various functional relationships far outweigh social groupings by sex. In fact, Lowie (1948) was one of the few modern theorists to discuss groupings by sex at all, and he used such pallid distinctions as those among bachelors, spinsters, and married persons. Although most kinship distinctions include sexual criteria, some do not, and, in general, most kinship groups have not one but several criteria for admission. Clubs and societies have on occasion been sex limited, as in Melanesia, but there is no reason to believe that this limitation has promoted homosexual behavior in these social, economic, or sometimes ritual settings—or indeed that such behavior exists at all in such instances.

Holmberg, in his monograph *Nomads of the Long Bow* (1950), about the Siriono of Eastern Bolivia, has noted that, in the hand-to-mouth existence of these South American Indians, anxieties about food gathering and sharing occur regularly but seem to be divorced from sexual matters. The Siriono practice nudity, chiefs have many wives, and there is no question that young males see "mothers" and are aware of menstrual functions. Although, in our modern Western European cultures, both male and female paranoid schizophrenics typically show evidence of both overt and "latent" homosexuality, if the theory were transculturally valid, the paradigm of incomplete Oedipal repressions followed by male castration fears and female fears of seduction would have a flying start among the Siriono. In actuality, the Freudian anxiety of Oedipal origins, the projective conversion of "I love him" to "I hate him," and its later defensive generalization to paranoid persecutions do not find ready analogues in Siriono culture. We suspect that what have been left out of account are other massive processes of social and self-identification.

In our belief, not only do self-, social-, and sexual-identification processes co-exist and interweave, but also, with self-identification chronologically consolidated in the first stages, social identification doubtless impinges on the cognitive processes associated with language. In this manner, areas labeled "social" and "learned" have a curious way of invading the other two from the outer cultural and family environments. Only a total life-cycle perspective would ever give weight to social-identification processes as such. Piaget (1952), Sullivan (1953), and Fromm (1955) have initiated trends in this direction from child studies, life-cycle, and social-identity theory respectively. The epidemiological interests of social psychiatry have already proved this point on a different frontier in a multitude of studies on variations in every form of mental disorder by age-sex or class-cultural analyses. To suppose, against this massive evidence, that we have one model of human development, male or female, or one process of ego adaptation to describe is to set the scene only for psychologically based theories of sexual adaptation or self-identification. Both exist but not alone. *Their existence is essentially meaningless unless social identification is immediately added as a concomitant in the life cycle.*

REFERENCES

Benedict, Ruth F. *Patterns of culture.* Boston: Houghton Mifflin, 1934.

Bogoras, W. The Chukchee. *Jesup Exped. Rep.* (New York: American Museum of Natural History, 1904–1909), 7 (Memoir 11).

Brenner, C. *An elementary textbook of psychoanalysis.* New York: Internat. Univer. Press, 1955.

Calhoun, J. B. A behavioral sink. In E. L. Bliss (Ed.), *Roots of behavior.* New York: Harper & Row, 1962.

Driver, H. E. *Indians of North America.* Chicago: Univer. Chicago Press, 1961.

Erikson, E. H. *Childhood and society.* New York: Norton, 1950.

Erikson, E. H. The problem of ego identity. *J. Amer. psychoanal. Assn.,* 1956, 4, 56-121.

Ford, C. S., & Beach, F. A. *Patterns of sexual behavior.* New York: Harper & Row, 1951.

Freud, S. Psychoanalytic notes upon an autobiographical account of a case of paranoia. *J. Brit. psychoanal. Psychopath.,* 1911, 3, 9-68.

Freud, S. *Totem and taboo* (1913). London: Routledge & Kegan Paul, 1950.

Freud, S. *The ego and the id.* London: Hogarth Press and Institute of Psychoanalysis, 1927.

Fromm, E. *The sane society.* New York: Holt, Rinehart & Winston, 1955.

Goldman, I. *The Cubeo, Indians of the northwest Amazon.* Urbana: "Ill. Stud. Anthrop. No. 2," Univer. Illinois Press, 1963.

Harlow, H. F. Love in infant monkeys. *Scient. Am.,* 1959, **200** (68), 40, 63-74.

Holmberg, A. R. *Nomads of the long bow.* Washington, D.C.: "Smithsonian Inst. soc. anthrop. Publ. No. 10," 1950.

Lowie, R. H. *Social organization.* New York: Holt, Rinehart & Winston, 1948.

Mead, Margaret. *Male and female.* New York: Morrow, 1949.

Opler, M. E. *An Apache life-way.* Chicago: Univer. Chicago Press, 1941.

Opler, M. K. The southern Ute Indians in Colorado. In R. Linton (Ed.), *Acculturation in seven American Indian tribes.* New York: Appleton-Century-Crofts, 1940.

Opler, M. K. The influence of ethnic and class subcultures on child care. *Soc. Prob.,* 1955, **3**, 12-21.

Opler, M. K. Cultural perspectives in research on schizophrenics. *Psychiat. Quart.,* 1959, **33**, 506-524. (a)

Opler, M. K. (Ed.) *Culture and mental health.* New York: Macmillan, 1959. (b)

Piaget, J. *The origins of intelligence in children.* New York: Internat. Univer. Press, 1952.

Radcliffe-Brown, A. R. *The Andaman islanders.* New York: Free Press, 1948.

Rado, S. *Psychoanalysis of behavior.* New York: Grune & Stratton, 1956.

Steward, J. H., & Faron, L. *Native peoples of South America.* New York: McGraw-Hill, 1959.

Sullivan, H. S. *The interpersonal theory of psychiatry.* New York: Norton, 1953.

7 | Legal and Moral Aspects of Homosexuality

THOMAS S. SZASZ

Ever since the Freudian revolution, and especially since the Second World War, it has become intellectually fashionable to hold that homosexuality is neither a sin nor a crime but a disease. This claim means either that homosexuality is a condition somewhat similar to ordinary organic maladies, perhaps caused by some genetic error or endocrine imbalance, or that it is an expression of psychosexual immaturity, probably caused by certain kinds of personal and social circumstance in early life.

I believe it is very likely that homosexuality is, indeed, a disease in the second sense and perhaps sometimes even in the stricter sense. Nevertheless, if we believe that, by categorizing homosexuality as a disease, we have succeeded in removing it from the realm of moral judgment, we are in error. I make this claim not only because the concept of disease itself involves a value judgment, distinguishing some states of bodily and mental functioning from others, but also because every society attaches certain additional value judgments of both a legal and a moral sort to particular diseases. In ancient times, for example, epilepsy was considered a holy disease, and today venereal diseases are considered very unholy indeed.

It is a social-psychological fact that, in our society as in most contemporary Western societies, homosexuality is neither legally nor morally neutral. On the contrary, homosexual acts and persons labeled "homosexual" are subject to a variety of legal and moral sanctions. Homosexuality is thus a legal and a moral problem as well as a particular behavioral manifestation.

The Distinction between the Legal and the Moral

The similarities between law and morals are often more keenly appreciated than the differences between them. To be sure, both are systems of social control, concerned with conduct deemed good and bad, right and wrong. In a theocracy, the laws are regarded as upholding moral principles. Even in such a society, however, there may be moral wrongs for which there are no specific legal sanctions (for example, violating dietary laws).

In a secular society, the distinction between law and morals is of great importance (St. John-Stevas, 1961). The two differ first in the type of sanction imposed. In law, the sanction is imposed by the state and is usually physical—typically, deprivation of property or liberty. The moral sanction is imposed by conscience and is usually psychological—typically, deprivation of "inner freedom" produced by feelings of guilt and worthlessness. Occasionally, moral sanctions may be imposed externally by individuals or groups, as in social ostracism.

Second, the law is normally concerned with conduct, although, of course, it cannot ignore motives altogether. Morality, on the other hand, is concerned equally with actions and motives. In Christian ethics especially, motives determine the ultimate moral values of actions. And similarly, in psychoanalysis, motives determine the ultimate psychological meaning of actions (for example, actions that are externally heterosexual may be internally homosexual).

Third, the purpose of law is generally conceded to be the good of the community. Laws are necessary to ensure the integrity of the social order. Especially in the United States, offenses are often designated *ad hoc* to meet particular social problems—for example, prohibition or the "sexual psychopath" laws. Morality, on the other hand, has a larger scope and is less utilitarian: its aim is to promote the widest possible adherence to an ethical ideal (everyone should be a Christian, a heterosexual, and so forth).

These distinctions, although of course not absolute, are important, especially in connection with laws regulating sexual conduct. In no other area is there a greater attempt to impose moral values through legislation.

Homosexuality as a Legal Problem

I shall present, first, a brief review of the laws pertaining to homosexuality in America and Europe and shall then offer some comments on them.

In the United States, homosexual acts between males, though not between females, are offenses in every state. The specific types of act that are punishable and the nature of the punishments vary greatly from state to state, however. In many jurisdictions, it is not homosexual conduct as such but so-called "sexual acts against nature" that are proscribed. Finally, although consent between adult parties is nowhere an excuse, the degree of force applied by one person to another is often an important aspect of the offense. New York State, for example, recognizes three types of sodomy, depending mainly on the degree to which one party is assaulted by the other.

In California, the law prohibits "crimes against nature." There is, however, no clear definition of what constitutes such crimes. The punishment is imprisonment for a period of from one to ten years. Sexual perversions are also offenses and are punishable by imprisonment not exceeding fifteen years. In addition, California has statutory provisions for so-called "sexual psychopaths," who may be subjected not only to criminal sanctions but also to deprivations of liberty by means of involuntary mental hospitalization.

As a rule, the term "crimes against nature" is not clearly defined, but it usually implies sexual penetration *per anum* or *per os* with "either man or beast." Such acts are listed as offenses in Colorado, Florida, Idaho, Kansas, Louisiana, Maine, Michigan,

Missouri, Montana, Nevada, North Carolina, Oklahoma, South Dakota, Tennessee, Virginia, Washington, and West Virginia.

In Arizona, homosexual acts fall into the category of "sodomy," which is a crime punishable by imprisonment for one to five years. "Said crime may be committed by the penetration of the mouth or rectum of any human being by the organ of any male person." Intercourse *per os* or *per anum* is thus considered an offense regardless of whether it occurs between members of the same or opposite sex, between adults and children, or between consenting or nonconsenting parties.

In most of the states in which the statutes do not speak of "crimes against nature," the offense is also "sodomy," defined, in Georgia for example, as "the carnal knowledge and connection against the order of nature, by man with man, or in the same un-natural manner with woman."

In addition to being punishable under the laws prohibiting crimes against nature and sodomy, homosexuals may be included in the category of sexual psychopaths and may thus be subject to the controls of the "sexual psychopath" statutes. Most of the states have enacted statutes of this sort. It should be noted, how-ever, that this type of legislation aims mainly at curbing sexual acts against children or sexual acts constituting assaults. Sexual conduct in private between consenting adults is not likely to be brought within the scope of these statutes.

In England, as in America, homosexual conduct is still a crime. In 1885, the Criminal Law Amendment Act "provided that any male person, guilty of committing or procuring, or attempting to procure, an act of gross indecency with another male, 'in public or private,' should be guilty of a misdemeanor, punishable with a maximum term of two years imprisonment, with or without hard labour" (St. John-Stevas, 1961, pp. 209-210). This law has re-mained substantially unchanged. Attempts to prohibit female homosexuality, however, have failed.

The law against homosexuality has recently been subjected to significant legislative criticism in England. In 1954, a special committee was appointed by the House of Lords, under the chair-manship of Sir John Wolfenden, to study the problem. The report of this committee, known as *The Wolfenden Report* (Home Office, 1957), strongly criticized the view that homosexuality is a disease and proposed that "homosexual behavior between consenting adults in private should no longer be a criminal offense" (p. 25). This conclusion, the committee pointed out, follows inevitably from adherence to the principles of a free society in which "there must remain a realm of private morality and immorality which is, in brief and crude terms, not the law's business" (p. 24). Nevertheless, when in 1960 a motion was made in the House of Commons to implement the relevant findings of *The Wolfenden Report,* the proposal was defeated by 213 votes to 99.

In contrast to England and the United States, the majority of European states do not proscribe homosexual acts between consenting adults. Austria, Germany, and Norway are the only European countries that do so, but in Norway the law is not enforced. In Belgium, homosexual conduct is punishable only if there is assault, if the sexual object is a minor, or if there is violation of public decency. Similar situations obtain in Denmark, Greece, Italy, the Netherlands, Sweden, and Switzerland. In France, homosexuality between consenting adults has not been a crime since the *Code Napoléon* went into force in 1810 (St. John-Stevas, 1961, p. 216).

For many years on both sides of the Atlantic, jurists and physicians have, in the main, agreed that homosexual acts taking place in private between consenting adults should not be subject to the criminal law. This view by American and English leaders in law and medicine has, however, so far not been reflected in remedial legislation.

There can be little doubt that present legislation on this subject is, to say the least, utterly irrational. In many of the statutes, acts as different as impairing the morals of a minor and oral–genital intercourse between man and wife are placed in the same logical class and called "sodomy" or "crimes against nature." As long as people seek, through their legislators and by means of the criminal law, to influence the private sexual conduct of adult members of society, it will be impossible to differentiate adequately between sexual acts that offend the public safety and welfare and those that do not.

The laws we have surveyed suggest a few general conclusions:

First, male homosexuality is a greater crime than female homosexuality. This attitude seems to be a direct carry-over from rabbinical law, which regarded male homosexuality as a serious crime but female homosexuality only as a disqualification for marriage with a rabbi (St. John-Stevas, 1961, p. 204). Our present laws against male homosexuality reflect the ancient view, evidently not yet outgrown by the modern community and its legislators, that women, like children, are inferior beings; grown men need not have much interest in what they do among themselves.

Second, homosexuality is a crime because it is unnatural. In many jurisdictions, the offense is not homosexuality as such but any act included under such headings as "unnatural intercourse" or "acts against nature." These laws incorporate and reflect the traditional Judeo-Christian concept of "natural law." All types of so-called "unnatural" sexual activity—from oral–genital intercourse between married couples to sexual acts with animals—are thus brought within the purview of the law.

Third, the male homosexual is also penalized as a member of a minority group. The discrimination to which he is subjected is best illustrated by the treatment accorded him by the federal government. Although subject to the draft during the Second World War, homosexuals could be separated from the service for their homosexuality by means of a so-called "blue discharge," which was neither honorable nor dishonorable but was undesirable. Although homosexuality was technically defined as a medical, and more specifically as a psychiatric, condition, it was nevertheless treated with punitive sanctions:

> These soldiers and sailors were told that they were being treated like sick people, and not criminals. They had committed no wrong, but were ill, and if other ill soldiers were allowed benefits after the war, these men would receive the same.
>
> Such promises were later brushed aside when, by executive order of a Veterans Administrator . . . anyone having a blue discharge for homosexuality was barred from receiving any and all government benefits under the G.I. Bill of Rights, except those specifically granted by Act of Congress. Thus no government-subsidized education, no business or home loans, no bonus. Once again only broken promises. But the important fact here is that no other medically discharged men, including those disassociated from the army as psychoneurotics under Section Eight of the Medical Dis-

charge regulations, were barred from such benefits. Only the sexual invert! (Cory, 1951, p. 44).

In peacetime too, the federal government has shown dread of homosexuals. For purposes of employment, the Civil Service Commission places homosexuals in the same category as criminals and persons engaging in "infamous, dishonest, immoral, and notoriously disgraceful conduct" (Cory, 1951, p. 269).

Fourth, the homosexual is mentally ill. How much homosexuality is dreaded in our society is illustrated by the fact that this condition is considered not only a crime but also a disease. On the one hand, the homosexual may be treated as a sexual offender, while, on the other, he may be defined as mentally ill and subjected to involuntary "hospitalization" and "treatment." Thus changing an important moral and social problem into a medical one has loosed on the homosexual the sanctions, or the threat of sanctions, that psychiatrists are in a position to exercise *vis-à-vis* mental patients (Szasz, 1960a).

In many states homosexuals are technically committable. Although such persons are probably rarely committed merely because of their sexual conduct, this fact does not alter the intent of the legislation or its potential threat. In Massachusetts, for example, a person is considered a fit subject for involuntary hospitalization if he conducts himself "in a manner which clearly violates the established laws, ordinances, conventions or morals of the community" (Mass. Ann. Laws, 1957, 123-1). Accordingly, the homosexual is the subject of repressive legislation as a member not only of the class of criminals but also of the mentally ill.

The homosexual is also subject to the penalties of the so-called "sexual psychopath" laws. A homosexual act, forbidden by law, is by definition a "sex crime," punishable by indeterminate incarceration in a mental institution.

Homosexuality as a Moral Problem

One of the differences between legal and moral rules is that the former are explicit, whereas the latter must usually be inferred from what people do and say. The moral aspects of homosexuality may be inferred from observing three spheres of life: law, psychiatry, and everyday life.

Antihomosexual legislation is an attempt to regulate personal morality by criminal sanctions. If such legislation were limited to the control of homosexual prostitution or the corruption of minors, it could be argued that its aim was to protect society from certain kinds of harm. But when the law defines as criminal all homosexual contact between consenting adults, it becomes clear that its aim is no longer social but moral. Antihomosexual legislation thus reflects deep-seated abhorrence and condemnation of homosexual practices.

Many observers of the contemporary social scene have pointed out that, despite appearances to the contrary, our culture remains strongly antisexual. Nowhere is this bias better illustrated than in our laws on sexual conduct. As we have seen, most of the statutes that prohibit homosexuality prohibit other types of sexual conduct as well. Implicitly, sexuality is treated as an evil, justified only if it is "natural" (heterosexual and genital) and if it leads to conception. The connection between laws against homosexuality and other "perversions," on the one hand, and those against contraception and abortion on the other, is obvious: Both reflect our antisexual morality (Szasz, 1960b).

It is often claimed that our morality is permissive toward heterosexuality and is hostile only to homosexuality. This claim is a deceptive half-truth. Much of what seems permissiveness toward heterosexuality is inspired by dread of homosexuality; the heterosexuality it promotes is compulsive, not spontaneous. There is an impressive similarity between the prohibition of alcoholic beverages and our present laws and mores about sex. One might say, for example, that the Volstead Act did not prohibit the use of alcohol but only its misuse. Drinking for mere pleasure was regarded as wrong ("perverse") and was therefore prohibited. At the same time, the proper or biologically "normal" use of alcohol was not only permitted but encouraged. Just as Prohibition reflected a moralistic condemnation of drinking, so our sex laws reflect a moralistic condemnation of fornication. Sex laws prohibit not only homosexuality but also all sorts of so-called "heterosexual perversions," as well as contraception and abortion (Lindman & McIntyre, 1961). That they allow or even encourage "normal"—heterosexual, procreative—unions should not blind us to the moral implications of these legal regulations.

Although there is no reliable information on the subject, it seems likely that most psychiatrists—like most educated persons —look with disfavor on the kind of repressive legislation against homosexuals that still remains on our statute books. Probably no educated person today really believes that private homosexual acts between consenting adults are crimes. Many persons, however, and perhaps especially psychiatrists believe that homosexuality is an illness. As an illness logically requires treatment, the question arises whether homosexuals ought to be treated. The problem then is to decide not only whether homosexual acts should be punishable but also whether homosexuals should be forced to submit to psychiatric treatment against their wills. In other words, we must be careful lest, by defining homosexuality as illness, we merely shift the methods by which we control homosexual conduct. The sanctions of the criminal law are judicial and "punitive," whereas the sanctions of legal psychiatry are medical and "therapeutic" (Szasz, 1963).

To argue that homosexuality is abnormal and heterosexuality normal is to cast various types of sexual conduct into the framework of health and disease. Health and disease are useful concepts. For instance, to suffer from cancer of the colon is to be sick; it is more healthy to have an anatomically and physiologically intact colon. Of course, this statement is true only if we base our judgment on the proposition that the human body is for living. In defining heterosexuality as normal and homosexuality as abnormal, what is the basis for our judgment? The main reason for adopting this standard is the value of heterosexuality for procreation and therefore for the survival of the species. In this biological sense, intercourse that is heterosexual and genital is an appropriate norm.

But, from an ethical point of view, such a decision begs the question; the survival of the human species today does not depend on the procreative performance of every man and woman. On the contrary. Our biological survival is now threatened by too much procreation, not by too little.

The issue, in fact, is not so much whether or not, as psychiatric theoreticians, we conceptualize homosexuality as a type of disease. The issue is what we *do* on the basis of our concepts. Freud was evidently keenly aware of this problem—that is, of the difference between the sorts of psychiatric *idea* we have about homosexuality and the sorts of *action* we base on them. The following discussion between Freud and Wortis is illustrative:

"There are plenty of people who are ready to call any unusual behavior neurotic," I [Wortis] said, "like the students at my college who thought there must be something wrong with anybody who read poetry."

"Unusual conduct isn't necessarily neurotic," said Freud.

"Many people take it for granted too," I said, "that homosexuals are neurotic, though they might be perfectly capable of leading happy and quiet lives if society would tolerate them."

"No psychoanalyst has ever claimed that homosexuals cannot be perfectly decent people," said Freud. "Psychoanalysis does not undertake to judge people in any case."

"Still," I said, "it makes a difference to homosexuals whether they are considered neurotic or not."

"Naturally homosexuality is something pathological," said Freud. "It is an arrested development (*eine Entwicklungshemmung*)."

"But plenty of valuable qualities could be called the same: you might call the simplicity of genius a kind of childishness or arrested development too," I said.

"Of course," said Freud, "the fact that a person is a genius doesn't prevent his having pathological traits: if he is only five feet tall instead of six, that would have to be called pathological."

"The question, though," I said, "is whether one ought to undertake to *cure* homosexuals as if they were diseased, or make their lot easier by making society more tolerant."

"Naturally," said Freud, "the emphasis ought to be put on social measures; the only homosexuals one can attempt to cure are those who want to be changed."

"But that might only have the effect of making them discontented heterosexuals instead of honest homosexuals."

"Certainly," said Freud. "One often has the experience of starting an analysis with a homosexual who then finds such relief in being and talking just as he is that he drops the analysis and remains homosexual" (Wortis, 1954, pp. 55-56).

Certainly, it is not surprising to read that Freud eschewed the idea of treating homosexuals (or anyone else) who did not want to be treated. Yet herein lies the crux of the ethical problem in the modern psychiatric approach to homosexuality. The idea that homosexuality is an arrest in psychosexual development or a mental disease (related to paranoia and schizophrenia) is one thing; to make this notion the basis of compulsory hospitalization or treatment is another. When psychiatrists diagnose homosexuality in a setting in which the diagnosis becomes public property—for instance, in the military, in government service, in prisons, and so forth—their work is psychiatric in name only; actually, those psychiatrists act as judges, condemning people for being homosexuals.

Let us now consider certain popular attitudes toward sex, other than those reflected in the practices of law and psychiatry.

The popular attitude toward sex in the United States is a mixture of compulsive heterosexuality and religious antisexuality. The former is frequently mistaken for sexual "freedom," the latter for medical and psychiatric "insight" into "normality." In many ways, our culture encourages heterosexuality. Dating begins early. In advertising there is an ever-present heterosexual motive; cars, cigarettes, cosmetics, and countless other products are promoted in this fashion. And, above all, marriage is extolled. An unmarried man or woman past thirty must justify his or her single status, as if it were a defect or a dereliction of duty. At present, in the United States, the median ages for marriage are twenty-one for men and eighteen for women. Still more amazing, there are more than 20,000 children fifteen and under who are married. It is a telling commentary on our sexual morality that the concept of teen-age marriage is not rejected as strongly as are a host of other sexual practices. To be sure, such marriages are often regarded as foolish but rarely as "sick"! Yet the social implications of this sort of sexual conduct are more farreaching than are those of homosexuality (Shearer, 1962).

Let us consider a fairly typical situation. At sixteen or seventeen, a girl marries a boy her own age or a few years older; by the time she is nineteen, she has two children; by the time she is twenty or twenty-one, she is divorced. Such marriages are veritable factories of social deviance, especially what we call "schizophrenia" and "delinquency." Such unions are ill-suited for child-rearing. This judgment prevails among workers in three important agencies of contemporary society—the police, psychiatry, and social work; in their experience, more problems stem from such juvenile marriages than from others. It is incontestable then that at least this type of "normal," heterosexual, procreative sexuality does more demonstrable harm to society than do homosexual practices between consenting adults.

It is important to appreciate that the homosexual does not threaten society by his actual behavior but rather by the symbolic significance of his acts. Like the political subversive who undermines the value of established political institutions or the religious subversive who undermines the value of established religious institutions, the homosexual undermines the value of heterosexuality. In my opinion, this symbolism explains society's attitude toward the homosexual. He is treated as if he were "subversive"; for example, it is widely assumed that he is a greater security risk than a nonhomosexual. In a way, he is, for he subverts one of the favorite "games" of Western society—heterosexuality.

Because he rejects heterosexuality, the homosexual undermines its value. So, of course, does the priest. The homosexual, however, rejects one type of sexual conduct in favor of another, whereas the priest eschews the pleasures of the flesh to emphasize the value of the spirit. The homosexual thus threatens the heterosexual on his own grounds. He makes the heterosexual fear not only that he too may be homosexual but also that heterosexuality itself is not as much "fun" as it has been made out to be. Many people behave as if sexual satisfaction were one of their main interests in life. If the value of their favorite game is undermined, they may lose interest in it, and then what will they do?

The Christian religions and (classical) psychoanalysis lend credence to a parochial obsession with sex. It is implicit in their orientation to human conduct that sexuality is one of the most important and most interesting facets of life. But is it?

Of course, the homosexual himself is a victim of this sexual obsession. Preoccupied with and intent on homosexual cravings and gratifications, he is the mirror-image of the ever-lustful, ever-frustrated heterosexual.

Psychiatry, Sex, and Values

Psychiatrists perform two fundamentally different tasks in our society: they analyze the values people profess to hold and the games they like to play, and they promote certain values and instruct patients in how to play certain games (Szasz, 1961). These two activities are frequently combined and confused, for example, in psychoanalysis.

Ideally, psychoanalytic therapy is a purely "analytic" enterprise; the therapist's activity is limited to helping the patient learn about himself, others, and the world about him. The goal of converting homosexual to heterosexual conduct is incompatible with such a concept of psychoanalytic treatment. As a theory of personality, however, psychoanalysis holds that man "develops" through certain stages of psychosexual organization and that heterosexual genitality is the "normal" end stage of this developmental process. It is implicit in this scheme that the psychoanalyst will try to help his patients reach this stage of "normality."

We delude ourselves, however, if, because of its biological value, we accept heterosexuality as a social value. The jump from biological value to social value is the crux of human morality.

I do not want to belabor the problem of the role of values in psychiatry. Nevertheless, for a meaningful examination of the legal and moral aspects of homosexuality, the issues must at least be presented. The biological "naturalness" of heterosexuality (which can be easily exaggerated for higher primates) does not, in itself, justify adopting it as a social or moral value. Killing one's enemy is also biologically natural and effective, but it does not justify warfare. Or let us consider a more sophisticated example. In times of famine, Hindus will starve to death in the midst of a herd of cattle. To argue that eating beef is more "natural" than believing in the Hindu religion would not be value analysis but value promotion. Similarly, psychotherapeutic efforts to change homosexuals into heterosexuals must be clearly defined as attempts to change the patients' values.

But if this sort of thing is what we—psychiatrists and psychotherapists—do, the question arises: What sexual values should we advocate? There are several possibilities. We might take the position that sexual activity is only one among many things that men find interesting. Accordingly, we should oppose defining sexual activity as extremely interesting or important. Or, without special reference to sex, we might advocate an autonomous morality (Szasz, 1960b, 1961). Or we might advocate procreative heterosexuality. Or, we might encourage nonprocreative heterosexuality to lessen the danger of overpopulation. We might even advocate homosexuality over heterosexuality; this choice could be supported as a contraceptive technique, especially for women intellectually or artistically gifted, for whom the value of traditional feminine heterosexuality is a barrier to achievement.

Conclusions

In a modern industrial society, the attitude of people toward sexual activity in general and homosexuality in particular reflects many influences and interests. Religious teachings or their absence or an emphasis on scientific atheism are one such influence. Economic considerations are a second, political and military factors a third, and ideas about medical and psychological health a fourth.

When human beings engage in sexual acts, they do not simply discharge sexual tensions. Only some animals do that. For men and women, the performance of the sexual act—whatever it may be—is complex and symbolic. No simple generalization about it can be valid.

Similarly, no simple generalization can explain why some people foster, others tolerate, and still others violently condemn certain kinds of sexual practice. Whatever their sexual preference may be, people will have little difficulty creating a morality to rationalize and support them and laws to enforce them.

In the United States today, why is homosexuality a problem? Mainly because it presents, in sexual form, the classic dilemma of popular democracy: How much diversity should society permit? Many people, eminent psychiatrists among them, do not distinguish between democracy and what Tocqueville called "the tyranny of the majority." In his book *Sex Offenses*, Manfred Guttmacher, one of the outstanding American forensic psychiatrists, expressed the following view:

I have great faith in the democratic process. If it is the considered will of the majority that large numbers of sex offenders, most of whom admittedly have a high social nuisance value, be indefinitely deprived of their liberty and supported at the expense of the state, I readily yield to that judgment (1951, p. 132).

There is little meeting ground between those who "readily yield" to such a judgment and those, like myself, who repudiate such democracy as the quintessence of totalitarian oppression.

The importance of the political aspect of the problem of homosexuality cannot be exaggerated. Guttmacher stated that, if sex offenses—among them homosexuality—are condemned by the majority, one's loyalty to the group requires supporting that condemnation and the legal sanctions backing it. Why stop at homosexuality? If the majority finds Jews, Negroes, or atheists offensive, should it be free to harass them also? This logic is behind many of our present views and practices concerning homosexuality. As long as attorneys, legislators, and psychiatrists find this logic acceptable, their protests against specific measures, on the grounds that they are "unscientific," are doomed to fail.

There is, of course, another conception of democracy. According to it, democracy is not simply a political organization in which the majority tyrannizes the minority but one in which the freedom of minorities from such oppression is a foremost consideration. John Stuart Mill (1859) was one of the ablest champions of this classic idea:

There is a limit to the legitimate interference of collective opinion with individual independence; and to find that limit, and maintain it against encroachment, is as indispensable to a good condition of human affairs, as protection against political despotism (p. 7).

In our day, homosexuality is a moral, political, and social problem. It is not enough, therefore, for psychiatrists to concern themselves with abstract notions of psychosexual health and disease and to disregard the more general problem of conformity versus diversity in a complex human society. Coercive measures aimed at reducing diversity of opinion or action, whether in the sexual or in the intellectual sphere, are destined to constrict society and thus the human personality.

I think we are more likely to find the answer in the other direction. Only through intellectual freedom can we achieve intellectual self-discipline. Similarly, we cannot expect to promote sexual self-discipline (if that is what some of us want) by our present methods, which combine, in a single package as it were, heterosexual titillation with dread and prohibition of specific sexual acts.

Men have always feared that sexual freedom would result in sexual license. Accordingly, they have put their faith in external controls—that is, in prohibitions and punishments. Intelligent measures to ensure sexual freedom would perhaps foster sexual self-discipline rather than sexual license. Without adequate inner controls, in the sexual as well as in other spheres of life, the outlook for modern man is dim indeed.

REFERENCES

Cory, D. W. *The homosexual in America.* (2nd ed.) New York: Castle, 1960.

Guttmacher, M. S. *Sex offenses.* New York: Norton, 1951.

Home Office. *Report of the committee on homosexual offences and prostitution (the Wolfenden report).* London: Her Majesty's Stationery Office, 1957.

Lindman, R. T., & McIntyre, D. J., Jr. (Eds.), *The mentally disabled and the law.* Chicago: Univer. Chicago Press, 1961.

Mill, J. S. *On liberty* (1959). Chicago: Regnery, 1955.

St. John-Stevas, N. *Life, death and the law.* Bloomington: Indiana Univer. Press, 1961.

Shearer, L. Date early! marry late! *Parade,* May 13, 1962, pp. 6-7.

Szasz, T. S. Civil liberties and the mentally ill. *Cleveland-Marshall Law Rev.,* 1960, **9**, 399-416. (a)

Szasz, T. S. The ethics of birth control: or, who owns your body? *Humanist,* 1960, **20**, 332-336. (b)

Szasz, T. S. *The myth of mental illness.* New York: Hoeber-Harper, 1961.

Szasz, T. S. *Law, liberty, and psychiatry.* New York: Macmillan, 1963.

Wortis, J. *Fragments of an analysis with Freud.* New York: Simon & Schuster, 1954.

8 | Historical and Mythological Aspects of Homosexuality

GORDON RATTRAY TAYLOR

The materials necessary for an exhaustive historical study of homosexuality do not exist. Even in the culture for which we have more historical material than any other—Europe in the last thousand years—they are inadequate. Legal and ecclesiastical prohibitions of such behavior caused homosexuals to conceal their activities as a rule, while the polemics of the moralists tended, we may be sure, to exaggerate the actual state of affairs.

The presentation of a balanced picture is made more difficult by a second factor, our inevitable tendency to judge all sexual behavior, including homosexuality, by the standards of our own culture. In addition to the need to suspend moral judgments, we need to know a great deal about such matters as family structure and religious beliefs before we can make much sense of the data. When these elements are taken into consideration, a much more interesting situation emerges than one would expect, to judge from the rather crude historical sketches usually found in encyclopedias of sexual knowledge.

I propose, therefore, to start with a short account of the history of homosexuality in Western culture; then to outline some of the significant features of the Mediterranean cultures from which Western culture sprang; and finally to present the available data concerning homosexuality against this background.

Western Culture

It is not until we reach the seventeenth century that the kind of source material we really need becomes freely available, that is, diaries and travel books in which the social scene is reported frankly and in detail. As soon as it does, we find reports of the existence of homosexuality.

William Lithgow (1906), for example, a Scot who traveled (by his estimate) some 36,000 miles in a series of journeys in Europe and the Middle East between 1609 and 1622, during which he was at one stage imprisoned and tortured by the Inquisition, makes a number of references to homosexuality. The Turks, he says, are "generally addicted, besides all their sensuall and incestuous lusts, unto Sodomy, which they account as a daynty to digest all their other libidinous pleasures." We may detect some Protestant bias in his accusations of "Romish priests" whose "continuall pleasure and practise" is sodomy, but the following passage on the situation in Padua seems matter-of-fact:

> The Schollers here in the night commit many murthers against their privat adversaries, and too often executed upon the stranger and innocent, and all with gun-shot or else stilettoes: for beastly Sodomy, it is as rife here as in Rome, Naples, Florence, Bullogna, Venice, Ferrara, Genoa, Parma not being exempted, nor yet the smallest Village of Italy: A monstrous filthinesse, and yet to them a pleasant pastime, making songs, and singing Sonets of the beauty and pleasure of their Bardassi, or buggered boyes.

As he goes on to praise Venice and Genoa for their anti-Jesuit and anti-Jewish attitudes, his inclusion of these towns in the list can hardly have been motivated by a generalized bias.

Lithgow does not discuss England, but Pepys (1946) speaks of sodomy as general at court, and in 1698 the Duchess of Orleans wrote to a friend that "nothing is more ordinary in England than this unnatural vice." At the turn of the century, Dudley Ryder

was warned that it was dangerous to "send a young man who is
beautiful to Oxford," for "among the chief men in some of the
colleges sodomy is very usual." In 1729 the anonymous author
of *Hell upon Earth: or the Town in an Uproar* wrote:

> They also have their Walks and Appointments, to meet and pick up
> one another, and their particular Houses of Resort to go to, because
> they dare not trust themselves in an open Tavern. About twenty of
> these sort of Houses have been discovered, beside the Nocturnal As-
> semblies of great numbers of the like vile Persons, what they call the
> *Markets,* which are the Royal Exchange, Lincoln's Inn Bog Houses,
> the south side of St. James's Park, the Piazzas in Covent Garden, St.
> Clement's Churchyard, etc.
>
>   It would be a pretty scene to behold them in their clubs and
> cabals, how they assume the Air and affect the name of Madam or
> Miss, Betty or Molly, with a chuck under the chin, and "Oh, you bold
> pullet, I'll break your eggs," and then frisk and walk away.[1]

In mid-century, such tracts as *Satan's Sowing Season* (Est,
1611) alleged that sodomy was increasing, a view supported by
Smollett (1843) in *Roderick Random,* where he declared that
homosexuality "gains ground apace and in all probability will
become in a short time a more fashionable device than fornication." A number of allegedly sodomitical groups were uncovered
following the royal *Proclamation against Vice* in 1788.

Toward the end of the century, the puritanical views of the
middle classes began to gain the ascendancy, and an increasing
number of prosecutions and cases of blackmail are to be found.
Public scandal was caused by the prosecution of one Cook for
keeping a house of resort in Vere Street in 1811, for he named
several prominent men among his customers. The Home Secretary intervened, and Cook was sent to the pillory. "It was not
intended that you should have come back alive" the turnkey told
him afterward. A solicitor who, though opposed to homosexuality, was indignant at the treatment accorded to Cook made an
investigation. He recorded with naïve astonishment, "It is not
effeminate men but butchers, blacksmiths, coal merchants, police

---

[1] *Cf.* also J. Dalton (1728).

runners, who do it . . ." and added that there were many houses of this sort in town.

By the middle of the nineteenth century, supposedly an era of Victorian rectitude, things had reached the point at which "it is not long since that, in the neighborhood of Charing Cross, they posted bills in the windows of several respectable public houses, cautioning the public to 'Beware of Sods.' " Ryan, the secretary of the Society for the Suppression of Vice, asserted that there were brothels in which not only girls but boys as well could be obtained—and at a cost of only ten pounds.

The Yokel's Preceptor, a cheap guide for visitors published at about the same time, warned its readers to be careful because of the "increase in these monsters in the shape of men, commonly designated Margeries, Pooffs, etc." and goes on to describe the signs by which they made themselves known to one another. These signs, interestingly enough, were precisely the same as those G. Parker (1789) had described in the previous century.

Enough has been said to indicate clearly that the notorious trial of Oscar Wilde was no isolated phenomenon nor any indication of *fin de siècle* decadence. (The fact that the case came to trial at all was due to factors of quite another kind.)

When we turn further back to the medieval period in England, direct evidence is almost nonexistent, and we must infer what we can from indirect material. It was only when eminent persons displayed overtly homosexual traits that history recorded the fact. We learn that King Rufus and Edward II were homosexuals. The chief forms of indirect evidence are the ordinances and penitentials issued by successive church councils. The earliest of these include penalties for incest but do not refer to homosexuality. Penalties for the latter gradually made their appearance and almost wholly displaced references to incest by about the twelfth century. Presumably, there was a marked increase in homosexuality in England during the period, an assumption that the cases of Rufus and Edward II seem to confirm.

The period saw an increasingly severe attitude toward sex generally on the part of the Church. In particular, the penitentials anathematized priestly sodomy. The Church was becoming increasingly strict about priestly celibacy, which may have driven priests into homosexual alternatives. It is also possible, however, that the less masculine type of individual was attracted to the priesthood, for it was the only profession in which aggressive or acquisitive behavior was not a desideratum.

Before Christianity came to Britain, there was a free sexual morality there, based on a system of group marriage, as was true also on the Continent. Alcuin (1941), flaying the vices of the ninth century, complains about widespread adultery and incest but does not mention homosexuality. What he called adultery and incest were, of course, the consequences of the group-marriage system; in point of fact, there were strict rules of exogamy. This point also explains the earlier complaint of Boniface (1940) that the English "despise matrimony" and "utterly refuse to have legitimate wives but continue to live in lechery and adultery."

A major difficulty in interpreting the data arises from the doubtful interpretation of the word *sodomia*. It appears to have denoted anal intercourse rather than homosexuality. The Cathars, for example, were accused of *sodomia*. The Cathars (or pure ones), a heretical group in the South of France, held that the spirit had become enmeshed with matter and that the path of development was to escape from material existence to pure spirituality—a doctrine derived from the Gnostics and by them from India. Ascetic in all things, the Cathars eschewed sexual intercourse and practiced a form of chaste marriage. The Christian Church accused them of *sodomia* with their wives—that is, of avoiding procreation by anal intercourse. The doctrine had supposedly reached France via Bulgaria, and its proponents were called "Bulgars"—a term subsequently corrupted to "buggers." Similar accusations were brought against the Templars and with as little basis.

The failure to distinguish between homosexuality and buggery is also embedded in current British law, which prescribes, under one act, severe penalties for anal intercourse (whether heterosexual or homosexual) and, under another much later act, lesser penalties for "gross indecency"—meaning oral or masturbatory practices between males. Similar practices among women are ignored.

Interestingly enough, the church equated sodomy and heresy. Heretical sects were regularly accused of sodomy, as were witches. The essence of witchcraft was that it depended on worshiping the Devil—and all deities other than the Christian God were regarded as avatars of the Devil. Today we tend to think of a witch as one who works magic, but in the Middle Ages magic was commonplace. What mattered was whether one worked by appealing to God or by appealing to the Devil. Furthermore, witches did not function in individual isolation; they were members of covens or groups that met regularly to worship the Devil. Some form of debased fertility worship seems often to have been involved. The desire to associate heresy and sodomy led to witches' being accused of various practices, notably the "obscene kiss." According to some accounts, the Devil is equipped with a forked penis so that he can commit both buggery and fornication at the same time.

All we can safely say of the period was that the Church was intensely preoccupied with homosexuality. To what extent it constituted a genuine social problem is hard to say, but in all probability the menace was vastly exaggerated. When the system of control cracked in the Renaissance, there apparently was not any marked efflorescence of homosexuality, although we do find men (in Elizabethan England, for example) adopting some feminine practices, like wearing earrings, while remaining fully virile.

What appears to have replaced preoccupation with homosexuality was preoccupation with incest. This theme is rather common in the Elizabethan drama and is treated in an atmosphere of horror. Homosexuality is mentioned in a tone of mockery if at all. The spirit is well expressed in the joke coined when James I ascended the throne of England: "Elizabeth was King; now James is Queen." In Italy, where a general breakdown of morality seems to have occurred, homosexual assaults were recorded but were not particularly outstanding in the general pattern of amorality and law-breaking. Sigismondo Malatesta attempted to assault his son but was also convicted of "murder, rape, adultery, incest, sacrilege, perjury and treason, committed not once but often."

We must add that the Church's condemnation of homosexuality was merely an aspect of the general condemnation of sexual pleasure and indeed of all sexual activity not directly necessary to ensure the continuation of the race. Even within marriage, sexual activity was severely restricted, and virginity was declared a more blessed state than matrimony. Homosexuality was thus condemned as much because it was a source of pleasure as because it was "unnatural."

The Ancient World: Temple Prostitution

Most accounts of homosexuality in ancient times are bedeviled by misunderstanding of a specialized manifestation known as temple prostitution, and it is useful to clear up confusion on this point.

Primitive religion is shot through with myths based on the idea of union between a woman and a deity. Often it was the moon that was held to fertilize women; later the sun or the rain was held responsible. By the time of the Periclean Greeks, this belief was mythologized in the story of Zeus's visiting Danaë in the form of a shower of gold. Such notions reflected the observation that the sun and rain cause vegetation to sprout.[2] Paradoxically, such intercourse was often held to restore virginity. In more advanced societies, in which the worship of the deity had become institutionalized and was attended by a priesthood, women visited the temple at least once in their lives to await the attention of the deity, who turned up in the form of one of the priests. The participating women were undoubtedly aware that the physical presence was that of the priest but regarded him as the vessel of the deity.

Conversely, where the deity worshiped was female and the attendants therefore also female, men would visit the temple to have intercourse with the deity on a similar basis. Herodotus says that nearly all people except the Egyptians and the Greeks observed this practice. Although some travelers reported this as a form of prostitution, such a conception entirely misrepresents the character of the transaction, which was sacramental.

Sex in ancient times was regarded as a great generative force to be venerated and worshiped. The Greeks called the sexual parts

---

[2] In more sophisticated times, it was often held that deities might still visit favored women and that the offspring would be heroic figures. Such origins were often attributed to heroes. The same concept underlies the story of Jesus' being born of a virgin by divine intervention.

aidoion—inspirer of holy awe. Phalli were carried in processions at fertility ceremonies, the culminating feature of which was usually the performance of the sexual act by all concerned. To later ages, these saturnalia have sometimes appeared to be bestial and degrading orgies; those who took part in them, however, considered them uplifting and purging and found in them reunion with the spirit of life. The experience was, in fact, a religious one.

Homosexuality, too, was seen in a "good" frame of reference rather than in a "bad" one. It was considered a natural form of self-indulgence, and, if it was condemned at all, it was only in terms analogous to those in which one might condemn gluttony.

To understand the matter further, we must also recall that marriage as we know it did not exist. Marriage was primarily an economic association, often impermanent in character, and was not regarded as the exclusive field of sexual gratification. Men maintained concubines for the latter purpose; among the Jews, it was considered good form for a wife to obtain a new concubine to please her husband when he had been away on a journey. In some societies, marriage was on a group basis, a man having access to all the women in the group—or, in a more restricted form, to all the sisters of the woman he had married. Among the Celts it was a compliment for a married woman to offer herself to a valiant knight as a reward, and, when Cuchulainn visited Ulster, the Queen and all the ladies of her Court came to meet him, raising their skirts "so as to expose their private parts" in order to show how greatly they admired him. Homosexual indulgence in these times did not have, as it does with us, the character of a threat to marriage or of an alternative to it. As with the Arabs, the maintenance of both homoerotic and homosexual relations was quite compatible with successful marriage.

There were also circumstances in which a female deity might come to be served by male as well as by female attendants. Usually, perhaps invariably, such males wore female costume and were considered to have adopted the life of women. Consequently, when men visited the temple to perform ritual intercourse with the deity, if the hierodule was biologically male, the intercourse was technically homosexual. Some historians have described this practice as homosexual prostitution—a doubly misleading descrip-

tion, as the attitudes involved were appropriate neither to homosexuality nor to prostitution.[3]

Patrist and Matrist Societies

At this point I shall outline a system of ideas that may be helpful in interpreting the historical material to be presented subsequently.

As I have sought to show elsewhere (Rattray Taylor, 1954;
Rattray Taylor, 1958), in societies that conceive of their deities as
mother-figures, incest is regarded as the overwhelming danger and
is hedged with taboos, whereas homosexuality has little importance. Conversely, in societies that conceive of their deities as
father-figures, homosexuality is regarded as the overwhelming
danger and is surrounded with taboos and condemnation; incest
may also be tabooed, but it falls far behind homosexuality in importance. I have proposed the terms *matrist* and *patrist* for these
two patterns. (I do not regard "matriarchy" and "patriarchy" as
satisfactory, for reasons that need not concern us here.)

As anthropologists have long noted, these two forms of society
differ in other respects also. The patrist society tends to depress
the status of women, the matrist to elevate it. The patrist society
treats all sexual activity and even all pleasure as matters to be
regulated; asceticism is regarded as a virtue. The matrist society,
in contrast, treats sexual activity as positively good, even sacred,
and admires complete abandonment to impulse. Its ceremonies
include frenzies and saturnalias, whereas those of the patrist
society involve self-mortification and self-discipline. The patrist
society regards offenses against chastity as more serious than
offenses against the food supply; the matrist society takes the
reverse position.

In the Mediterranean world in the pre-Christian period, we
find religions predominantly based on a mother-deity figure; to
the Phoenicians she was Astarte; to the Phrygians, Cybele; to the
Babylonians, Ishtar; to the Thracians, Bendis; to the Cretans,

---

[3] I speak of the general case; no doubt such ceremonies sometimes became
degraded. There is, however, very little direct evidence.

Rhea; to the Ephesians, Artemis; to the Canaanites, Atargatis; to the Persians, Anaitis; to the Cappadocians, Ma. Although her eponyms differed, her attributes were the same; she was always the mother who succored and helped and who represented fertility. Accordingly, we can infer—and such facts as are available bear out the inference—that these societies were generally tolerant of homosexuality but were more seriously concerned about incest.

Although our information about most pre-Christian cultures is sufficient for us to say only that these patterns can be detected, in the case of the Jews we have such a comparative wealth of information that we can confirm the diagnosis in detail and even trace a process of change from one attitude to the other.

The Hebrews, with their arbitrary and vengeful father-deity Jahweh, appear to us the paradigm of a father-identifying society. It is not always realized that the culture was originally matrist, as were the other Semitic groups.

The "four matriarchs," Sarah, Rebecca, Rachel, and Leah, originally occupied a more important position than the "three patriarchs," Abraham, Isaac, and Jacob. If we read the Old Testament closely, we find women founding cities and metronymic tribes, and we observe marriage into out-groups on a matrilocal basis, as in the case of Jacob. The temple of Jerusalem was simultaneously dedicated to Jahweh and to the Queen of Heaven, and at its doors stood the asherah, a symbolic tree associated with mother cults all over the Middle East. Furthermore, Adon, the Lord, was not the spouse of the Queen of Heaven but, like Dionysos, was her son. Subsequently, the two deities Jahweh and Adon were fused; it was the vocalizing of the tetragrammaton JHWH with the vowels from Adonai by ignorant translators in the Renaissance that gave rise to the barbarism "Jehovah."

Israelites were surrounded by tribes worshiping Baal, a deity that had but recently attained pre-eminence over a mother deity, Anat. Baal was a rain and vegetation god, a fertilizer. Anat was a fertility figure, allied to the moon and hardly distinguishable from the Phoenician Astarte and the Semitic Ashtaroth. Sometimes Anat appeared as the sister-wife of Baal, sometimes as his mother. These deities were worshiped by a cult involving "temple prostitution," including homosexual attendants who were known as *qedeshim.*

The worship of the fire and mountain god JHWH (originally confined to Mount Sinai) gradually permeated Israel, although there were many relapses against which the prophets fulminated. (*Cf. Jere.* xliv. 17*ff.*, where the people tell the prophet that they will certainly burn incense to the Queen of Heaven and make cakes and pour out drink offerings to her, as they and their fathers and kings have long done. *Cf.* also *Jere.* vii, 17, 18.)

We should therefore expect to find in the earliest Hebrew records that sexual activity was free and homosexuality acceptable and that the second became forbidden as the father-deity became dominant. Such was the case. Sexual activity prior to marriage was unrestricted in pre-Exilic times. The only sexual injunction in the Ten Commandments is that against adultery or the coveting of a neighbor's wife. Proscription of "adultery," however, did not mean that a man should restrict his sexual attentions to his wife; indeed the Bible constantly reminds us that men had many concubines or mistresses. It meant only that he should not interfere with another man's wife; to do so would have confused paternity and would have transgressed her husband's property right in her.

By the same token, sodomy was not a crime except when committed as part of the worship of non-Jewish gods. As we can see from *Genesis* xix. 5 and *Judges* xix. 22, it was regarded as a natural, if rather vulgar, form of debauchery. It was the obligation to protect strangers that impelled Lot to offer his daughters to the men of Sodom. The ban in *Deuteronomy* xxiii. 17 refers only to the religious form, and the word *qadesh*, translated as "sodomite" in the King James version of the Bible, means a priest concerned with temple prostitution.[4] Similarly, many references to "harlots" actually refer to priestesses of the rival cult.

By the time of *Leviticus*, however, homosexuality was specifically proscribed as an abomination (xviii. 22) and had been

---

[4] In general, writers have been misled on this point. *Cf.* R. Wood: "Sodomy, it would seem, was considered a very serious offence from early times. The stories of Sodom and Gomorrah reflect the belief that it was preferable that an innocent girl . . ." (1961, p. 128).

made a capital offense (xx. 13). Female homosexuality, though disapproved, did not carry any penalties until a later date. Homosexuality thus came to have for the Jews the character of heresy, and, in view of the medieval repetition of this pattern, it is permissible to wonder whether or not there was more than chance involved. It is precisely because homosexuality alarms the father-identifier that the Jews found it a particularly objectionable feature of the worship of Baal. Equally, only because it offers a solution to the mother-identifier could it become a regular feature of the worship of mother-deities.

The tolerance of homosexuality in early Judaism was a feature of the whole early Mediterranean world, wherever the leading deities were feminine. It was common in fifth-century Greece and among the Dorians, and the Persians were believed to have learned it from the Greeks. It became common in Rome as the patrist influence declined after the Greek conquests (Hopfner, 1938). It was a recognized feature of Arab cultures.

Gender-Role Changes in the Ancient World

But these Mediterranean societies, for all their unrestrictive attitudes toward sexual matters, were not without their psychopathologies. This point is vividly revealed by Lucian (1905). He describes how, at the festivals of the Syrian goddess, great crowds gathered at the temples and worked themselves into frenzies with music, singing, and self-flagellation. At this point, young men "who have resolved on the action, rush forward and castrate themselves with swords kept there for the purpose." Each man then "runs wild through the city, bearing in his hands what he has cut off. He casts it into any house at will, and from this house he receives women's raiment and ornaments." He adds, however, that many who came as mere spectators afterward were found to have committed the great act. Similar reports are made of the priests of Ishtar, of the Kouretes, the priests of Pessinos, the Hittite priests, and those of the Ephesian Artemis.

Permanent role changes of this kind are found in many other societies, especially among the Indians of Northwest America. Characteristically, the moon (or a mother-deity) appears in a dream and offers a choice of two gifts, one typifying the male

existence (for example, a spear or bow) and the other the female
existence (a distaff or quern perhaps). If the dreamer chooses
the second, he assumes female attire and lives the life of a woman.
Among the Chukchee he enters into marriage with a man. Such
societies thus offer institutionalized outlets for those who genuinely desire a change of sexual role. Indeed to refuse the role
after it had been thrice indicated in dreams would be to court
death (Eliade, 1951).

Such customs are not found only in the ancient world. In the
eighteenth century, they were reported from Ethiopia and North
America, as from Madagascar in the seventeenth century. They
are found today in New Mexico, the Marquesas, and Tahiti.
Tacitus reported them among the ancient Germans. Clearly,
many societies have offered suitable niches for mother-identifying
deviates.

Such persons are often, in fact, regarded as peculiarly the
representatives of the deity and are credited with powers of
divination and of magic. They are shamans. Far from being de-
spised, they are respected and feared.[5] The analogy with the
castrate who becomes the priest of the mother-deity, the source of
magical power, is very close. (The corresponding change, in
which a woman takes on a male role as the servant or representative of a male deity, though less common, is not unknown.

This prestige explains why history and anthropology offer
countless instances of men adopting female attire temporarily
when it is necessary for them to act in magical roles. Zulu chiefs
don petticoats when they conduct rain-making ceremonies, and
in the Pelew Islands any man taking part in the ceremonies adopts
female attire.

Priests too characteristically adopt female attire. The priests of
Ishtar at Babylon wore female attire, as did the priests of Artemis
at Ephesus. Among the ancient Germans male priests dressed as

---

[5] *Cf.* Marquette: "[S]ome Illinois as well as some Nodowessi, while yet
young assume female dress and keep it all their lives. There is some mystery
about it, for they never marry, and glory in debasing themselves to do all
that is done by women; yet they go to war, though allowed to use only a club.
. . . They attend councils and nothing can be decided without their advice.
Finally . . . they pass for 'manitus' and persons of consequence" (1846,
p. 34).

women. This practice is still a world-wide phenomenon, as prevalent among the Indians of the Northwest as it is in Indonesia. Some writers have interpreted it as the result of the gradual infiltration of a female cultus by males during a period of transition from a matrist to a patrist society. The evidence suggests, however, that the throwing down of the old deity and its replacement by a new cult are more usual features of such a change. It seems more probable that men adopted women's attire on such occasions from a deep sense that women were the true custodians of divine power, even when they no longer sought actually to identify themselves with women. It is for precisely this reason that Christian priests in the West today still wear the cassock or soutane, a robe of female type.[6]

This point sheds light on why those men who felt impelled to adopt a female role, the berdaches, in so many cases became shamans or priestesses. Such men were deemed to have been chosen by the goddess as her servants. Many writers have assumed that they practiced unnatural vices, but there are many cases in which we can be sure that they did not—for instance, among the North American Indians. It seems reasonable to suppose, however, that, where the cult of the goddess in question involved temple prostitution, the male who joined her service would have to fulfill a similar function.

Further evidence of disturbed psychic states in the Near East may be found in the story Herodotus tells of the Scythian Enarëes, who were afflicted with "the feminine disease." Hippocrates says they were impotent and dressed as women, and attributes such behavior to their riding horseback, but Herodotus claims it was a divine punishment on ancestors who had pillaged the temple of Aphrodite. Like shamans, the Enarëes had the gift of divination.

There is also more indirect evidence that the mother-image was seen as dominating and oppressive as well as supportive and loving. If we are right in assuming that mythologies provide us with important clues to unconscious preoccupations, then we must certainly attend to the powerful and popular myth associated in

---

[6] The frequent association of brothels with religious houses in the early Middle Ages may also have been a relic of this tradition.

Greece with the name of Dionysos, which has many parallels throughout the Mediterranean world.

In this myth, the central figure is a young man, the son of a mother goddess. He fertilizes his mother and is subsequently killed or castrated. Generally he then descends into hell or the underworld, whence he is rescued by his mother, only for the cycle to be repeated. We find him under such names as Tammuz, Dumuzi, Adonis, and Attis, associated with such mother-figures as Inaana-Ishtar, Astarte, and Cybele in Babylonia, Syria, and Mesopotamia. In Canaan he appears as Baal, the son of Anat. Hittite beliefs seem to show a parallel combination, as do those from Crete.

Clearly these myths reflect a mother–son relationship of an incestuous kind, in which the penalty for incest is castration or death. Following castration the son can safely be reunited with his mother. These young gods were usually effeminate in appearance and were served by priestesses. (Normally, male deities were served by priests.) Dionysos at one point donned women's attire and in one account was brought up as a girl. Nevertheless, Dionysos is an embodiment of male fertilizing power, and one of his epithets was "the Testiculous." His object in dressing as a woman was to gain the confidence of the maenads, frenzied women who were apt to tear men to pieces. It seems fair then to infer that many young men in the ancient world were preoccupied with the mother relationship and saw the mother as both a threatening and a protective figure.

The myth that ultimately replaced that of Dionysos and his homologues was that of a young man, a son, whose preoccupation was with his father. He was killed according to the will of his father, then descended into hell and was subsequently reunited with his father. We may thus assume that the unconscious preoccupations of young men had changed by the time of this myth.

These considerations may seem to have led us away from our theme, but in fact they are closely related. Let us now consider in more detail the question of the Greeks and their attitude to these matters.

Greek Homoerotism

It is sometimes said that homosexuality was institutionalized among the Greeks, but the statement is incorrect as long as the term is defined, as it is in legal systems based on canon law, by the occurrence of intercourse.

In Athens and Sparta, every man was expected to take to himself a boy to whom he should act for a time as mentor, helping him to find his place in life. The man was called the inspirer, the boy the listener, and each such arrangement was made by prior agreement with the boy's parents. While a strong emotional relationship was normal between inspirer and listener and embraces and a common couch were permitted, the performance of sexual acts (referred to as *stuprum* or vile behavior) was strictly forbidden and, in the code of Lycurgus (*c.* B.C. 825), was made a felony punishable by death. For this unusual system, the term "homoerotism" has been suggested.

The Greeks were, of course, aware of the existence of homosexuality as a sexual perversion and called it "pedomania" to distinguish it from "pederasty" or "homoerotism." It is unfortunate that in modern times the word pederast has come to have the meaning of pedomaniac. The Greeks not only condemned pedomaniacs but ridiculed effeminate youths.

Plato (1947) clearly distinguishes the two: "The one love is made for pleasure; the other loves beauty. The one is an involuntary sickness, the other a sought enthusiasm. The one tends to the good of the beloved, the other to the ruin of both. . . . The one is virile, the other effeminate."

It was a disgrace for a boy not to be chosen by anyone. Plato declared that the highest form of human existence was philosophy combined with pederasty, and Xenophon said pederasty was part of pedagogy. The picked band of lovers who fought at Chaeronea fell to a man. Philip of Macedon shed tears as he beheld the scene and said, "Perish any man who suspects that these men either did or supposed anything that was base."

In Sparta the relationship was actually prescribed by the government. A boy who had no lover was punished, and if he chose a rich lover over a poor one he was fined. There are indications that the practice was derived from Crete. It was found primarily among the Dorian peoples.

The existence of male prostitution is referred to by Aristophanes and others but was generally condemned.[7]

It should be added that female homosexuality, also of a rather idealized type, was practiced in Greece, though how widely is not known. Apart from the case of the poetess Sappho of Lesbos, whose few poems have associated her with the topic and from whose home the term "Lesbianism" has been derived, little is known; instruments (*olisboi*) for enabling women to imitate the heterosexual act with one another have been found.

It may be easier to understand the development of homoerotism when we recall that the Greek pantheon contained both male and female deities. As Jane Harrison (1921) has shown, the primitive Greek deities were earth-mothers. It was probably the Dorian invaders who brought in sky-father deities, of whom Zeus was the paradigm. The two streams were finally unified in the cult of Dionysos. Such evidence as exists suggests that, in early Greece, the social pattern was matrist; genealogies, for instance, were derived through the mother, house property was transmitted through the daughter, and so on. In Sparta, often regarded as the embodiment of Hellenic civilization, the social organization was purely matriarchal; marriage was matrilocal, and fraternal polyandry was practiced.

As we might expect, therefore, Greek sexual life represents an unusual attempt to synthesize the two contrasting attitudes that I have called "patrist" and "matrist." In sexual relations, the Greeks maintained both the paternal family (in which the wife's liberty was much restricted) and the "heterae," or sexually free and independent women. The heterae must not be confused with mere providers of sexual outlets, for the Greeks recognized the latter as a third function. (Hence the saying of Demosthenes: "We have wives for child-bearing, heterae for enjoyment and concubines for daily needs.") Classical Greece does, however, present us with another sexual phenomenon of quite a puzzling character.

---

[7] See R. Flacelière (1960) for details.

Greek Bisexuality

Many Greek myths describe men dressing as women and women dressing as men. On closer examination these myths usually specify that such cross-dressing was associated with the moment at which intercourse first took place, frequently on the wedding night. The customs give expression to the idea that potency is ensured by cross-dressing.

In Sparta, for example, the young bride's head was shaved, and she was dressed in men's clothes and laid on the bed without a light; the husband then came to her in the dark. At Argos, the bride wore a false beard on the wedding night. At Cos, however, it was the husband who put on women's clothes to receive his wife.

Similar customs were associated with various Bacchic and Dionysiac festivals, that is, festivals at which sexual intercourse took place. In Bacchic feasts, those who escorted the phallus and those who performed the dance called "ithyphallos," all wore the dresses of the other sex. Similarly, at the feast of Hera at Samos, men "donned long white robes sweeping the ground, their hair loose in golden nets, and wore . . . feminine bracelets and necklaces." In the Hybristika, men dressed as women and vice versa.[8] A number of vases of this period show women dressed as men and men dressed as women.

Attempts are sometimes made to explain the donning of female attire as a strategem to outwit a foe, but this explanation does not stand up to examination, as can be seen from some of the stories just noted.

As all these occasions were marked by strong heterosexual activity, it seems clear that the cross-dressing involved was not a homosexual manifestation; on the contrary it appears actually to have intensified or guaranteed the success of heterosexual intercourse. This point is so remarkable as to deserve further discussion.

The case of the Roman Hercules and the Greek Herakles is especially interesting, as the hero is famed for his courage and

---

[8] For many further instances see Marie Delcourt (1961).

virility. According to Plutarch, Herakles wore a robe embroidered
with flowers on the occasion of his marriage, and it was for this
reason that newly married husbands in Cos put on feminine attire to receive their brides. In Rome, too, men had to don
women's attire before they could take part in the rites of Hercules, who was venerated at these ceremonies as the giver of
health.

When the Emperor Commodus went into the amphitheater
at Lanuvium to do battle with wild beasts, he wore a lionskin
on his head but also a long robe tied with a girdle. Modern writers have supposed that this dress proved him effeminate or in-
sane. Actually his object was to assert himself as the reincarna-
tion of Hercules Victor and thus to draw on his strength.

We may find a clue in the legend of Omphale: Hercules was
obliged to compensate for his murder of Iphitus by serving the
imperious Queen Omphale dressed as a woman, and later writers and painters have dwelt on the shamefulness of his position.
But in early versions of the legend, neither he nor the Queen
seemed to think it shameful; on the contrary, he departed laden
with presents, having provided Omphale with one or more children. Here the cross-dressing was again regarded as a factor in
virility. But the matter goes further. Omphale's name (from *om-
phalos*, the umbilicus) denotes the cord that binds a child to its
mother and is the root of life. The myth seems to represent the
overcoming of subordination to the mother and the assumption
of manhood.

In point of fact, initiation ceremonies throughout the world
display these same features. The initiates are dressed as women
or girls before finally emerging as full-fledged men.

In his *Symposium*, Plato tells how humankind consisted originally of double beings, male and female, united back to back,
and how they were cut in two, after which each half sought
to unite again with its counterpart. (In Christian myth, Eve was
originally part of Adam, and Eusebius thought Plato must have
derived his story from *Genesis*.)

The Greeks, we may infer, were deeply preoccupied with understanding the experiences of the other sex. Several legends
tell of beings who, in the course of their lives, changed their sex.
The best-known story is that of Tiresias, born a male, who spent

seven years as a woman and later was turned back into a man again. (Sithon also seems to have changed sexes.)

The Greeks also had a number of bisexual or androgynous deities, of whom Hermaphroditos is the prime example. In late Greek art, Hermaphroditos appears as an effeminate youth, but in earlier representations he is either a bearded and virile figure with breasts or a massively maternal figure with prominent male sex organs. The figure represents not a neutral canceling of sexual powers but the fullest possible expression of both aspects of sexuality.[9] Greek iconography shows many hermaphrodites of this kind.

Dionysos is often depicted as hermaphroditic in this sense. It is only in Roman and especially Christian times that he is depicted as effeminate. The archaic painters depict him with a full growth of beard, and his key epithet is *Diphues,* of double nature. The Greeks feared genuine hermaphrodites and put them to death.

Other myths describe women who wished to be men. Pindar tells of Kainonis, who induced Poseidon to turn her into a man; then she planted her spear upright in the middle of the market place and ordered everyone to pay it divine honors. Zeus, shocked by this impiety, called on the centaurs, who beat Kainonis to the ground with trees (also phallic symbols, of course). Female "penis envy" and the assertion of male dominance could hardly be more graphically illustrated.

Furthermore, the legends in which Greek heroes—Herakles, Achilles, Dionysos, Theseus, and others—spend part of their time clad as women always lead either to their carrying off women or to their overcoming Amazonian women. The myth seems to depict the gradual establishment of male dominance after a period of female dominance. It is also to the point that the Amazons were associated with Dionysos, who was portrayed as conquering them.

Cross-dressing remained a conspicuous feature of the frag-

---

[9] It is interesting that the Phrygian deity Agdystis, whose devotees are described as castrating themselves and assuming women's clothes, was actually a bisexual deity, who was forced by the gods to emasculate himself to prevent his marrying the king's daughter. This deity is also found in Lesbos, the classic home of female homoerotism.

mentary fertility ceremonies that persisted in Europe under
Christianity right down to modern times. It was a feature of the
medieval feast of fools, as it had been of the Roman saturnalia,
and it was practiced at the harvest festival certainly as late as the
eighteenth century. The Phrygian ceremonies were incorporated
in the Roman state religion under Claudius and became the
hilaria or festivals of joy, celebrated in Rome with universal license and masquerading.

Gender Role-Changes in Europe

It is not widely known that in the early Christian church many
female saints and holy women dressed themselves in men's attire
and lived as men. What is remarkable is that the Church approved such actions, despite the injunction in *Deuteronomy*
against them.

The *Acta Sanctorum* includes accounts of "Brother Marinos,"
whom the other monks supposed to be a eunuch from his voice
and beardlessness, who was even accused of seducing a local girl,
and who turned out at death to be female; of *frater* Pelagius
monachus et eunuchus, also a girl; of Marina, Margarita, and
others. Other instances noted by Delcourt (1961) include Ath-
anasia of Antioch, Eugenia of Alexandria, Apollinaria, Papula of
Gaul, and Hildegonde of Neuss.

Hagiography includes such stories of girls dressing as men
as those of Thekla and Glaphyra. An especially striking instance
is that of Joan of Arc; her refusal to resume female attire was the
primary cause of her condemnation to death.

In general, of course, the Church strongly opposed any attempt
by women to escape from their role; it condemned women who assumed male roles as strongly as it condemned men who adopted
effeminate practices. In the eighteenth century, however, when
pressures on women were less severe, there was a quite astonish-
ing number of cases of women dressing as men. The *Annual Reg-
ister* reports fifteen cases between 1761 and 1815, and many
more must have gone undiscovered. One of the women had been
married three times in the guise of a man. Another became an
officer in the Spanish army. A third was wounded at Pondicherry
and underwent 500 lashes without revealing her sex. A fourth

was wounded at Fontenoy. Mrs. Ann Bousted, alias Heslop, performed as a wrestler and ploughman; after her husband left her,
she kidnaped and married a Mr. Sewel. As late as 1835, a woman
passing under the name of Bill Chapman appeared in court; she
was living as a male ballad singer.

In addition to these cases of permanent role change, there
were many temporary ones. Charlotte Clark (1888) records in
her autobiography how on various occasions she dressed as a
man, and the theme was popular in the novels of the period. At
the end of the century, moralists were complaining of the horsy
girl who stood before the fire with her legs wide apart like a man.

At the same time, there were many attempts by men to sample
the role of women, although their efforts were in general less public because they were more strongly condemned. But in France
the Chevalier d'Eon (from whom Havelock Ellis derived the term
"eonism") made no secret of his phases of feminine impersona-
tion. Philippe d'Orléans, the Abbé de Choisy, the Abbé d'En-
tragnes, and such others as Saralette du Langues did the same.
When the "homosexual" clubs in London and Exeter were raided,
men dressed as women were discovered, and there was evidence
that they had enacted marriages and even the births of babies—
dolls and other "props" were found. As late as 1833, an actress
named Eliza Edwards turned out on her death to have been a
man. She had shared a room with another girl, without arousing
any suspicions.

Preoccupation with the role of the other sex was a marked
feature of the German Romantic movement. Karl Varnhagen von
Ense, the biographer, wrote to his wife (1874): "You are a great
man. I am the first woman who ever lived." The theologian,
Schleiermacher (1860), toyed with the idea of becoming a
woman, and his wife wrote to him, "You are not a man to me, but
a sweet, pure, virgin." Bettina von Arnim (1959), the author-
ess, wrote in 1807 that she had ordered "a skirt? No, a pair of
trousers. Hurray, now another era begins to dawn; and a jacket
and an overcoat besides." Goethe's heroes and heroines were
"delicate and dreamy men, free and daring girls." The roles of
the sexes were becoming interchangeable.

Such a phenomenon was not peculiar to the eighteenth century. The seventeenth-century mystic Antoinette Bourignon ar-

rived at a conception of fused sexuality not unlike the one that Auguste Comte advanced in the nineteenth century. Similar ideas are found in the sixteenth-century German mystic Boehme, who described Adam as a *mannliche Jungfrau,* and also in Paracelsus. The evidence has never, I believe, been thoroughly reviewed.

Conclusion

This sketch has left much ground uncovered, chiefly because the data are too scant. Nothing has been said of homosexuality in the Orient, for instance. As it is my thesis that attitudes toward homosexuality can change within a few generations, isolated observations do not provide a basis for generalizations. The Hindus, for example, are reported to have held homosexuality in abhorrence and, in remote times, to have punished it. In modern times, however, homosexual prostitution has often been noted, and a sect of boys, the Jinras, was regularly prepared for this purpose by stretching the anal opening with conical objects of wood and metal.

Similarly, sexual life in China has recently been studied with care by Van Gulik (1961). He declares that, while homosexuality is believed to have been more common in China in recent times, it is actually only more open than it formerly was. There are traces of many changes in the position. Under the North Sung Dynasty, for example, there was a class of male prostitutes. Soon afterward, penalties were imposed on them, but, under the succeeding South Sung Dynasty, they were organized into a guild and appeared on the streets in female attire.

The isolated fragments of information we possess about other cultures, often imprecise and uncorrelated with other social or religious data, are therefore more misleading than useful. All we can say is that there is probably no culture from which homosexuality has not been reported.

Historical analysis also indicates that the incidence of homosexuality is unlikely to be changed radically by individual therapy, however widely it may be applied. Homosexuality, like the divorce rate and other phenomena, is no more than a symptom of an underlying state of psychosocial distress. The "cure" of this state on a broad scale can be effected only by altering the relevant social conditions.

REFERENCES

Alcuin. In W. S. Howell (Trans.), *The rhetoric of Alcuin and Charlemagne.* London: Oxford, 1941.

Boniface. In E. Emerton (Trans.), *The letters of Saint Boniface.* New York: Columbia Univer. Press, 1940.

Clark, Charlotte (Mrs. C. O. Van Cleve). *Three-score years and ten.* Minneapolis: Harrison & Smith, 1888.

Dalton, J. *Genuine narrative of the streets, etc.* London: Gilliver, 1728.

Delcourt, Marie. *Hermaphrodite.* London: Studio Books, 1961.

Eliade, M. *Le shamanisme et les techniques archaique de l'extase.* Paris: Payot, 1951.

Est, W. *Satan's sowing season.* London: Okes, 1611.

Flacelière, R. *L'amour en Grèce.* Paris: Hachette, 1960.

Harrison, Jane E. *The religion of ancient Greece.* London: Constable, 1921.

Hopfner, T. *Das sexualleben der Greicher und Römer.* Prague: 1938.

Lithgow, W. *Rare adventures and painefull peregrinations.* Glasgow: MacLehose, 1906.

Lucian. In F. G. Allinson (Ed.), *Selected writings of. . . .* Boston: Ginn, 1905.

Marquette, J. Recit. des voyages. *Hist. Coll. Louisiana,* 1846.

Parker, G. *Life's painter of variegated characters in public and private life.* London: Ridgeway, 1789.

Pepys, S. *Diary of Samuel Pepys.* New York: Random House, 1946.

Plato. *Euthyphro, Apology, Crito, Phaedo and Phaedrus* (Loeb Classical Library). London: Heinemann, 1947.

Rattray Taylor, G. *Sex in history.* New York: Vanguard, 1954.

Rattray Taylor, G. *The angel-makers.* London: Heinemann, 1958.

Schleiermacher, F. *Aus Schleiermachers leben, in briefen.* Berlin: G. Reiner, 1860.

Smollett, T. G. *Roderick Random and other works.* London: Bohn, 1843.

Van Gulik, R. H. *Sexual life in ancient China.* Leiden: Brill, 1961.

Varnhagen von Ense, K. *Briefwechsel zwischen Varnhagen und Rahel.* Leipzig: Brockhaus, 1874.

von Arnim, Bettina. *Werke und briefe.* Frechen: Bartmann, 1959.

Wood, R. Sex life in ancient civilizations. In A. Ellis and A. Abarbanel (Eds.), *The encyclopedia of sexual behavior.* Vol. I. New York: Hawthorn, 1961. Pp. 119-131.

A Note on Male Homosexuality and the Role of Women in Ancient Greece

9

SAUL H. FISHER

The phenomenon of homosexuality and its determinants in ancient Greece have engaged the interest of numerous students of the problem of male homosexuality. Kinsey (1948) uses it as an argument for the bisexuality of men, and Freud (1962), in his *Three Essays on the Theory of Sexuality* (1905) uses it to buttress his libido theory. A fundamental question arises: What were the historical and social conditions in ancient Greece that gave rise to so much homosexual behavior? This paper is an attempt to answer that question, with full recognition of the fact that it is not a complete answer but merely represents one factor in the problem.

A few words about chronology: The Bronze Age in the Aegean area began about B.C. 3300. The beginning of Greek immigration was about B.C. 1800. The fall of Troy occurred in B.C. 1184. The year B.C. 1050 represented the beginning of the Iron Age and coincided with the Dorian invasion from the South and the Ionian colonization of Asia Minor. The *Iliad* and *Odyssey* of Homer were composed between the years B.C. 900–800. The outbreak

of the Peloponnesian War was in B.C. 431, and the death of Peri-
cles was in B.C. 429. Athens was defeated by Sparta in this war,
and the Spartan garrison entered Athens in B.C. 403.

The origins of the Greek people can be traced to about B.C.
1800 with the first immigration from the North of a branch
of the Indo-Europeans, consisting of a number of tribes who
came in successive waves and gradually occupied the whole
peninsula to the South. The land had already been settled by
Aegean peoples with rather highly developed cultures. There
is considerable evidence that the Indo-European tribes were
pastoral and hunting societies and strongly patrilineal, whereas
the conquered Aegean societies, particularly those in the southern part of the peninsula, were agricultural and strongly matrilineal. There was thus present in ancient Greece a clash of cultures, a conflict between matrilineal and patrilineal succession.

The early social organization was derived from the clan or
tribe, in which the concept of private ownership of property was
unknown in the sense we know it today. When the Homeric
chieftain counted his possessions, he enumerated his household
goods, his slaves, and his livestock, but he did not mention the
pastures on which his cattle grazed. In fact, land was tribal and
divided by lot for use, not for ownership. This procedure was
also followed for booty obtained in wars and for food—in other
words, communal ownership and sharing prevailed. Military exploits, however, were rewarded with especially valuable land,
the *temenos,* which was not liable to redistribution and could be
enclosed and so better protected; the chief who owned it could
cultivate it with the labor of slaves brought home from the wars.
His supply of slave labor was limited, but after the Dorian in-
vasions cheap hired labor was available from thousands of de-
tribalized and demoralized outcasts, who could be put to work
on the harvest and then turned adrift for the winter. It was not
long before the ownership of land began to be concentrated. By
loans of seed and stock after a bad season, the big landowner
became a creditor of the small. Then a point was reached where
the smallholder could only redeem his debt by surrendering his
holding or tying himself to his creditor by some system of annual
tribute. He lost his land or became a serf. With these develop-

ments we see the beginnings of nobility, ownership of real property, and serfdom—the characteristics of a feudal society.

By the seventh and sixth centuries B.C., there had occurred
a growth of trade, the rise of a merchant class, and the building
of towns, all of which were intensified by a technical advance of
farreaching significance, a change that those developments had
themselves promoted: the invention of coinage. With the spread
of coinage and the increase in commerce, there arose a powerful
merchant class, which soon challenged the political privileges of
the old nobility, who drew their power from birth and their
wealth from the land. Faced with the competition of these *nou-
veaux riches,* the landowners recouped their fortunes by intensi-
fying their exploitation of the peasantry. This pressure led to a
great crisis in Attica in the sixth century B.C. The peasants were
on the verge of insurrection. The lowest classes were permitted to
retain only one-sixth of their produce. Preyed upon by usurers,
whose rates of interest soared to 50 per cent, they had been
forced to sell their land, their children, and their very selves.
Many had been driven overseas, and many became beggars or
slaves, homeless in fields once their own. The Eupatridai, a rul-
ing group of nobility, enlisted the cooperation of the merchants, and, accordingly, Solon, a member of the Eupatridai who
had been actively engaged in trade, was entrusted with dicta-
torial powers (B.C. 593). He introduced a constitution with several reforms, and Greece entered on a period of rapid development, commercially and culturally, which is still extolled as one
of the outstanding periods in human history. This greatness is all
the more remarkable when we consider that, in the year B.C.
431, the year before the great plague that killed almost one-
fourth of the inhabitants, the total population of Athens consisted
of 172,000 citizens and 115,000 slaves. There were also resident
aliens (metics), who were not full citizens but who enjoyed certain privileges of work. Some slaves were drawn from those dis-
possessed of land, but most were the spoils of war. Slaves, metics,
and women had no political rights.

All this background leads us to the question: What conditions
gave rise to homosexuality in ancient Greece? It must be emphasized that homosexuality was not an isolated and hidden

phenomenon. It was widespread among the citizens of Greece, practiced by many of the outstanding men of the time. It took the special form of pederasty, that is, love of boys, and the literature of the time is rich in eulogies of this love as the highest form of wisdom. Socrates declared his philosophy to be one of love, and his love was homosexual love. In the dialogues of Plato, love is always pederasty or homosexual love. Homosexuality was legally recognized. Solon, himself a homosexual and the man who introduced the so-called "democratic" constitution, issued important laws for the regulation of pederasty, providing, among other things, that a slave must not have connection with a free-born boy.[1]

Many explanations have been put forth for the intense devotion to pederasty among the Greeks. The fact that it aided them in war by promoting intensely loyal comradeship and outstanding military exploits, is one such explanation. Another is that in the religion of the Greeks pederasty was fostered by initiation rites at puberty. Yet another is the marked devotion to body that made up so much of the educational training of the Greek youth, who wrestled and ran races in the nude. Freud attributed it to the fact that youths were brought up by male slaves. It has been suggested, too, that the leisure in which the governing class lived, supported by crowds of slaves, rendered it peculiarly liable to

---

[1] It is true, as Rattray Taylor states (see page 155), that the Greeks idealized the man–boy relationship, that it was a teaching relationship, and that pedomania was not encouraged, for it meant "frenzied, uncontrolled passion for boys." It is also true that Lycurgus was a law-giver to the Spartans; but he is not fully known as a person. Furthermore, the laws of Sparta were far more stringent than the laws of Athens.

But to state that physical relations were not part of the homosexuality of the Greeks (Athenians) is to deny a mass of data to which I have had access. My main sources have been *Sexual Life in Ancient Greece* by Hans Licht (1950) and *Aeschylus and Athens* by George Thomson (1950). Not everyone in Athens favored this practice, for some were disturbed by the marked prevalence of male prostitution, described at great length by Licht. Socrates cannot be cited as representative of the institution, for he personally practiced abstinence as a means of achieving perfection, although he found boyish companions indispensable. But he was an exception. And Thomson states flatly (p. 366), ". . . a relationship which, in the conditions of Athenian city life, became predominantly sexual . . ." referring to the origins from initiation rites.

preoccupation with passion and pleasure-seeking. Certainly sensuality played a very important role in Greek upper-class life. Heracleides Ponticus, a pupil of Plato and himself a famous philosopher, wrote a book *On Pleasure* (1887–1890), many passages of which have been preserved. In it he argues that luxury is *the* conduct of life and that voluptuousness is a right reserved for the governing classes, whereas work and toil fall to the lot of slaves and the poor. All who prize luxury and voluptuousness are broad-minded men of fine character and therefore more to be esteemed than others.

Yet the fact remains that homosexuality had not always been so prevalent in Greek history. Homer knew nothing of pederasty, although he did sing of close friendships in the *Iliad* and *Odyssey*. The evidence is strong that homosexuality in the form of pederasty came later and flourished in the historic period, from the sixth century B.C. on, coinciding with the development of a monetary, commercial, and slave form of society.

Of course, homosexuality in Greece did not preclude heterosexual relationships and marriage, and, at this point, it is appropriate to ask what the status of women in ancient Greece was. The answer is a startling one because, in a culture as advanced as this one, we might expect at least a humane and liberal attitude to have existed. The truth is quite the opposite—the position of the woman was a degraded and depreciated one. She had no political or economic rights, except those brought by her dowry. Her education was minimal, including only elementary knowledge in reading and writing and skill in such female handiwork as spinning and weaving. Her function in marriage was to procreate and to raise children, but even the second part of her function was largely usurped by slaves. Because of her poor education and her lack of function, there was no common ground between man and woman, and she was excluded from the cultural activity of the times. Her life was circumscribed by the walls of her home, and, in the words of Euripides (Licht, 1950, p. 29), "just that brings blame upon a woman, if she will not remain at home." It is written that, at the news of the fearful defeat of Chaeronea, the women of Athens only ventured as far as the house doors, where, half senseless with sorrow, they inquired after husbands, fathers, and brothers—but "even that was considered unworthy of them and their city" (Licht, 1950, p. 29). The tortoise, on which the foot of the Aphrodite Urania of Pheidias in Elis rested, was regarded as the symbol of the woman's life shut up in the narrow limits of the house, "that unmarried girls in particular need to be guarded, and that housekeeping and silence befit married women (Licht, 1950, p. 29). Solon thought such matters worthy of regulation by law, and there actually were laws regarding the clothes and money and food a woman might have when she went to a funeral.

It is of interest that the heterae, high-class prostitutes, without families but with better educations, had higher status than the family women and exerted much more influence on the men. The experience of a young wife is touchingly expressed by Sophocles:

> Now I am nothing and left alone; I have often observed that such is the lot of womankind—that we are a mere nothing. When we are young, in our father's house, I think we live the sweetest life of all; for ignorance ever brings us up delightfully. But when we have reached a mature age and know more, we are driven out of doors and sold, away from the gods of our fathers and our parents, some to foreigners, some to barbarians, some to strange houses, others to such as deserve reproach. And in such a lot, after a single night has united us, we have to acquiesce and think that it is well (Licht, 1950, p. 39).

Plato, in his *Timaeus*, explains the existence of women and the other lower animals by a doctrine of the progressive deterioration of men. "Those of the men first created who led a life of cowardice and injustice were suitably reborn as women in the second generation, and that is why it was at this particular juncture that the Gods contrived the lust of copulation" (1937, p. 67).

In the play *Medea*, Euripides has written of a tortured woman rejected by her husband Jason, and her desperate fury is dramatically portrayed. She cries, "O women, of all creatures that live and reflect, certainly it is we who are the most luckless. . . . And yet people say that we live in security at home, while the men go forth to war. How wrong they are! Listen: I'd rather be sent three times over to the battlefront than give birth to a single child" (1947, p. 206).

But this degraded state of women had not always been. In *Medea*, after she is ordered banished by King Creon, the chorus chants:

The Sacred rivers are flowing back to their sources!
The order of the world is being reversed!
Now it is men who have grown deceitful,
Men who have broken their sacred vows.
The name of woman shall rise to favor
Again; and women once again
Shall rise and regain their honor: never
Again shall ill be said of women! (1947, p. 211).

It was in the Attic tradition and known by the writers and thinkers of the time that, in earlier times, women had enjoyed greater liberty. Down to the reign of Cecrops, they had been allowed to vote with the men in the popular assembly, there had been no formal institution of marriage, each woman had been allowed to have children by several men, and the children were named after their mothers. Although before the historical period matrilineal societies had existed, with the change from tribal to feudal period to a monetary economy, that is, with the development of private property and its control by men, came the subjugation of women. In the *Iliad* and the *Odyssey* and in the tragedies dealing with the heroic age, women played roles of importance and respect. In the *Iliad*, when Hector takes leave of Andromache, the parting is described with great feeling and devotion. Similarly, Penelope in the *Odyssey* is portrayed as a person of great dignity and loyalty.

It is striking that, in the Homeric period, the absence of pederasty coincided with the more elevated status of women, whereas, in the historic period, the prominence of pederasty coincided with the degraded status of women. This pattern suggests that, in approaching the problem of homosexuality today, it is not enough to deal with so-called "instinctual" and interpersonal factors; social factors must be taken into account as well.

REFERENCES

Euripides, Medea. In D. Fitts (Ed.), *Greek plays in modern translation*. New York: Dial, 1947.

Freud, S. In J. Strachey (Trans.), *Three Essays on the theory of sexuality* (1905). New York: Basic Books, 1962.

Kinsey, A., Pomeroy, W. B., & Martin, C. E. *Sexual behavior in the human male*. Philadelphia: Saunders, 1948.

Licht, H. *Sexual life in ancient Greece*. London: Routledge & Kegan Paul, 1950.

Plato. Timaeus. In B. Jowett (Trans.), *The Dialogues of Plato*. Vol. 2. New York: Random House, 1937.

Ponticus, H. On pleasure. In G. Kaibel (Ed.), *Athenaei Naucratitae deipnosophistarum libri*. Leipzig: Teubner, 1887–1890. 3 vols.

Thomson, G. *Aeschylus and Athens*. London: Lawrence & Wishart, 1950.

PART III | THE VIEW OF THE CLINICIAN

A Critical Examination of the Concept of Bisexuality

10

SANDOR RADO

Historical Survey

Man and woman were once a single being. This entity was cut in two by an angry god, and ever since the halves have reached toward one another in love, out of a longing to restore their original state. So the story runs in Plato's "Banquet." Traces of it have been found, however, in older sources, including the Upanishads and the Old Testament, proving that Plato's fanciful conception was based on a far more ancient myth (Freud, 1924; Winthuis, 1928; H. H. Young, 1937).

This myth represents one of man's earliest intellectual approaches to the puzzle of the existence of two sexes. It offers a simple solution to this problem by creating an opposite concept, that is, the idea that man was formerly bisexual. To the primitive mind, however, this means that he still is. Consequently the myth is curiously equivocal, and manages to convey the exact opposite of the fact that it so ingeniously explains. It is as if the myth read: "I will tell you why there are two sexes. The truth is that they are one. Properly speaking we are all bisexual."

It is clear that ancient man must have had strong motives for

denying the differences between the sexes. He may have found
support for his comforting solution in the occurrence of hermaphrodites. The two other elements of the myth are traceable to
simple and profound human experiences. The image of violent
separation is reminiscent of the event of childbirth, culminating
in the cutting of the umbilical cord, while the concluding idea of
a partial reunion brings to mind the pattern of the mother
holding the child in her arms.

The conception of bisexuality was sanctioned by religious authority. Embodied in a system of belief, the idea had the power
to eclipse the facts. Certain Egyptian gods were notoriously bisexual and Hermaphroditos, a favorite Greek god and highly
popular subject for painting and sculpture, still carried an implication of deity in the Roman Empire. The advent of Christianity wiped out the religious significance of this foremost symbol of bisexuality, but the idea itself remained, to be revived in
less spectacular form throughout the ages. Nor was its diffusion
by any means limited to cultures touched by the heritage of the
classical world. Anthropologists have found it to play a vital role
in the cults, customs, and folklore of primitive societies of our
time, the Dutch Catholic missionary and anthropologist, J. Winthuis, even making it the title and central theme of his book
Das Zweigeschlechterwesen (1928). To what can we attribute
the extraordinary range and tenacity of this myth? This question, involving as it does the history of civilizaton, obviously
reaches beyond the province of psychoanalysis. We have, however, an experimental approach to the problem. Through the analytic study of children and neurotics we are familiar with the
emotional conflicts associated with the discovery of the differences between the sexes. Since many of these reactions are
elementary, it is reasonable to assume that they are also ubiquitous and that they are a part of the aboriginal matter from which
the concept of bisexuality has arisen.

These scanty references may suffice to show that the idea of
bisexuality far antedates the scientific era and owes its origin to
primeval, emotional needs of animistic man. It is important to
bear this in mind in our examination of the part played by the
same concept in modern science.

In about the middle of the nineteenth century, it was discov-

ered that the urogenital systems of the two sexes derive from a
common embryonic origin. The question of whether this *Uranlage*
should be considered neutral or hermaphroditic was at first a
subject of debate. When it was found to contain cellular material of both gonads (Wittich, 1853; Waldeyer, 1870), it was
definitely labeled hermaphroditic (Waldeyer, 1870). This unfortunate appellation of an undeveloped embryonic structure
marked an historical turning point, as it opened the door to indiscriminate speculations on man's bisexuality. These speculations, resting on generalizations drawn from biological findings
in lower animals, seemed to offer at last what appeared to be a
scientific basis for the explanation of homosexuality and it was
because of medical interest in this subject that the concept of bisexuality found its way into psychiatry. The first attempts in
this direction were made by Kiernan (1884; 1888), Frank Lyd-
ston (1889; 1892), and the Frenchman Chevalier (1893). The
writings of these men stimulated the Viennese psychiatrist Krafft-
Ebing (1931) to expound the neuropsychological aspects of bisexuality in the following theory: Since the peripheral part of the
sexual apparatus is of bisexual predisposition, this must be true
of the central part as well. Thus one must assume that the cere-
brum contains male and female centers whose antagonistic action and relative strength determine the individual's sex behavior.
Homosexuality results from the victory of the wrong center.
Krafft-Ebing realized that hermaphroditic developmental abnormalities of the genitals and homosexuality are rarely associated.
So he went on to the further assumption that the central part of
the sex system is autonomous and therefore independently subject to developmental disturbances. Not a trace of neurological
evidence was then or is now available to give credence to Krafft-
Ebing's chain of hypotheses.

From 1896 on, Krafft-Ebing's views on bisexuality were included in his *Psychopathia Sexualis* (1931) and thus gave the
first impetus to the vogue which the concept has enjoyed even to
the present time. Two other writings during the 1890's also
contributed to its popularity: Havelock Ellis embraced the idea
in his eclectic tenets, and Magnus Hirschfeld, who engaged in a
lifelong defense of homosexuals against the harshness of a medieval law (1914) became a devoted partisan of the concept of

bisexuality. The latter gave a new slant to the subject implicit in his view of homosexuality as an inborn characteristic brought about by a specific proportion of male and female substances in the hereditary composition of the brain. This version places the burden of proof primarily on the shoulders of geneticists, who, however, have not yet fulfilled this obligation.

In 1905 Freud published his *Three Essays on the Theory of Sexuality* (1962). Here he followed the lead of Krafft-Ebing in applying the notion of bisexuality to the central as well as to the peripheral part of the sex apparatus. However, he was aware of the futility of ascribing to the brain hypothetical properties and functions not yet ascertainable by neurological research and claimed that the central manifestations of sex, i.e., psychosexuality, must be studied by psychological means. This was in line with his general attitude in regard to all the psychologically accessible functions of the brain, and it was precisely for this purpose that he had evolved the method of psychoanalysis. In the desire to remain free and unbiased in the evaluation of his findings, Freud intentionally kept himself apart from the other medical sciences. He was obliged however to use as points of orientation a few of the basic assumptions of biology, and it was as one of these that he introduced into psychoanalysis the concept of bisexuality. This borrowed concept, formulated as a general characteristic of every human individual, came to play so important a role in psychoanalytic theory that younger men in the field dealt with it, not as a postulate or convenient frame of reference for interpretation, but as an established fact. Freud himself had no pretensions on this score; as recently as 1933 he reiterated that he had merely "carried over the notion of bisexuality into mental life" (1933); he spoke significantly of "constitutional bisexuality," and, as he of course always maintained that constitutional factors were beyond the reach of psychoanalytic investigation, the phrase explicitly disclaims for psychoanalysis all responsibility as to the validity of the assumption. Psychological data alone have never been, and could not be, conclusive in this respect. If the hypothesis were abandoned in the field of biology from which it had been taken, the data accumulated by psychoanalysis would have to be reinterpreted. In any case, verification rested, and quite rightly, with biology.

This state of affairs is somewhat disconcerting to a psychoanalyst, as grave doubts have arisen as to the psychological value of this concept, doubts substantiated by certain observations made in its application to medical practice. The analyst therefore has an urgent theoretical and practical motive to seek clarification of this subject, and for this he must turn to a field other than his own.

Sex and Bisexuality in Contemporary Biology

We shall now glance briefly at the actual status of the idea of bisexuality in the biological field (H. H. Young, 1937; Allan, 1939; Steinach, 1940; Bard, n.d.; Weiss, 1939; Hartmann, 1933, 1939; Meisenheimer, 1921). What has happened to this idea since its first appearance as a scientific generalization? On examination one finds that a truly enormous amount of relevant data has been assembled, leading to new formulations and terminology, and that as a result the old speculative notion of bisexuality is in the process of withering away. These developments are due, not only to the greater body of available facts, but also to an increasingly scientific attitude, less animistic, dedicated to a finer logical precision, and coinciding with a definite shift of emphasis from the morphological to the functional point of view. This trend is clearly indicated by Frank R. Lillie in the following passages:

> There is no such biological entity as sex. What exists in nature is a dimorphism within species into male and female individuals, which differ in respect to contrasting characters; it is merely a name for our total impression of the differences. It is difficult to divest ourselves of the prescientific anthropomorphism which assigned phenomena to the control of personal agencies, and we have been particularly slow in the field of the scientific study of sex characteristics in divesting ourselves not only of the terminology but also of the influence of such ideas. . . . Sex of the gametes and sex in bodily structure or expression are two radically different things. The failure to recognize this elementary principle is responsible for much unsound generalization (1939).

From the biologist we learn that sex in the gametes refers to their differentiation in form and function relevant to their reciprocal action of fertilization. In the somata, carriers of the gametes, sex refers to their differentiation in form and function relevant to or associated with their reciprocal action of ensuring proper functioning of the gametes and the development of the embryo, giving birth to and caring for the child. If we combine these, we see that sex in its entirety refers to the differentiation in the individuals as regards their contrarelated action systems of reproduction. Taking these considerations now in reverse order, we start from the fact that, insofar as concerns their reproductive action systems, individuals are of two contrarelated types. It is precisely this differentiation that constitutes the character of the sexes. Each of the two systems may be dissected into a multitude of structures, substances and functions, of which it is composed. The sex aspect of every one of these constituent parts is derived from the fact of its participation in the system as a whole.

From this definition of sex it follows that it is not permissible to single out any one element no matter how conspicuous, such as the gonad, and make it the sole criterion of sex. To attempt to determine "maleness" or "femaleness" by the relative percentage of male and female hormones in blood or urine is obviously to carry this error to an extreme. Sex can be determined only by the character of the reproductive action system *as a whole*. The human being is not a bundle of cells or tissues but a complex biological system, in which new system properties appear on every hierarchical level of integration. And sex is not a small bundle of cells and tissues within a larger one, but a component system of the total system—the individual. The relative significance of the various elements in each of the two sex systems has still to be established. The usual distinction among primary, accessory, and secondary sex characteristics is one-sided and inconsistent, and misleading when applied in medical practice. This is a problem to be approached from different theoretical and practical angles and to which there is accordingly more than one solution.

Reproductive activity of course presupposes reproductive maturity. What then is sex, in terms of this biological conception, in the infant, the embryo, the zygote? The answer is obvious: differential development, directed toward the construction and perfection of the reproductive system. At this point, however, the picture becomes more complicated. Biologists today agree in the assumption that every zygote has the intrinsic capacity to give rise to an individual with either a male or a female reproductive system. The developmental process is shunted into one or the other direction by the successive action of determining factors, such as genes and endocrine substances. It may even happen, as demonstrated in animal experiments, that the initial direction is reversed by the action of a later determinant. Also important is the fact that, although by its gene composition the zygote is already earmarked for one sex, the traceable developmental process is at first identical for both sexes; and even when visible differentiation begins there may still appear two sets of discrete *primordia* for some parts of the genital apparatus, as if a choice of direction still remained. Thereafter, one set of *primordia* develops further while the other degenerates, regresses, or remains in a rudimentary state. In accord with these facts, the zygote as well as the early embryonic stages are no longer referred to as bisexual, but are said, more accurately, to possess bipotentiality of differentiation. Under normal developmental conditions, as differentiation proceeds and one type of reproductive action system grows to completion, the original bipotentiality ceases to have any real significance. It is true that in some classes of mollusk, such as oysters, certain gastropoda and pteropoda, every individual has as standard equipment two complete reproductive systems, one male, one female, and actually engages in fertilization in both ways. The individuals of these species are truly hermaphroditic, i.e., bisexual in the only legitimate sense of this term. However, from the existence of species so organized nothing whatsoever may be deduced in regard to the organization of the human species or of the higher vertebrates in general. The standard developmental pattern of our species provides for each individual only one reproductive action system. The two inherent potentialities of the zygote are thereby mutually exclusive.

In humans the complicated embryological past of the reproductive system has no detectable influence on the efficient reproductive functioning of the normal individual. It can, however, play a part in disturbances of embryonic development or later in the life cycle. Embryonic differentiation of the reproductive system may be hampered by abnormally changed genes or hormonal or other factors, which foster a rival development on the part of the contrasting set of discrete *primordia*. The stimulation of tissues which produce hormones of the opposite sex is an important element in these disturbances. The result is anatomic malformation ranging from a marginal inconsistency in the ultimate differentiation of the sex system to a bizarre fusion and confusion of parts and characteristics of both systems. In such individuals, the capacity of reproductive functioning is often hindered or lacking; they are sexually crippled, but obviously not bisexual. Derangement of a normally built sex system in later life may be observed in the female. Certain tumors of the ovarian medulla, of the adrenal cortex, or of the pituitary entail an excessive output of male sex hormones that rouse the male embryonic rudiments to belated developmental activities. As in the case of embryonic malformations, this conflicting growth impedes or destroys one form of reproductive functioning while creating no new capacity to function in the opposite way. Similar changes can also be brought about artificially in animal experiments in so-called sex reversal. With or without removal of the animal's own sex hormone-producing tissues, hormones of the opposite sex are injected at various stages of embryonic development or later. Although in Mammalia this has resulted only in the derangement of the established sex system, in lower species complete and successful reversal has been obtained. Partial reversal means that the individual is sexually incapacitated; in complete reversal the sex is changed but there is still only one.

To sum up this biological survey: Using the term bisexuality in the only sense in which it is biologically legitimate, there is no such thing as bisexuality either in man or in any other of the higher vertebrates. In the final shaping of the normal individual, the double embryological origin of the genital system does not result in any physiological duality of reproductive functioning. This double origin is of significance only in developmental disturbances and reversals resulting in an admixture of structural characteristics of the opposite sex and thus recognizable as inconsistencies of sex differentiation. In such abnormally built individuals reproductive activity may be impaired or impossible, but the presence in their genital structure of fragments of the opposite sex does not confer on them the reproductive capacity of that sex.

The Problem in Psychoanalysis

Reverting to the psychological study of reproductive activity we are at once struck by the element of pleasure, a feature that necessarily eludes the physical methods of the biologist and which seems at first to lead us into another world. Must we now abandon the dictum of biology, that sex is a matter of the reproductive action system? Let us glance briefly at the decisive psychological facts. It is man's practice to engage in genital activity regardless of reproductive intent. He may even abandon any possibility of reproduction by evading in this pursuit the genital organ of the opposite sex. But how then is the pleasure yield of genital activity obtained? What is its nature? It is, of course, orgasm, a reflex effect of the reproductive action system. Having so identified genital pleasure, we see that it is precisely the orgasmic element of the reproductive system that forms the basis of the genital pleasure function. Orgasm is a pivotal point, being also the point of insemination. Considering the enormous variety of man's sex practices it seems at first incredible, but on second thought quite natural, that they can all be reduced to a simple formula: in deviating from the standard pattern of genital activity man derives excitation from stimulating the sensitive spots available in his mind and body; he may even be driven to seek excitation by dramatizing himself in terms of the opposite sex; yet all this preparatory excitation culminates in genital excitation and is discharged by way of the orgasm reflex. To repeat, the common denominator in all clinical pictures of genital psychopathology is that they represent abnormal conditions of stimulation; yet all the stimulation derived from whatever sources, and by whatever means, acts upon a single physiological pleasure-effector, the orgasm reflex. This reflex partakes of the differentiation of the two reproductive action systems, for it involves different anatomic structures and performs different mechanical duties in each. Physiologically, genital pleasure activity in an individual with male organs is always male, and the same applies to the female. Whatever man does or fancies, it is just as impossible for him to get out of the confines of his biological sex as to get out of his skin.

At this point there of course arises the question of the extragenital pleasure functions, discovered and explored by psychoanalysis: oral, anal, tactile, etc. These are rooted not in the reproductive system but in the alimentary or some other basic biological system. They interact and combine with one another and with the genital pleasure function to make up the individual's entire pleasure organization. The latter is obviously neither sexual nor nonsexual, but an entity of a new order, brought about by integration on a higher level. It undergoes typical changes during the life cycle and is characterized at every stage by a measure of functional flexibility, working in the service of one and then another of the underlying biological systems. If pathologically disturbed it of course hampers rather than benefits the utility function of the system involved. This pleasure organization requires a term that reflects its biological nature and avoids confusion between the superior entity and its component parts. The identification of pleasure and sex made by classical psychoanalysis is at any rate biologically untenable; though originally a dynamic source of inspiration and unparalleled in popular appeal, it led eventually to hopeless confusion and doomed the psychoanalytic study of sex to scientific frustration.

Thus the biological status of the genital pleasure function, heretofore wrapped in ambiguities, is definitely established; inseparable from the reproductive action system, it is also integrated on a higher level into the pleasure organization in the individual.

This clarification was a prerequisite to any examination of the use that has been made of the concept of bisexuality in psychoanalysis. Essentially the procedure has been as follows: Certain types of behavior, or attitudes, or even mere fantasies have been interpreted in the male as "feminine," and analogously with the female, and taken as manifestations of the individual's "negative Oedipus complex" or "homosexual component." Such a component has been assumed, on the basis of the concept of bisexuality, to be present in every individual. It is not pleasant to have to admit that a closer scrutiny reveals no less than six major flaws in this procedure.

(1) The designation of masculine or feminine can be made with reasonable certainty only in the case of a relatively small group of fantasies referring either to the individual's possession of one

or the other type of genital equipment, or to impregnation, pregnancy, or childbirth. Where no possession or reproductive use of genital equipment is implied, as is the case in the vast majority of fantasies, attitudes, and types of behavior, such a designation, though perpetuated by convention and routine, has rested on purely arbitrary grounds. Freud was always aware of this stumbling-block and in 1905 (1962) suggested as the psychological definition of male or female the pursuit of active or passive goals. However, in 1933, he was forced to retract this suggestion and to admit the futility of any such attempt.

(2) In diagnosing psychic manifestations as masculine or feminine, no distinction has been made between adults and the youngest children, in total disregard of the differences in information and intellectual maturity. A fantasy whose content is unquestionably male or female in an adult, might in a child reflect nothing but complete ignorance or deliberate misinformation. The inheritance of knowledge and ideas, first envisaged by Plato and lately revived in psychoanalysis, must obviously be left out of consideration in the absence of any factual basis for such a claim.

(3) Equally unwarranted is the idea that these so-called masculine and feminine manifestations are the direct expression of a constitutional component of the opposite sex. It is well known that fantasies draw their content from experience and therefore to a large extent reflect environmental influences, but this has been lost sight of in the field of sex. A fantasy, even though influential in attitude or behavior, may or may not be the expression of a particular constitutional component. Inspired by birds, man has dreamed for millennia of flying under his own power, but no one has ever suggested that this implied a flying component or predisposition in his constitution. It is also noteworthy that pure fantasies devoid of any driving force and behavior indicative of a strong motor urge have been considered equally representative of a constitutional component.

(4) The constitutional component itself has been a subject of further ambiguity and error. In general theoretical formulations as well as in practice it is indiscriminately referred to either as a homosexual component, or as the female component in the male and the male component in the female. This is all the more remarkable as it is a matter of general knowledge that in some forms

of homosexuality behavior is in no way related to the behavior pattern of the opposite sex. Obviously no knowledge is immune to the truly narcotic effect of an appealing generalization.

(5) Even aside from this confusion, the term "homosexual" has been so stretched as to become almost meaningless. Any relationship between two individuals of the same sex, domination, submission, competitve struggle or friendly cooperation, has readily been interpreted as a manifestation of "unconscious homosexuality," regardless of whether it has any conscious or unconscious bearing on the patient's sexual life. We have already seen the inconsistency and inaccuracy of the term "sex" as used in psychoanalysis; the term "homosexuality" has been even more grossly misapplied.

(6) The assumption of a "homosexual" or "opposite sex" component in the constitution has not served as a challenge to discover what such a component might actually consist of, and in what specific ways, if at all, it influences man's sexual behavior. On the contrary, it has been relied on as if it were the outcome of research which in reality has never been made or even attempted.

It should now be apparent that the vague notion of biological bisexuality and the incredibly loose manner in which it has been used in psychoanalysis have had deplorable consequences. It has acted like a will-o'-the-wisp, always and everywhere luring our attention so that it was impossible to see where the real problem lay. And it has seriously detracted from the benefits to be derived from the unique method of research possessed by psychoanalysis. This could not but have the effect of lowering our therapeutic efficiency. The idea that he is up against a homosexual component in his constitution has often produced in a patient needless discouragement or panic, if not more serious complications.

Free from the preconception of bisexuality, we must of course take new and more reliable bearings in the field of genital psychopathology. The position outlined on biological grounds then inevitably becomes our point of departure. The basic problem, to state it briefly, is to determine the factors that cause the individual to apply aberrant forms of stimulation to his standard genital equipment. Following this line of inquiry, we find that the chief causal factor is the affect of anxiety, which inhibits standard stimulation and compels the "ego action system in the individual" to bring forth an altered scheme of stimulation as a "reparative adjustment" (Rado, 1936–1940; 1939). Both the inhibitory and the reparative processes begin far back in early childhood, leading up to the picture which we encounter in the adult. The reparative adjustment may allow the individual several alternatives of morbid stimulation, or may take the form of a rigid and inexorable pattern on which he depends for gratification. This approach, of which we can give here only the barest suggestion, has in practice unfolded a wealth of clinical details leading to a theory that is free of inconsistency and that serves as a reliable guide to treatment.

It also demands a change in outlook toward the underlying problem of constitution. If we assume, as we must, that constitutional factors may have an influence on morbid sex developments, we are now justified in considering this influence to be of two kinds: one preparing the ground for the inhibitory action of anxiety, the other modulating the course of the reparative adjustment. In considering the factors so involved we must not overlook the possibility of general, i.e., nonsexual factors, as well as innate defects of the sexual action system of as yet unknown character. It is well to recall, lest we underestimate this eventuality, that we are still in the dark even as regards the physiological mechanism of such an elementary phenomenon as sexual attraction. Still another possibility is of course the presence of elements of the action system of the opposite sex such as reflexes, or rather chains of reflexes, susceptible to resuscitation by hormones or other agents (W. C. Young & Rundlett, 1939). However, not until somatic research has disclosed such elements shall we be able to determine by psychological methods their role in shaping morbid sex behavior. Meanwhile unbiased psychological analysis can offer invaluable clues to the somatic investigator in his search for predisposing somatic factors. Any such contribution was obviously out of the question as long as we employed fictitious constitutional factors as a means of psychological explanation. This methodological error not only trapped us in a vicious circle, but also deprived somatic research of a lead not obtainable elsewhere.

In conclusion it is imperative to supplant the deceptive concept of bisexuality with a psychological theory based on firmer biological foundations. Reconstructive work of this nature is more than an invitation; it is a scientific obligation for psychoanalysis. It is also an obligation to the founder of our science, Sigmund Freud, who left us not a creed but an instrument of research.

REFERENCES

Allan, E. (Ed.) *Sex and internal secretions.* (2nd ed.) Baltimore: Williams & Wilkins, 1939.

Bard, P. The hypothalamus and sexual behavior. *Res. Publ. Assn. nerv. ment. Dis.,* 20 n.d.

Ellis, H. Sexual inversion. In *Studies in the psychology of sex.* New York: Random House, 1956.

Freud, S. *Beyond the pleasure principle* (1920). New York: Liveright, 1924.

Freud, S. *New introductory lectures on psycho-analysis.* New York: Norton, 1933.

Freud, S. In J. Strachey (Trans.), *Three essays on the theory of sexuality* (1905). New York: Basic Books, 1962.

Hartmann, M. *Allgemeine biologie.* Jena: 1933.

Hartmann, M. *Geschlecht und geschlechtsbestimmung im Tier- und Pflanzenreich.* Berlin: 1939.

Hirschfeld, M. *Die homosexualität des mannes und des weibes.* Berlin: Marcus, 1914.

Krafft-Ebing, R. von. *Psychopathia sexualis.* New York: Pioneer, 1931.

Lillie, F. R. General biological introduction. In E. Allan (Ed.), *Sex and internal secretions.* Baltimore: Williams & Wilkins, 1939.

Meisenheimer, J. *Geschlecht und geschlechter im Tierreich.* Jena: 1921.

Rado, S. Lectures at the New York Psychoanalytic Institute. 1936–1940.

Rado, S. Developments in the psychoanalytic conception and treatment of the neuroses. *Psychoanalyt, Quart.,* 1939, 8, 427-437.

Steinach, E. *Sex and life.* New York: 1940.

Waldeyer, W. *Eirstock und ei: ein beitrag zur anatomie und entwicklungsgeschichte der sexualorgane.* Leipzig: 1870.

Weiss, P. *Principles of development.* New York: Holt, 1939.

Winthuis, J. *Das zweigeschlechterwesen.* Leipzig: 1928.

Young, H. H. *Genital abnormalities, hermaphroditism and related adrenal diseases.* Baltimore: 1937.

Young, W. C., & Rundlett, B. The hormonal induction of homosexual behavior in the spayed female guinea pig. *Pyschosom. Med.,* 1939, **1,** 449-460.

Reprinted from *Psychosomatic Medicine,* 2 (1940), 459-467.

Passing and the Continuum of Gender Identity

11

ROBERT J. STOLLER

In studying problems of gender identity, we are constantly confronted by patients' identifications with members of the opposite sex. The results of these identifications have been most obvious in transsexuals and transvestites.[1] Yet people whose gender identifications are manifestly less confused have also revealed psychodynamics and vestiges in character structure or in dreams that are qualitatively similar to those found in patients with more ambiguous identities. Identification with aspects of members of the opposite sex is present in all human beings.

Koff (1961) puts this point very clearly:

> . . . [T]he boy regularly identifies with his father. But the logical consequence of the theory of identification is that the boy should also identify with his mother, since she is the main object that is aban-

---

[1] A transsexual is a person who actively seeks a sex-transformation operation, that is, a surgical procedure to change primary or secondary sex characteristics to the appearance of those of the opposite sex. A transvestite is a person who habitually prefers to wear clothes of the opposite sex. All transsexuals are overtly transvestic; transvestites are not transsexual except for occasional fantasies of sexual transformation.

doned, so far as direct libidinal gratification is concerned. Likewise, the girl should have some accentuation of masculine traits out of identification with her father, when she abandons him as an object. Actually, clinical observations indicate this does occur so regularly that we should recognize this as inevitable, instead of necessarily considering feminine identification in boys and masculine identification in girls, as evidence of distortion in development, as is often mistakenly done. Glover observed and commented on this in his paper, "Neurotic Character," first published in 1925 (p. 363).

There are continua along which particular aspects of gender identification can be measured. For example, there is a continuum in men between frank effeminacy of voice, posture, and gestures and total absence of such mannerisms. Similarly, there is a continuum of reaction formations against showing such tendencies, a series that extends from no attempt to exaggerate attributes of one's own sex to movie-queen or muscle-beach caricatures. Such continua are almost countless. People react intuitively to others, grading them grossly in terms of these continua, as "He is manly" or "He is effeminate."

Work with transsexuals and transvestites has revealed a rare and dramatic phenomenon: *passing*, that very risky adaptation in which an individual chooses to cross a forbidden line from one clearly ascribed status in society to another, despite the severe punishments he faces if caught. Although passing is familiar enough to laymen, sociologists, and psychiatrists, surprisingly little systematic work has been done on it. The more we look, the more we become aware of its fascination for people. Books, plays, and films are filled with individuals who are passing. Of the various areas of life in which passing can be observed, the one we shall consider here is "gender passing."

The purposes of this chapter are several: hopefully to focus more attention on passing and to stimulate recognition that passing is not peripheral to psychiatric observation but a significant process deserving more study. It is also worth pointing to the need for future work to probe and enlarge the problem of passing and its relationship to psychodynamic theory and to problems of identity formation and character structure.[2] The main focus of

---

[2] One aspect of this problem, how the dread of being homosexual helps to

this preliminary study, however, is on clinical material on the confusion in gender caused by impulses to change gender and on whether these cross-gender impulses differ in those who have passed and those who have not.

This chapter does not attack many of the issues, especially sociological, that the phenomenon of gender passing raises. Instead, it underlines the presence in society of this phenomenon, in order to begin its examination through the concept of the continuum of gender identity and to come to some understanding of what is meant by "gender passing."

Subjects

Without trying to list all the continua that might be considered in describing degrees of identificaton with aspects of the opposite sex, we present a rough generalization of such a continuum. To formulate this graded series, vignettes from the case histories of a number of patients who range along this spectrum are utilized.

Case 1. A thirty-year-old bachelor who is successfully building a career in his profession, has been in psychoanalysis for a year. His unremitting complaint has been a severe feeling of inadequacy in the presence of most men. This feeling is accompanied by a worshipful attitude toward a particular leader in his profession and toward his psychoanalyst and hidden but conscious rages toward his employers and his father. He feels inept in his sexual relations. In the course of describing for the first time his feeling that his penis is too small, he said that his girlfriend would not agree with that statement. To quote him, "She says that my vag—, penis is just right." Calling his attention to this slip produced a flood of associations about the beauties of a vagina and the disgusting, infecting quality of his "little dangling noodle." That night he dreamed that "Someone offered me a glazed fruit—a candy. It was very small and long, like an orange peel in marmalade, about four inches long. I bit into the fruit, and it went gooey in my mouth and stuck in my teeth."

---

motivate the transsexual's behavior, is being explored by Greenson (1963).

His associations went from the piece of candied fruit he had actually been given at his parents' house that evening; to his excited fear of a young girl he was trying to date; to his constant daydreams of being a great hero; to the cotton rolls his dentist packs in his mouth; to his fear of the dentist's needle and the syringe with the finger-holders on each side; to venereal disease, which he caught in the service and which was treated with syringes of penicillin; to the prostitute who gave him the venereal disease after refusing to perform fellatio; and finally to the homosexual pun on the word "fruit." This chain of associations was followed by many hours of work on his feminine identifications and fears of being homosexual.

Case 2. The second patient is an adolescent boy whose fantasies, masturbatory and otherwise, are exclusively directed toward his being loved by a handsome athlete. He has never had any overt sexual relations, although he is exclusively (consciously) directed toward a homosexual object. He shows no overtly effeminate behavior. He feels himself to be weak, however, in constant danger of breakthrough of unmanly emotion, and consciously desires only to make a powerful man happy. He reported the following dream: "I am watching without any feeling a car driving down the street near where I lived when I was little. The car is being chased by a boar." In the patient's associations, the car was a little car; the boar was a large wild animal with tusks with which it was trying to attack the car from the rear; a boar was related to a pig, which is a milder domesticated version of this wilder animal; and the patient's last name (which he has received from his father) is also that of a wild animal that is related to a domesticated animal. He continued that his father is a cold and unfeeling man interested only in his work, to which he attends all day at his office and throughout the evening at home. The therapist said. "He is a bore," and the patient responded, "That's exactly what I was thinking last night," before recognizing the pun in surprise. He then added that his father is not only a bore but also persistently questions him, goads him, criticizes him, and bores into him. The associations in the hour ended with the patient revealing for the first time that in his homosexual fantasies he pictures anal intercourse being performed on him. At that moment, he recalled that the little car had a tail pipe at which the boar's tusks were aimed in the dream.

Case 3. This woman, with no demonstrable genetic or biological defect, has dressed exclusively as a man for many years and in childhood dressed and acted as a very marked tomboy. If one were to meet "him," "he" would stir no suspicion that there is a problem in gender identity. "He" works in an electronics plant with men and is accepted as an equal by them. With "his" boots, jeans, lumberjack shirt, crew-cut, man's name, and comfort with swearing, "he" is accepted as a man in ordinary social situations. "His" difficulties, like those of similar patients, arise in such situations as physical examinations and the use of toilets. To direct inquiry, "he" never denies that "he" is female.

Case 4. The fourth patient is one step further along the continuum of increasingly overt identification with the opposite sex. This person is transsexual. "He" has lived throughout "his" adult life as a man and is known only to intimate friends as what "he" is biologically, a woman. Over the years, "he" has involuted "his" pelvic organs piece by piece by means of surgery, has replaced the lost estrogens by externally administered testosterone, and had even developed a breast carcinoma, which required bilateral mastectomy. Against the recommendations of the surgeon, the patient insisted on having only a simple mastectomy, as the plastic result of that procedure alone complied perfectly with one of "his" wishes throughout adult life, to have a masculine appearing chest so that "he" could sit in bathing trunks at the beach. This fantasy was more powerful than even the fear of death from metastases if a radical mastectomy were not performed. These surgical transformations plus the hormones have produced a "man" with a beard that requires daily shaving, a deep voice, a hairy "masculine" chest, and other paraphernalia that make it easier to appear in public as a man. "He" has only a mild interest in gaining a phallus, less than that of the urologist who has promised the surgery when the patient is ready.

Case 5. The fifth patient (Schwabe, Solomon, Stoller, & Burnham, 1962; Stoller, Garfinkel, & Rosen, 1960) goes still further.

This young "woman" was born and developed till puberty as a biologically normal boy but with a very feminine bent. Beginning at puberty, he developed the typical secondary sex characteristics of an amply endowed, attractive female, which flowered in adolescence. The quality of this biologically induced transformation from one sex to the other, which accompanied psychological disturbance in gender identity, was marred by the presence of normal penis and testes. To this patient, the feminine characteristics seemed natural, and the male genitalia were not merely superfluous but disgusting. In late adolescence, the patient left home, returning several weeks later dressed and behaving as a girl. In the years that followed, "she" froze into permanent feminine behavior in a manner no different to observation from that in which an awkward adolescent girl develops her more comfortable femininity. "She" moved from home to another community, lived as a girl with girls, held the sort of job typically held by women, went on dates, and finally became engaged. The intimacies of engagement brought with them frightening questions from "her" fiance about the "growth" between "her" legs. These questions resulted in a clear-cut single-minded determination to have the "growth" removed. After the operation, the source of estrogens was discovered to have been in "her" testes, and "she" developed a typical menopause, for which "she" has to the present been receiving estrogen-replacement therapy. The man-made vagina was at first a mixed blessing, but it has come to serve its purpose, as the patient was recently married. The marriage was legal, for the patient had managed, sometime before the operation, to persuade the authorities of the state in which "she" was born to change "her" birth certificate to read "female" instead of "male."

As contrasts to these patients, two others can be described.

Case 6. The first (Stoller & Rosen, 1959) is a man who had to reverse his direction along the continuum, who had to find his way back to identifications appropriate to his correct biological sex. This man, in fact a male hermaphrodite, was considered at birth to be a female and was brought up as one, although he was an unusually masculine "girl" in his behavior. In his teens, his

"enlarged clitoris" was removed. For many years afterward, he
lived exclusively as a "butch" homosexual, adopting the mannerisms, dress, voice, thinking, and other societal camouflage required of tough females. Only after psychiatric treatment were
his doubts about his sex and gender clearly focused in consciousness. He then began the difficult process of pumping life into the
vestigial masculine identifications that had been deposited in his
childhood and had been dormant within his personality for
many years. For this man, there were considerable problems related to "passing" to his biological sex. Everyone knew him as a
"butch" homosexual, and it has not been easy for him to maneuver his life in order to transform himself safely into the male
that he actually is. After several years' work, he has succeeded in
doing so completely, even in his profession. Because he had
worked with the same people for so many years, he delayed
longest before taking the risk of telling them who he really is. At
this late date in life, he has finally been married.

Case 7. The second of these contrasting patients appears toward the pole on our continuum at which people with essentially
normal identification with their biological sex appear. She is a
young woman involved in the typical problems of a girl her age
in our society. She is not any more or less free of neurotic symptoms and neurotic ego structures than are other people, nor can
her gender-role behavior be distinguished from that typical of
women in this society who have not yet been married. She is mentioned here for only one reason: She is a genetic male who, for
unknown reasons, did not develop *in utero* a male genital apparatus. She confirms Jost's theory (1958) that the *anlage* of sexual
apparatus in both male and female has a predilection toward female anatomical structure, which tendency is counteracted in
the male by the production of an unknown substance in the fetus,
probably produced by the fetal testes. As this patient did not
have testes, this tendency was permitted to progress unchecked
in a feminine direction, with the result that she developed feminine external genitalia, a broad ligament, but no internal genitalia
or gonads. Without any estrogens or testosterone, except the minimal amounts produced by the adrenals, the patient's eunuch-

oid physique permits her to appear feminine. The only reason she came for medical treatment was that breasts had not developed and menses had not begun.

Discussion

It is worth pausing at this point to say more about gender identity, for it is a key concept in gender passing. The term "gender" connotes psychological aspects of behavior related to masculinity and femininity. It does not have the same meaning as "sex." A person's sex is the result of a number of factors: chromosomes, external genitalia, internal genitalia, hormonal status, the secondary sex characteristics produced by estrogens and testosterone, and the gonads. There are biological attributes of both sexes in everyone, but the sum of these attributes falls in most people decidedly toward one or the other pole of the continuum between male or female. "Sex" is biological, "gender" social. Most often, the two are relatively congruent, that is, males tend to be manly and females womanly. It is clear, however, that there is no natural law governing this congruence (Joan G. Hampson, 1955; Hampson, Hampson, & Money, 1955; Money, 1955; Money, Hampson, & Hampson, 1955a; Money *et al.*, 1955b; Money *et al.*, 1956; Novak, 1948); sex and gender may be independent of each other, as some of our cases demonstrate. "Gender" connotes behavior learned from a tremendous pool of cues present in every culture and from a massive, intricate, though usually subtle, system of rewards and punishments in which every person lives from birth on. (The first questions a woman asks at the moment of delivery are, "What is it—boy or girl? Is it all right?")

It is therefore more precise to talk of "gender identity" than of "sexual identity." [3]

It is important to distinguish gender identity from gender role. A clear-cut gender identity leads to a habitually clear-cut con-

---

[3] The reader is referred to a most important study by Lichtenstein, "Identity and Sexuality" (1961), for a discussion of the meaning of the term "identity" as well as for a superb review of the literature of this concept.

frontation of society that is called "gender role." [4] The behavior
that reflects this culturally determined role is gender-role behavior. It is possible to shift gender role, even while gender identity
is constant (although it seems likely that playing a consistent
role long and hard enough may cause some changes in gender
identity). For instance, the gender identity developed by the
hermaphroditic male brought up as a girl (Case 6) is a rare one
found in intersexed people, in which the patient is uncertain if
he is either male or female. This uncertainty is as much a part of
his identity as certainty is a part of the more normal identity.
Such people can successfully shift their gender roles (Berg,
Nixon, & MacMahon, 1963; Brown & Fryer, 1959; Brown & Fryer
1964; Burns, Segaloff, & Carrera, 1960; Kraft, 1963; Norris & Keettell, 1962), while their gender identities, permanently uncertain
(Stoller, 1964b; Stoller, 1964c), do not change.

In brief, one plays a role but possesses an identity.

What produces gender identity? Normally, at the moment
when the child is delivered, its mother receives the ascription of
sex from society's delegated authority, the doctor. The mother
confirms this ascription with her first look at the infant's genitalia,
tells the father, and the necessary information is broadcast. The
machinery of society is set in motion. Myriad cues from everyone
who comes in contact with the child funnel the culture's gender
criteria in upon him. The way these expectations are presented
is very specifically modified by the child's mother—by her own
gender identity, her relationship with her husband, her experience with other children or the lack of it, the way she handles
the child's body and helps to define its body ego, and many
other aspects of the mother–infant relationship. Some of what the
mother conveys to her baby is evident only to the careful eye. For
instance, some mothers cuddle or feed or make noises at a little

---

[4] "By the term, gender role, we mean all those things that a person says or
does to disclose himself or herself as having the status of boy or man, girl or
woman, respectively. It includes, but is not restricted to sexuality in the sense
of eroticism. A gender role is not established at birth, but is built up cumula-
tively through experiences encountered and transacted through casual and
unplanned learning, through explicit instruction and inculcation, and through
spontaneous putting two and two together to make four and sometimes,
erroneously, five" (Money *et al.*, 1955b).

girl differently from the way they perform the same actions toward a little boy. Other activities are blatant, although not necessarily more formative, as choosing colors for the infant's blankets and clothes. At any rate, these cues are given in vast amounts all day long.

These elements the environment provides. But the child contributes its part too. Genital sensations, both those arising spontaneously and those provoked by the environment (diapers, mother, and so forth), gradually produce in the child an increasingly intense awareness of these curiously pleasure-giving tissues. Part of the infant's awareness of its existence and separateness from the rest of the world (body ego), like its awareness of being a one-headed, four-limbed creature with sensitive openings and exits, comes from this growing awareness of the external genitalia (Brierly, 1932; Brierly, 1936; Casuso, 1957; Deutsch, 1933; Greenacre, 1948; Greenacre, 1950; Greenacre, 1952; Greenacre, 1953; Greenacre, 1955; Horney, 1933; Kestenberg, 1956a; Kestenberg, 1956b; Kramer, 1954; Lowenstein, 1950; Mahler, 1958). These sensations confirm the ascription of maleness and femaleness by society (Greenacre, 1955; Horney, 1933; Stoller, 1964a). With greater mobility, language, experience, and independence, the child learns not only to consider genitalia very important but that genitalia distinguish two (and only two) classes of humans (and other creatures).

Later issues like penis envy, castration fears, and the Oedipal conflict and its resolution, especially through identification with the parent of the same sex, cannot be discussed here, although they are essential to the growing complexity of gender identity. Our description deals only with the earliest stage of the development of gender identity, which results in a *core gender identity.* In almost all people, this core identity is simply an unshakable conviction that "I am a male" or "I am a female." This conviction is established by the age of two or three years (Hampson, Money, & Hampson, 1956; Money, 1960; Money *et al.*, 1955b; Money *et al.*, 1957). Attempts to reverse the child's sex and gender are increasingly less successful as the child grows beyond this relatively critical period (Joan G. Hampson, 1955; Hampson, Money, & Hampson, 1956; Money, 1960; Money *et al.*, 1955b; Money *et al.*, 1956; Money *et al.*, 1957).

In addition to the core gender identity, there are later vicissitudes in gender-identity development. Although a child may know unequivocally that he is male, he will wish that he had one attribute or another of the female. A gross example of this wish is seen in the adult transvestic male. As Fenichel (1930) has described him, he is a man who fantasies himself a phallic female. He knows he is a male and knows he has a penis, but by a process of make-believe that can reach almost the intensity of delusion, he wishes himself and plays at being a woman with a penis.

So far, two determining factors in gender identity have been mentioned: parental (cultural) attitudes and the infant's external genitalia. There seems to be a third, a "biological force," an undercurrent urging a male toward masculinity and a female toward femininity (Stoller, 1964a). If it does exist, its effects can nonetheless be overcome by rearing,[5] though not always. Cases have been reported (Stoller, 1964a) in which the effects of rearing, including those very subtle ones involved in the process of identification—the parents' own gender identities and the secret permissions for cross-gender impulses that some parents give— are not present to account for a child's apparent overwhelming rejection of its gender of rearing. In adolescence, secondary sex changes have first revealed that biological forces are present that are in complete agreement with the child's insistence on acting as a member of the opposite sex. Suggestive of a different aspect of this possibility that in some people a "biological force" may influence gender role is the report by Lief and his associates of a young man whose gender behavior was more masculine or more feminine in direct and not coincidental relation to shifts in sex hormones (Lief, Dingman, & Bishop, 1962).

Although it would be of value to discuss what gender identity consists of now that we have looked into its origins, such discussion must be deferred for a separate study. It can be very briefly stated, however, that, in addition to the body ego, the gender identity is made up of all sorts of identifications (good and bad

---

[5] Money *et al.* have described how, in two biologically identical pseudo-hermaphrodites, one raised from birth as a boy and the other as a girl, the appropriate gender roles developed regardless of the biological state. That is, the child raised as a girl was an unremarkable feminine girl and the one raised as a boy as masculine as any other boy (1957).

representations of parts and attributes of people of both sexes), starting with the mother and eventually taking in a large part of the available objects in a culture.[6] In the normal case, the selection process eventually results in a choice of objects of the same sex much more than of the opposite sex, although by no means exclusively. For example, the first person available (and essential) for identification in a boy is his mother, and only if this relationship is not too badly disturbed will the later crucial identification with his father be possible.

Now let us return to our seven cases and the continuum of gender identity they illustrate. We know that cross-gender impulses are ubiquitous (for example, couvade; penile subincision; Halloween and Mardi Gras transvestism; the feminization of Hercules; gender passing in many of Shakespeare's plays and in Gênet's *The Balcony* and *Our Lady of the Flowers;* the mana of bisexual or intersexed shamans; the many Greek Hermaphroditos statues in the museums of Europe; *Charley's Aunt* and *Some Like It Hot;* children's games of dressing up; analytic patients' dreams; the myth of Tiresias; Schreber's delusion of impregnation by God; and Christ's feminine appearance in so many paintings). The woman in the audience watching Rosalind pass as a boy in *As You Like It* resonates to the theme partly because it is a possibility inside herself.

As we progress along our continuum, however, we begin to deal with increasingly active impulses and fantasies. We finally reach the transsexuals, who, like our fourth patient, believe themselves to be females trapped in male bodies, or vice versa, or the intersexed patients like our sixth, who are uncertain to which gender they belong and can therefore shift gender roles at any time without disastrous effects (Stoller, 1964b; Stoller, 1964c). In order to better understand this continuum, it is suggested that the less well established the gender identity, the more intense the cross-gender impulses. The earlier in the life of the child that uncertainty is introduced into the gender identity, the more intense the cross-gender impulses will be. When a person's core gender identity has been invaded, he may truly not adequately know to

---

[6] See Koff (1961) for an excellent review of the psychoanalytic literature on identification.

which sex and gender he belongs. To resolve this identity dilemma, such a person may attempt to pass.

People who pass have a very rare condition: an uncertain core
gender identity. This developmental defect, produced very early
in life, seems to appear in three kinds of people: biological nor-
mals whose mothers have in some as yet unknown manner[7] made
their children uncertain of their own sex and gender; some but
not all people who have genitalia that can be taken for either
male or female (intersexed); and some but not all people with
apparently unambiguous genitalia who nonetheless belong biologically to the opposite sex from the one indicated by their genitalia (intersexed) and in whom a "biological force" congruent
with the correct but hidden sex overpowers the normally tran-
scendent effects of rearing.

The cases that have been described suggest that there exist
from childhood on certain areas of psychic life in which an individual feels what might be called "cross-gender impulses," that
is, desires to be like members of the opposite sex. There is good
evidence (Fenichel, 1926; Koff, 1961) that these impulses result from identifications with people of the opposite sex starting
in earliest childhood. In some cases, these identifications are
reinforced by events in later childhood, adolescence, and adulthood. In others, they lie dormant and become overt only with
special shifts in instinct, loss of ego control, or strong external
pressures from individuals or society. In still others, most of these
cross-gender identifications atrophy through disuse and are
never apparent again or appear only in vestigial form. It is our
concern in this chapter, however, in addition to demonstrating
the continuum of gender identity, to show the similarities and
differences between those who tend to act more and those who
tend to act less on these cross-gender impulses.

In our seven patients, the phenomenon of gender passing and
its relationship to gender identity are of special interest. As with
secret members of political undergrounds, spies, Negroes who become white, Jews who become Gentiles, impostors, and so forth,

---

[7] Some workers on schizophrenia who have studied the infant's relationship
with its mother may have clues to solving this question (Searles, 1961), as
have those working in the area of gender identity (Greenacre, 1953; Greenacre, 1955).

there are people who pass from their originally ascribed gender roles to the opposite ones. Our fifth patient, for instance, was a male from birth to adolescence and believed himself (correctly though reluctantly) to be one. Then he changed into a "woman" and has remained a "woman," undetected by society, ever since. Our sixth patient, although a biological male, believed himself a female from birth on, as did everyone else. For him, the dangerous change was the move from what he was not in the most concrete biological reality (a homosexual woman) to what he was (a heterosexual male). He too had to pass, to go from the status society ascribed to a new and forbidden one, even though this new role was a genetically and biologically proper one. Our seventh subject is biologically neuter, yet she has lived all her life unquestioningly as a female. She has no knowledge of maleness, only of defective femaleness (no breasts, sterility, and an inadequate vaginal vault). She is not passing, for she is expending no effort to overcome the effects of carrying a consciously held secret.

There is, of course, much more to the psychodynamics of passing than an understanding of gender identity and of identification. All that we can do here, however, is to indicate other areas for later work.

First, there is the great problem of society's ways of defining ranges of gender normality and the cues available to people who are passing.

Second, how is identification like and different from imitation? What are the relations of identification and imitation to acting? How does imitation become identification in infancy, childhood, and adulthood? What do games or silent fantasies contribute to identification, identity formation, and passing? Under what circumstances does practice make perfect? What is the process of identification in an impostor? What changes have occurred when a homosexual who doubts his masculinity becomes a public figure because of success in film cowboy roles, with his earnings buys a ranch, and, as a hobby, becomes an excellent cowboy (Abraham, 1925; Deutsch, 1955; Greenacre, 1958a; Greenacre, 1958b)?

Third, what part does passing play as a massive defense against identity diffusion? Loss of the sense of identity is probably at the bottom of impending psychosis (panic states) and of the nightmarish quality of the paranoid conditions. Not until such loss is threatened, until the feeling that one's *self* is being swept away, does panic result. The tidal-wave and falling-off-a-cliff dreams of women who fear orgasmic loss of control are an example. For such women, orgasm is feared as a loss of identity. As a defense against such identity loss, passing seems quite successful; despite the massive modification of character structure necessary to pass, none of our patients who are seriously engaged in it is psychotic, on the borderline, or even suffering from a diagnosable neurotic state.

One point is clear: A person who is the *real thing* knows he has the potential (in aspiration, resources, and above all in legitimacy) to fulfill his gender role, but the person who is passing does not and knows it. Even if the passer is comfortable in his role and is safe from detection, he cannot *really* be what he seems. He can only approximate it, and, although his approximation may be so beautifully performed as to avoid detection, to himself he is still not what he appears but only a representation.

It may be that passing cannot be absolutely defined but is rather a "more-or-less" state. It shares features in common with other points on our continuum, being simply the most intense of them all. It is certainly true that, the more willing a person is to be caught,[8] the less the way he lives his life approaches passing. For example, our third subject, a biological female, is to all appearances a man. When visiting "his" brother in another state, "he" went into the local grocery store, where the clerk immediately asked "him" if "he" wasn't Mr. J's brother. It pleased the patient to answer, "No, I'm not *his* brother, but he's *my* brother," leaving the clerk very puzzled. "He" thus showed that "he" is willing to suggest "he" is something other than a man. If "he" is looking for a job, "he" always admits openly (but only if specifically asked) that "he" is a woman. "He" has gone a long way in appearance and behavior toward making others feel that "he" is a man—but not all the way. Compare this subject with our fourth, the transsexual who has had "his" breasts and pelvic organs removed. When "he" looks for a job, "he" states at the first

---

[8] Including unconsciously motivated slips of tongue and behavior.

interview that "he" is a man, but the threat of more careful questioning or of physical examination makes "him" drop the game in despair, with a feeling that such is "his" fate (that he may never be able ultimately to escape detection that "he" is really a female). "He" has gone even further than the third patient but still admits not being a man if caught. In contrast to these two, there is the "female" with the feminine secondary sex characteristics and the "growth." The first two admit to their biological gender in certain public situations; the third does not do so under any circumstances in society. For example, if a physical examination is required, "she" does not run but submits. Only if "she" is confronted with a pelvic examination does she quit the game, and even then she does not reveal that there is a problem. The examining physician may be left puzzled at "her" unexpected exit, but "she" never leaves any clue that would make him suspect that "she" is not fully a woman.

It may indeed be that passing is only an extreme point on the continuum of gender identity. In some ways it definitely is. Nonetheless, there is one crucial area in which the issue is not simply one of degree. That one area is the relationship of a person to reality. In passing, the aspect of reality that is critical is society and its attitudes toward passing. It is possible to interrupt our continuum of gender identity at a certain point, beyond which it can be said that a person is passing. A person is actually *passing* if a qualitatively new element enters into his thought and behavior. He offers society a promise (of being a female, white, Gentile, or whatever he wants to be), knowing that he cannot fully satisfy claims made on the basis of this promise. He nevertheless attempts to achieve acceptance by society as a member of the class (gender, color, religion) contrary to the one to which he knows he has been "naturally" ascribed by society. This striving is endless. It is performed in secret and with the realistic conviction that disclosure would be disastrous.

We can therefore suggest that there is a fundamental difference between the expressions of cross-gender impulses in people who do not pass and in those who do. Some people may wish to pass and may act out some of these wishes in isolated areas of life or in character structure. But these people are not passing.

To pass, they need the overwhelming motivation that makes them willing to take great risks and permits them to go beyond imitation to actual gender identification.

Summary

Identification with aspects of the opposite sex, which expresses itself in cross-gender impulses, is found in everyone. Certain people in whom these impulses are very strong attempt to pass as members of the sex opposite to the ones they originally were assigned. People who do not pass share some of the same cross-gender fantasies and defenses. As these fantasies and defenses are so common, is there such an activity as passing, or is passing indistinguishable from previously described continua of gender confusion? Clinical material is available that has two elements, the identifications with the opposite sex that result in cross-gender impulses expressed by all subjects—a common denominator —and the internal and external effort to manage a role backed by a secret whose disclosure it is felt would be disastrous. Passing can be distinguished from other varieties of cross-gender impulses by the stand the subject takes about his "chosen" gender identity *vis-à-vis* sociocultural reality. The far greater sustained effort, motivation, thought, deliberation, and care that the person who is passing must use to live in his elected status distinguish him from those who are not.

REFERENCES

Abraham, K. The history of an impostor in the light of psychoanalytical knowledge. In Hilda Abraham (Ed.), *Clinical papers and essays on psychoanalysis: selected Papers of.* . . . Vol. 2. New York: Basic Books, 1955. Pp. 291-305.

Berg, I., Nixon, H. H., & MacMahon, R. Change of assigned sex at puberty. *Lancet,* 1963, 2, 1213-1216.

Brierly, M. Some problems of integration in women. *Int. J. Psychoanal.,* 1932, 13, 433-447.

Brierly, M. Specific determinants in feminine development. *Int. J. Psychoanal.*, 1936, 17, 163-180.

Brown, B. B., & Fryer, M. P. Hypospadias; complete construction of penis, with establishment of proper sex status after 13 years of mistaken female identity. *Postgrad. Med.*, 1959, 22, 489-491.

Brown, B. B., & Fryer, M. P. Plastic surgical correction of hypospadias with mistaken sex identity and transvestism resulting in normal marriage and parenthood. *Surg. Gynecol. Obstet.*, 1964, 118, 45-46.

Burns, E., Segaloff, A., & Carrera, G. M. Reassignment of sex: report of 3 cases. *J. Urol.*, 1960, 84, 126-133.

Casuso, G. Anxiety related to the "discovery" of the penis. *Psychoanalytic study of the child*. Vol. 12. New York: International Univer. Press, 1957. Pp. 169-174.

Deutsch, Helene. Homosexuality in women. *Int. J. Psychoanal.*, 1933, 14, 34-56.

Deutsch, Helene. The impostor. *Psychoanal. Quart.*, 1955, 24, 483-505.

Fenichel, O. Identification (1926). In *Collected papers of. . . .* Vol. 1. New York: Norton, 1953. Pp. 97-112.

Fenichel, O. Psychology of transvestism (1930). In *Collected papers of. . . .* Vol. 1. New York: Norton, 1953. Pp. 167-180.

Greenacre, P. Anatomical structure and superego development. *Amer. J. Orthopsychiat.*, 1948, 13, 636-648.

Greenacre, P. Special problems of early female sexual development. *Psychoanalytic study of the child*. Vol. 5. New York: International Univer. Press, 1950. Pp. 122-138.

Greenacre, P. Pregenital patterning. *Int. J. Psychoanal.*, 1952, 33, 410-415.

Greenacre, P. Certain relationships between fetishism and faulty development of the body image. *Psychoanalytic study of the child*. Vol. 8. New York: International Univer. Press, 1953. Pp. 79-98.

Greenacre, P. Further considerations regarding fetishism. *Psychoanalytic study of the child*. Vol. 10. New York: International Univer. Press, 1955. Pp. 187-194.

Greenacre, P. The impostor. *Psychoanal. Quart.*, 1958, 27, 359-382. (a)

Greenacre, P. The relation of the impostor to the artist. *Psychoanalytic study of the child*. Vol. 13. New York: International Univer. Press, 1958. (b)

Greenson, R. On homosexuality and gender identity. Paper read at 23rd Int. Congr. Psychoanal., Stockholm, 1963.

Hampson, Joan G. Hermaphroditic genital appearance, rearing and eroticism in hyperadrenocorticism. *Bull. Johns Hopkins Hosp.*, 1955, **96**, 265-273.

Hampson, Joan L., Hampson, J. G., & Money, J. The syndrome of gonadal agenesis (ovarian agenesis) and male chromosomal pattern in girls and women: psychologic studies. *Bull. Johns Hopkins Hosp.*, 1955, **97**, 207-226.

Hampson, Joan G., Money, J., & Hampson, J. L. Hermaphroditism: recommendations concerning case management. *J. clin. Endocrin. Metab.*, 1956, **16**, 547-556.

Horney, Karen. The denial of the vagina. *Int. J. Psychoanal.*, 1933, **14**, 57-70.

Jost, A. Embryonic sexual differentiation. In H. W. Jones, Jr., & W. W. Scott (Eds.), *Hermaphroditism, genital anomalies, and related endocrine disorders.* Baltimore: Williams & Wilkins, 1958.

Kestenberg, J. On the development of maternal feelings in early childhood. *Psychoanalytic study of the child.* Vol. 11. New York: Internat. Univer. Press, 1956. Pp. 257-291. (a)

Kestenberg, J. Vicissitudes of female sexuality. *J. Amer. psychoanal. Assn.*, 1956, **3**, 453-476.(b)

Koff, R. H. A definition of identification: a review of the literature. *Int. J. Psychoanal.*, 1961, **42**, 362-370.

Kraft, I. R. Psychological preparation of a five-year-old pseudohermaphrodite for surgical sexual change. *Ped. Clin. N. Amer.*, 1963, 257-263.

Kramer, P. Early capacity for orgastic discharge and character formation. *Psychoanalytic study of the child.* Vol. 9. New York: Internat. Univer. Press, 1954. Pp. 128-141.

Lichtenstein, H. Identity and sexuality. *J. Amer. psychoanal. Assn.*, 1961, **9**, 179-260.

Lief, H. I., Dingman, J. F., & Bishop, M. P. Psychoendocrinologic studies in a male with cyclic changes in sexuality. *Psychosom. Med.*, 1962, **24**, 357-368.

Lowenstein, R. M. Conflict and autonomous ego development during the phallic phase. *Psychoanalytic Study of the Child.* Vol. 5. New York: Internat. Univer. Press, 1950. Pp. 47-52.

Mahler, M. S. Problems of identity. In Panel report, problems of identity. *J. Amer. psychoanal. Assn.*, 1958, **6**, 131-142. (Abstract.)

Money, J. Hermaphroditism, gender and precocity in hyperadrenocorticism: psychologic findings. *Bull. Johns Hopkins Hosp.*, 1955, **96**, 253-264.

Money, J. Components of eroticism in man: cognitional rehearsals. In J. Wortis (Ed.), *Recent advances in biological psychiatry*. New York: Grune & Stratton, 1960.

Money, J., Hampson, Joan G., & Hampson, J. L. An examination of some basic sexual concepts: the evidence of human hermaphroditism. *Bull. Johns Hopkins Hosp.*, 1955, **97**, 301-319. (a)

Money, J., Hampson, Joan G., & Hampson J. L. Hermaphroditism: recommendations concerning assignment of sex, change of sex, and psychological management. *Bull. Johns Hopkins Hosp.*, 1955, **97**, 284-300. (b)

Money, J., Hampson, Joan G., & Hampson, J. L. Sexual incongruities and psychopathology: the evidence of human hermaphroditism. *Bull. Johns Hopkins Hosp.*, 1956, **98**, 43-57.

Money, J., Hampson, Joan G., & Hampson, J. L. Imprinting and the establishment of gender role. *A.M.A. Arch. Neurol. Psychiatr.*, 1957, **77**, 333-336.

Norris, A. S., & Keettell, W. L. Change of sex role during adolescence. *Amer. J. Obs. Gynecol.*, 1962, **84**, 719-721.

Novak, E. Congenital anomalies of the female reproductive organs. *Surg. Gynecol. Obs.*, 1948, **86**, 249-252.

Schwabe, A. D., Solomon, D. H., Stoller, R. J., & Burnham, J. P. Pubertal feminization in a genetic male with testicular atrophy and normal urinary gonadotropin. *J. clin. Endocrin. Metabol.*, 1962, **22**, 839-845.

Searles, H. F. Sexual processes in schizophrenia. *Psychiat.*, 1961, **24**, Supp. 87-95.

Stoller, R. J. A contribution to the study of gender identity. *Int. J. Psychoanal.*, 1964, **45**, 220-226. (a)

Stoller, R. J. Gender-role change in intersexed patients. *J. A.M.A.*, 1964, **188**, 684-685. (b)

Stoller, R. J. The hermaphroditic identity of hermaphrodites. *J. nerv. ment. Dis.*, 1964, **139**, 453-457. (c)

Stoller, R. J., Garfinkel, H., & Rosen, A. C. Passing and the maintenance of sexual identification in an intersexed patient. *A.M.A. Arch. gen. Psychiat.*, 1960, **2**, 379-384.

Stoller, R. J., & Rosen, A. C. The intersexed patient. *Calif. Med.*, 1959, **91**, 261-265.

I am indebted to my colleague, Harold Garfinkel, Ph.D., Associate Professor of Sociology at U.C.L.A., for pointing up the problems of passing in our research patients, for stressing the lack of discussion of this subject in the psychiatric and sociological literature, and for discussing with me the meaning and importance of passing as a social phenomenon.

Pseudohomosexuality and Homosexuality in Men: Psychodynamics as a Guide to Treatment

12

LIONEL OVESEY

Male patients, heterosexual as well as homosexual, frequently express, in the course of psychotherapy, wishes to be loved by other men, to be dependent on them, to be protected by them, to dominate or be dominated by them, and to establish physical—especially genital—contact with them. All these fantasies are lumped together in classical Freudian theory under the heading of "latent homosexuality." They are then attributed motivationally to a feminine component in an inherited bisexual constitution striving for gratification through a homosexual instinct. If we dispense with the instinctual frame of reference, however, and approach the fantasies from a purely adaptational point of view,[1] we can sort out three separate motivations: homosexuality, dependency, and power. The homosexual motivation

---

[1] The reasons for dropping such Freudian concepts as instincts, instinctual energies, and bisexuality are described in a series of papers delineating the differences between an adaptational frame of reference and the Freudian instinctual frame of reference (Kardiner, Karush, & Ovesey, 1959a; Kardiner *et al.*, 1959b; Kardiner *et al.*, 1959c; Kardiner *et al.*, 1959d).

211

is the only one of the three for which sexual satisfaction is the end goal. The dependency and power motivations, as their names suggest, have completely different, nonsexual goals, although the genital organs may be used to achieve them. In consequence, these goals are often misconstrued by the patient as sexual when in reality they are not. For this reason, I have designated the dependency and power motivations as *pseudohomosexual* motivations and the anxiety about being homosexual that accompanies them in heterosexual males as the *pseudohomosexual anxiety* (Ovesey, 1954; Ovesey, 1955a; Ovesey, 1955b).

The concept of pseudohomosexuality was originally devised to facilitate understanding of homosexual anxieties in heterosexual males suffering from dependency and power conflicts. The concept can also be used to reconstruct the psychodynamics of homosexuality during the treatment of male homosexuals. This chapter is therefore divided into two sections. In the first section, I describe the psychodynamics and therapeutic management of pseudohomosexuality in heterosexual patients. In the second section, I incorporate the concept of pseudohomosexuality into a psychodynamic formulation for male homosexuality. I then construct a theoretical model for psychotherapy from the formulation and, finally, demonstrate the clinical application of this model through description of a successful treatment with a follow-up of five years (Ovesey, Gaylin, & Hendin, 1963).

Pseudohomosexuality

Pseudohomosexual anxieties may develop in men at times of self-assertive crisis precipitated by failures in the masculine role in any area of behavior—sexual, social, or vocational. In such a crisis, a man may unconsciously represent his weakness through a symbolic equation: I am a failure as a man=I am castrated= I am a woman=I am a homosexual. The ideas in this equation are derived from cultural directives that delineate the relative statuses of men and women in a prejudicial way. In our society, masculinity represents strength, dominance, superiority; femininity represents weakness, submissiveness, inferiority. The former is equated with success, the latter with failure. The equation is a caricature of the social demand that every male fulfill certain "masculine" requirements and of the social judgment that "femininity" and homosexuality are failures for which a man must forfeit all respect from his fellows. Men with inhibitions of assertion who use this equation invariably invoke adaptive techniques involving dependency or power in order to repair the damage already done or to protect themselves from damage yet to come.

The unconscious wish for infantile dependency in adulthood is a confession of adaptive failure. The person who resorts to this wish is convinced that he lacks the adaptive equipment to satisfy his own needs and to ensure his own survival. The developmental prototype for the dependency relationship is the relationship between the child and the mother. It is this relationship that the dependent adult seeks to re-establish. To this end, he solicits help, support, protection. In extreme instances, he wants another person to take over all responsibility for his welfare, as his mother did when he was a child. At times of crisis, he regressively falls back on unconscious fantasies of magical repair (Karush & Ovesey, 1961). The most primitive of these fantasies is incorporation of the maternal breast. There is an alternative pseudohomosexual route to dependency, however, based on the equation, penis = breast. Its developmental prototype is the relationship between the child and the father. There are two ways in which this equation can be used. In the first, the father's penis appears as a feeding organ similar to the mother's breast, and the semen is equated with milk. The reparative fantasy is of sucking the penis. The second involves incorporation of the father's penis, usually by mouth or *per anum*. In this way, the dependent male undoes his castration, and the donor's "masculine" strength becomes available to him. These maneuvers are doomed to failure, not only because they are magical, but also because the fantasied acts of incorporation are misinterpreted by the patient as truly homosexual in their motivation and, paradoxically, serve only to perpetuate the very anxiety they were designed to alleviate.

The clinical examples that follow demonstrate the psychodynamics of pseudohomosexuality as they emerge in psychotherapy of heterosexual males. In the first example, the patient makes a direct, simple, and obvious equation between the penis and the breast:

> The patient was a young man who for weeks had been struggling with his desire to become as successful and powerful as the therapist seemed to be. In the midst of this struggle he suddenly reversed himself and launched a vitriolic attack upon the therapist as not only stupid and inadequate, but also cold and ungiving. He compared him with his hard-driving, ambitious, tyrannical mother, who always found him wanting and treated him with contempt. He began to complain he was getting no better and at the same time reported a rapid deterioration in his relationship with his mother. One day, after a particularly violent quarrel with her, he reported a dream: *He saw a penis and covered it with a handkerchief. Then he performed fellatio. There was an orgasm and a huge gush of milk that looked thin like skimmed milk. Next, he was talking to an analyst, who told him he saw 15 to 30 patients a day. He was amazed at the doctor's capacity and his large income.* The patient compressed a number of motivational and countermotivational ideas into this dream. In the wish to be fed and given his analyst's strength, he identifies the therapist with his mother. The penis functions as a breast and gives him milk, but he dramatizes his dissatisfaction by turning it into skimmed milk from which the richest portion is removed. The underlying envy of the analyst, therefore, continues unappeased in the second part of the dream. As might be expected the dream aroused intense anxiety about the homosexual implication of the symbolic use of the penis in place of the breast (Ovesey *et al.*, 1963).

The next example illustrates anal incorporation of a penis by a patient who symbolically misinterpreted his incapacities as castration:

> A dependent male involved in a competitive effort to expand his business became increasingly fearful that he would fail. He repeatedly sought reassurance from the therapist who, of course, did not guarantee his success. The patient thereupon resorted to a magical solution which he revealed in a dream: *He felt ill and went to a hospital. The office of the physician resembled the office of the therapist. The doctor examined him and told him he needed an injection. He was put on a couch face down. The doctor filled a huge syringe and plunged the needle into his buttock. He felt an excru-*

ciating pain and then found his penis swelling to an enormous size. He stood up and began to urinate. The stream emerged with such great force and in such gargantuan quantities that it swept everything before it and flooded the whole hospital. He felt immense pride in his power, but awoke in a state of anxiety. The dream is so obvious it needs no further interpretation except to note that the anxiety was not only a pseudohomosexual anxiety, but also reflected his fear of retaliation for his aggression (Ovesey *et al.*, 1963).

There are, of course, some heterosexual patients in whom true homosexual desires are latent. In such cases, the concept of pseudohomosexuality still applies, and it is necessary for the therapist to sort out the various motivations in order to make the patient's behavior understandable. This point is illustrated by another example of anal incorporation:

A young man developed an ambidextrous technique for simultaneous genital and anal masturbation. He manipulated his penis with one hand while he pumped a thermometer in and out of his anus with the other. In the fantasy that accompanied this act, he imagined himself sandwiched between his mother and father as they were having intercourse. The father's penis entered the patient's anus, emerged as the patient's penis, and then penetrated the mother's vagina. The incorporative fantasy here had a mixed heterosexual, homosexual, and pseudohomosexual motivation. The patient not only secured sexual gratification of both varieties, but he also incorporated the father's penis and magically made use of its strength to repair his own weakness, not just in sexual situations, but in nonsexual situations as well. The homosexual motivation was completely latent, for he had never had any homosexual experiences and engaged exclusively in heterosexual relationships. As one would suspect, however, he had an anxiety about being homosexual, but from the motivational breakdown of his fantasy it was clear that only a part of this anxiety was a true homosexual anxiety; the rest was a pseudohomosexual anxiety. The sexual motivations were primary during masturbation, but on other occasions the pseudohomosexual motivation of dependency took precedence. Nonsexual situations that called for assertion but generated severe anxiety were thus handled by the patient in a characteristic fashion. He would retire to the nearest lavatory, give his anus a few quick strokes with a thermometer, and then go out and try to assert himself. He always carried a spare thermometer with him for just such a contingency. While the use of a thermometer on such occasions might arouse erotic sensations, it was not primarily a sexual act; rather it was a magical attempt to achieve strength through magical dependency on the father. Here is a case, therefore, where the magical reparative fantasy of anal incorporation of the penis, when symbolically acted out, was at least temporarily "successful," but the cost was an accentuation of both the homosexual and the pseudohomosexual components of the patient's anxiety. This case is a good example of the motivational complexities of thoughts, feelings, and acts concerned with actual or symbolic homosexuality.

The unassertive male may attempt to deny his weakness by acting out its opposite, a compensatory striving for power. Dependency strivings and power strivings can thus be considered opposite sides of the same coin. The power-driven dependent male is continuously engaged in indiscriminate competition with other men. He structures such relationships in terms of dominance–submission. The relationships are then symbolically placed in a male–female context in which the weaker male is forced to submit as a woman to the stronger male. This unconscious conception of power struggles between men derives primarily from Oedipal rivalry with the father and, to a lesser extent, from sibling rivalry with brothers. Unfortunately, the unassertive male's conviction of inadequacy is so strong that he concedes defeat in advance. The result is a chronic pseudohomosexual anxiety that flares up acutely in self-assertive crises as a paranoid expectation of homosexual assault, usually in the form of anal rape.[2] The dream of a college instructor who lost out to a younger rival in promotion to a professorship reveals with remarkable clarity the unhappy effects of a competitive defeat:

I was sitting in a theater waiting for the show to begin. The management announced there was a celebrity in the audience. A

---

[2] This type of pseudohomosexual anxiety is particularly common in success phobias (Ovesey, 1962).

man got up and went to the stage where he was introduced as a world-famous figure. He got a big hand and then I realized it was my rival. I felt very depressed. Finally, the curtain went up and it was a burlesque act, a chase. A small comedian with baggy pants came running from the wing carrying a small wooden sword in his hand. After him came a bigger man with a bigger sword, and after him came a still bigger man with a still bigger sword. Suddenly the second man goosed the first man with his sword and it came out in front pushing up the small man's pants just like a penis. The audience thought this was terribly funny and roared with laughter. Then the third man goosed the second, but the sword, instead of coming out in the second man's pants, came out like a huge penis in the first man's pants. Now the audience really laughed. This was even funnier. I woke up laughing (Ovesey, 1954).

In this dream, the competitive defeat is perceived as a homosexual attack, but at the same time it is turned to reparative use through the magical acquisition of the victorious opponent's penis. The patient resorts to laughter, a mechanism of denial, to disguise his humiliation.

The fear of homosexual assault in a power struggle occurs again in the next example:

A patient involved in a competitive hostile transference began to complain that every afternoon a few minutes before his interview he became aware of a foul taste in his mouth that lasted throughout the therapeutic hour and disappeared only after he left the therapist's office. This symptom remained unexplained for several weeks until its meaning became clear in a nightmare. *He was sitting on a toilet moving his bowels. It was not an ordinary kind of toilet, but was shaped like a penis. He flushed the toilet but instead of the water going down, it shot up like a geyser. He tried to get off, but could not. Suddenly, he felt something in his mouth and spat out several brown pellets that he realized were feces. He woke up, terribly frightened, with the awful taste in his mouth.* The foul taste was a hysterical conversion symptom that represented his fear of anal rape, the symbol of competitive defeat by the therapist. The fear disguises a wish for the very act he rejects, because by it he would magically incorporate the therapist's more powerful penis. The oral symptom is especially interesting since the homosexual attack in the dream is an anal one; usually a bad taste in this motivational context is related to a fellatio fantasy. The symptom dramatically disappeared, as conversion symptoms occasionally do, immediately upon interpretation of the dream (Ovesey, 1954).

One more example will suffice to illustrate the pseudohomosexual elaborations of the power struggle:

A cartoonist who had had a series of cartoons rejected by a desirable magazine, reported the following dream: *The magazine printed one of my drawings, but under another artist's name, and they made the drawing so small you could hardly see it. Then a bull was attacking me. He had me impaled on his horns and was biting my thumb and running round and round with me on his head. I yelled for my cousin to act like a cow so the bull would get interested in him and let me go.* The bull that castrated and anally raped the patient represented his competitors, who had been more successful than he in getting their work published. His cousin, whom he exhorted to act like a cow, was an unskilled laborer, and in comparison with the patient, a complete vocational failure. Thus, vocational success was symbolically equated with masculine strength; vocational failure with feminine weakness. The penalty for failure was not only social humiliation, but also castration, rape, and subjugation as a woman by the victorious male competitors. The patient, of course, did not like such treatment in the least, and so he protested defensively that his cousin, a real failure, was more suited to the feminine role than he was. This dream, therefore, contained all the elements of the symbolic equation previously cited: a vocational failure led to social humiliation and then via the paranoid mechanism was simultaneously expressed in terms of homosexuality, castration, and femininity. The patient produced no homosexual motivation, nor in such a dream would any be expected. The motivation was solely that of power, and the associated anxiety was solely a pseudohomosexual anxiety (Ovesey, 1955b).

It is clear from these examples that anxieties about being homosexual need not be motivated by the erotic desire for homosexual gratification but are frequently symbolic reflections of failure in masculine aspiration, competitive defeat in power struggles, and fantasy of magical repair by incorporation of the penis. Clinically, the great majority of such anxieties in males whose overt sexual behavior is exclusively heterosexual fall into these three categories. The homosexual motivation, if present at all, is very much in abeyance. More often it appears to be entirely absent. The therapist should not be distracted by the patient's preoccupation with homosexuality. He should deal instead with the pseudohomosexual anxiety by directing the patient's attention where it belongs, to the motivations of dependency and power. It is here, particularly, that the classical Freudian constitutional approach, with its insistence on homosexual explanations, can do great damage. The interpretation of overt homosexuality as an expression of inherent bisexuality is discouraging enough to a homosexual patient, but to explain dependency and power strivings to a heterosexual patient on the same basis can be catastrophic. How can we expect a human being to come to terms with assumed innate tendencies that cannot be altered and to accept permanent deflation of his self-esteem? Worse yet, he is asked to make this sacrifice for socially unacceptable tendencies that he does not even have. The true problem lies in the integrative failure of self-assertion, not in homosexuality.

Homosexuality[3]

In this section, we shall formulate a compact psychodynamic framework within which any homosexual deemed suitable for psychotherapy can be fitted, understood, and treated. We shall focus on the narrow but definitive therapeutic goal of establishing and maintaining pleasurable heterosexual behavior in a homosexual patient. We are not concerned, therefore, with many related problems like family constellations, personality types, diagnosis, criteria for treatability, failures in treatment, and prognosis. Neither are we concerned with the issue of genetically determined imbalance in maturation potential that may underlie the tendency to homosexuality. I do not know what role, if any, genetic patterns play in the ultimate choice of sexual object. I do know, however, that arousal patterns can be readily influenced by cultural directives and individual experience. In clinical

---

[3] The material in this section, with some alteration, is taken from a recently published paper on the psychotherapy of male homosexuality (Ovesey *et al.*, 1963).

practice, all homosexuals have characteristic adaptive responses associated with the homosexuality. The theoretical approach to treatment is based on the motivational breakdown of those responses.

The homosexual seeks genital contact with other men primarily for sexual gratification, that is, for orgastic pleasure. The homosexual motivation, however, does not exist in isolation but always in association with the pseudohomosexual motivations of dependency and power. The latter two operate psychodynamically exactly as they do in the heterosexual, except, of course, that the reparative fantasies are not confined to the imagination but are overtly acted out. They not only enhance the motive force of the homosexual motivation, but their relative strengths determine the psychosocial structure of the homosexual relationship as well as the physical mechanics of the homosexual act. Pseudohomosexual anxiety is usually absent in confirmed overt homosexuals, for they have accepted their homosexuality as a fact and have come to terms with it. Anxieties about dependency and power strivings may therefore be experienced as such and need not be symbolically extended in the form of pseudohomosexuality. On the other hand, overt heterosexuals with latent homosexual desires, like the patient who masturbated anally with a thermometer, suffer from pseudohomosexual anxiety in the same way that totally heterosexual males do but to an even greater degree.

Let us add now to the earlier descriptions of the dependency and power motivations a brief review of the developmental history of the homosexual motivation.

Adaptationally, homosexuality is a deviant form of sexual behavior into which a person is driven by the intrusion of fear into the normal heterosexual function. The fear originates in excessive parental discipline in the developmental years of childhood. It may arise directly from actual intimidation of sexual behavior implicitly or explicitly, or it may arise indirectly from intimidation that inhibits assertion and undermines the growing boy's capacity to assume the masculine role. In either case, the child views heterosexuality as a dangerous transgression for which the fantasied punishments are castration and death. He perceives the source of these punishments as either the father or the mother, usually both. It makes little difference whether the initial focus of inhibition is sexual or nonsexual; ultimately, function in both areas will be impaired. This impairment occurs because inhibitions do not stay confined to the behavior areas in which they are originally laid down. The coincident loss of self-confidence tends to spread to other activities, and new inhibitions appear.

The child may respond to parental intimidation with a fear so great as to force a partial or complete withdrawal from sexual activity. Later, as the child grows, any heterosexual desires revive the earlier fear, and an inhibition of normal sexual behavior is established. Such an inhibition may result in a homosexual choice of object. The person reacts with such intense fear in relation to a heterosexual object that he either fails in performance, or he succeeds mechanically but experiences very little pleasure. His sexual need, however, continues unabated and is diverted to a "safer" object. This object is a homosexual one and derives its added safety from the reassuring presence of the penis, which allays the homosexual's castration anxiety.

Homosexuality, viewed in this light, is a symptom of a neurosis, a defense against castration anxiety by the phobic avoidance of the female genitals. The homosexual solution is only one of several solutions available to patients who suffer from this phobia. Other patients may retain their heterosexuality but make use of such protective devices as impotence, fetishism, exhibitionism, and so on. We cannot with certainty account for the specific choice of symptom, and it is not in the scope of this paper to explore the problem.

A theoretical approach to the treatment of male homosexuality derives logically from the understanding of the motivational basis for the homosexual patient's behavior. Variable combinations of the three motivations involved provide an adaptational formula by means of which the behavior of any particular patient suffering from homosexuality, either overt or latent, can be understood. The motivational component in ascendency at any given time can be inferred from the situational and emotional context in which the patient's behavior becomes manifest. It is a clinically observable fact that the three motivations interact one with the other and are mutually reinforcing. Any contact, either actual or fantasied, by a homosexual with another man's body, particularly his genitals, for purposes of heightening dependency or power, unfailingly acts as a sexual stimulant and cannot help but intensify the wish for homosexual gratification. In the opposite direction, homosexuality weakens the patient's masculine identification, inhibits his assertive capacities and thereby accentuates either passive strivings for dependency or compensatory strivings for power or some combination of both. The end result in every homosexual is a vicious circle in which each motivation leads to the other, regardless of the motivational impetus with which the circle may have begun.

The therapeutic task is to break this circle, to reverse the homosexual pattern, and to establish pleasurable heterosexual relations. This task can be accomplished by decreasing the intensity of the three motivations that propel the patient toward genital contact with male objects, while simultaneously enhancing his sexual interest in women. The primary focus of the therapy in terms of the ultimate therapeutic goal must, of necessity, be on the homosexual motivation and the phobic avoidance of the female genitals. There is only one way that the homosexual can overcome this phobia and learn to have heterosexual intercourse, and that way is in bed with a woman. In this respect, psychotherapy of homosexuality is essentially like that of any phobia. Sooner or later, the homosexual patient must make the necessary attempts to have intercourse, and he must make them again and again until he is capable of sustained erection, penetration, and pleasurable intravaginal orgasm. The achievement of these goals can be facilitated by helping the patient to gain insight into the unconscious fantasies that convert the vagina into a source of danger. We must emphasize, however, that such insights are the means to an end; they are not the end itself.

The secondary focus of the therapy falls on the pseudohomosexual motivations of dependency and power. In order to decrease the intensity of these motivations, the patient must become more "masculine" by learning appropriate patterns of assertion and increasing his self-sufficiency. Here again the process can be aided by insight into unconscious ideation. In some cases, a mere increase in nonsexual assertion may prove sufficient to initiate and maintain heterosexual behavior. This change may occur even in a brief therapeutic contact in which major reliance is placed on support, advice, and guidance, with little attempt either by the patient or the therapist to explore the unconscious basis of the homosexuality. In my clinical experience, however, the great majority of homosexuals do not respond to such a superficial approach, nor do they overcome their difficulties very quickly.

The clinical data in the case that follows[4] have been organized in a way to demonstrate best the psychodynamics as they emerge in the course of psychotherapy. The emphasis falls on the meaning of the patient's behavior as a basis for therapeutic technique, rather than on the technique itself. I shall try, however, to indicate at least some of the more important technical maneuvers, how they relate to the psychodynamics, and why they are undertaken.

A thirty-year-old, unmarried Jewish man, employed as a junior executive in an advertising agency, came to treatment because of mounting anxiety in his work. His difficulties arose from extreme competitiveness with his colleagues, particularly male authorities, which created so much overt hostility that his job was in jeopardy. In the course of the history, the patient casually revealed that he was an active homosexual. It was clear that he did not in any way associate his homosexuality with his problems, nor was it a factor in his seeking treatment.

The patient was short and slightly built but somewhat big of hip. He was dapper, good-looking, and meticulously dressed. His speech, manner, and dress were all studied, in the prep school tradition, which, however, was not part of his background. In his work at the advertising agency, he fitted all the generalizations attributed to Madison Avenue. He was the youngest of three boys from a middle-class family. The father was a moderately successful professional man but weak, inadequate, and totally intimidated by the mother, who was the dominant member of the household. She was sharp-tongued, aggressive, self-willed, and obviously brighter than the father. Despite this severe picture, the patient was much fonder of her than of the father, the implication being

---

[4] For additional examples of successfully treated homosexuals, see Ovesey (1956).

that strength at least could be respected. The weakness of his father aroused nothing but contempt.

Throughout his childhood, the patient had had a constant feeling that he was not "manly" like other boys. First, he was small and at a competitive disadvantage physically and, second, his mother resented never having had a daughter and attempted to feminize her sons, particularly the patient, as he was the youngest. She kept him in girls' clothes until he was three, insisted that he wear his hair long for several years more, and taught him to do such feminine chores as sewing, cleaning, and cooking. He dated girls all through high school, but, at the same time, began to be plagued by homosexual thoughts and feelings that he tried to push out of his mind. At the age of nineteen, he was drafted. The army was in every way a traumatic experience for him. He was frightened and bewildered and felt "different" from the other men, most of whom were large and more aggressive. Some of them taunted him about his hips and said that he was built like a woman. It was during this period in the army, when he felt particularly unmanly, that he had his first homosexual relationship. It followed a specific pattern, which was the prototype for all his subsequent activity. He insists first on satisfying his partner by manual masturbation. He then mounts the partner *per anum* and performs anal intercourse on him, but he does not permit himself to be anally penetrated. He thus plays the dominant masculine role in the relationship. In this way, he not only satisfies himself sexually but also enhances his deflated masculinity by making a woman out of his partner. His homosexual relationships have been mostly transient, although in a few instances they have lasted for several months.

The patient's heterosexual experience was limited to two occasions. In high school, he petted with a girl and gained pleasure from it, but there was no attempt at intercourse, and he never had an orgasm. His only experience with intercourse occurred at the age of twenty-three, when an older woman tried to seduce him. He was frightened and refused. At that point in his life, he was already an active and confirmed homosexual. She persisted until he reluctantly went to bed with her. They had intercourse one time, and he performed successfully, although mechanically and without pleasure. He had no further sexual contact with women until he entered therapy.

The patient was treated on the couch three times a week for three years for a total of 347 hours. The first major therapeutic maneuver occurred within the first few interviews and arose implicitly from the adaptational concept of homosexuality. As the patient was giving his history and registering his complaints, the therapist asked him why he did not list homosexuality as one of the symptoms he wished to have corrected. The patient seemed bewildered. It had never occurred to him that homosexuality was a neurotic symptom, nor that one went to a psychiatrist to have it cured. His brother, a homosexual like himself, was also in psychoanalysis, and his analyst believed that homosexuality was an inherited way of life that could not be altered and was therefore of no particular therapeutic interest. The therapist stated unequivocally that he could not agree with this position and that he considered homosexuality a psychiatric illness treatable by psychotherapeutic means. The patient seemed genuinely confused, anxious, yet delighted, as was evidenced by a dream he reported the following day: *He returned to the lobby of the building in which he lived only to find it completely rebuilt overnight. Everything looked elegant, shiny, strong, and new. He was amazed at the transformation.*

He felt the dream expressed his expectation that he might undergo a similar miraculous transformation, shed his homosexuality, and emerge from therapy a full-fledged heterosexual. The rather marked suggestibility of the patient was characteristic throughout treatment. It caused great difficulty in the later stages when he had to come to grips with his magical expectations, but at the beginning it served to mobilize intense activity toward a heterosexual existence. The assumption by a therapist that homosexuality is a developmental phenomenon and a treatable disease is basic to an adaptational therapy. Such an assumption, when communicated to a patient, can be a powerful therapeutic tool because it inevitably arouses hope that the deviant pattern can be altered.

In the second month of therapy, the patient spontaneously began to date girls, although he made no attempt to become sexually involved with them. The dating was accompanied by constant anxiety, which was invariably associated in the sessions with his father's weakness in the face of his mother's strength. He then became aware that there had been an earlier time in his childhood when he had viewed the father as a superman and when his disillusionment had produced great resentment. The therapist wondered what validity this view of his father's weakness had in his present life as an adult. Why did it still invoke the rage and frustration that it had stirred in his childhood? What possible effect could his father's strength or weakness have on his difficulties with women? Ultimately, such confrontations led the patient to recognize his own fears of standing up to his mother. He needed to enlarge his father, who would then protect him from the mother and by extension from all women. His present fear of women, therefore, not only recapitulated the original fear of his mother but also revived his anger with his father for failing to protect him. This insight led to increased anxiety, a feeling of depression, and a sense that he had "nobody."

He attempted to overcome his fear of women by forcing himself to engage in sex play with his dates. He was chagrined to find that fear so inhibited his aggressiveness that he felt more unmanly than ever. Nevertheless, he persisted and soon began to see a young woman, N., regularly. One night, aware of his failure to carry through sexually with her, even though she obviously was willing, he had the following dream: *He was with N. They were embracing. She petted his forehead and said, "Why don't you pluck your eyebrows?"*

This dream made clear to him for the first time how he equated a lack of "masculine" aggressiveness with femininity. He responded in his characteristic way by attempting to disprove this equation through intercourse with N. He could not sustain an erection, and the attempt proved a failure. Encouraged by the therapist, he continued to try, and finally, one month later, he successfully consummated the act. He exultantly described his success as a "real seduction," in which he took the "masculine, aggressive" role. His triumph ushered in a period of successful sexual relations with N. Except for occasional prematurity, he had no further potency problems, and he experienced increasing pleasure in his orgasms. At the same time, in therapy, he became more and more resistant. He tended to deny homosexual feelings and resisted discussions of those he could not deny. After six months of treatment, he felt that he was cured: He was ready to marry the girl, his problem on the job had disappeared, and he was free of anxiety. He said, "I look back on my homosexual life as something of the past. I guess I was just sowing my wild oats, and now I'm ready to settle down."

The patient's rapid improvement had all the earmarks of a transference "cure." In his opening dream he had already indicated his magical expectations from therapy. Apparently he had acted on them and, in the transference, had supplanted the original weak father with a stronger one represented by the therapist. Thus magically armed with the latter's strength, he sufficiently overcame his fear of women to embark on his heterosexual adventures, but the fear was hardly resolved, nor were its unconscious origins understood. None of these dynamics was interpreted to the patient during this period. As long as the transference was useful in mobilizing heterosexual activity, it was thought best to leave it alone. With sexual inhibitions of this kind, nothing succeeds like success, and, after his successful involvement, the transference would eventually have to be faced, as indeed it was.

In the period that followed, the patient began increasingly to complain about his girl friend, who began to emerge as a very aggressive type. Concomitantly, he expressed more and more hostility toward his mother, with whom unfortunately the girl had much in common. She also had a history of relationships with homosexual men and was aware of the patient's homosexual background. As time went on, the focus of the therapy became the aggressive woman, his involvement with his mother, and his increasing difficulties with N. All of these themes came to a head with a nightmare: *He was driving his car and skidded on some dog feces. He swirled around and around. N. was seated next to him. She was having a good time and enjoying it. Then he hit a lamp post, which broke in two. The top part fell away, but the bottom part shot up through the floorboard right under him, and he was in danger of being impaled on it. He woke up in great anxiety.*

The dream resulted from a bitter argument the patient had had with his girl, in which she disparaged his manliness and taunted him for being homosexual. That same day, while walking with her, he had stepped into some dog feces on the sidewalk. This dream was a key point in the patient's analysis because it revealed the unconscious fantasies responsible for his fear of women. He associated to the dream for weeks, producing peripheral, confirming dreams, until gradually he understood its meaning. The dream was couched in sexual terms and represented intercourse with a woman as a dirty, potentially dangerous act. It defined not only the penalties for sexual assertion with a woman but also, because it was prompted by a quarrel, for nonsexual aggression against her as well. In either case, the woman can castrate the man, appropriate the penis for herself, and then, as a phallic woman, force the man to submit in feminine fashion to her domination by shafting him *per anum* with her penis.

The patient felt disenchanted with N. and began to detach himself from her. She protested vehemently and became more abusive than ever. Her behavior stimulated renewed memories of his father's weakness, but now he saw the weakness as a product of his mother's destructiveness. She had castrated the father and usurped his role as a male. He feared that, if he continued his relations with women, the same thing could happen to him. For this reason, he felt ambivalent about becoming a man. Perhaps it was better to remain a homosexual after all. At least it was safer, as another man already had a penis and would not need his. In this period of disengagement from N., he explored his many fantasies of the woman as castrator and dominator. He dropped N., for a time avoided women altogether, and thought longingly of homosexuality but restrained himself from acting on the thought.

Up to that point, the patient had struggled mainly to free himself from the crippling distortion that all male–female relationships are duplications of the phallic mother-castrated father and the phallic mother-castrated child prototypes. His competitive difficulties with men had been checked and held in abeyance by his initial rapid success with women, but now, as he began to date again, his pseudohomosexual problem emerged in full force. He dated a great variety of women, seduced them as quickly as he could, and then discarded them. He returned in his sessions to the competition at work, talked of rivalry with his brothers, and of competition with men in general. Gradually, an Oedipal trend emerged, in which he saw himself in conflict over women not only with his father but also in transference with the therapist. He had repetitive dreams of rivalry with his father for his mother. The following castration dream was typical of this period in the therapy: *He saw a huge crocodile floating down a river. Suddenly it grabbed hold of a small snake. The next thing he knew he had his hand in a toilet and was pulling out the snake.*

He identified the crocodile as the father (huge penis) and himself as the snake (small penis). The penalty for attempting access to his father's territory, the river (mother's vagina), is castration and death. He saved himself by pulling his penis out of the mother's vagina (the toilet or "dirty hole").

As he examined his Oedipal rivalry, the patient began to talk of his father with less hostility and then turned to him for love. At the same time, he was surprised to find a rise in homosexual desire, despite the fact that he was eminently successful in his heterosexual life. He produced the first of several dreams of dependency on the therapist: *He was talking to the therapist and told him of his increased homosexual feelings. As he related them, he broke down and wept. The therapist said, "You better come home and spend some time with me," and he became one of a group of children who lived at the therapist's house.*

In his associations, the patient again expressed his old resentment toward the father, who had never satisfactorily taken care of him. He wished now that he could be dependent on the therapist, but, paradoxically, the idea of being dependent on a man, even though he wanted it, was distasteful to him and made him angry. It served only to confirm his sense of inadequacy and made him feel less masculine, more feminine, and, in the end, castrated. The validity of this symbolic sequence was bolstered for him by a number of dreams in which, through fellatio, he sucked strength from a stronger man's penis and so himself became more powerful. In another series of dreams, he was dissatisfied with his penis, saw it as deficient, and borrowed or stole new penes from more favored men. It became clear to him that homosexuality was not only a means of sexual gratification but also a magical way of borrowing another man's penis for his own use.

In the next few months, the patient came to grips with his ambivalence toward men—his competitiveness and his dependency. He explored their developmental origins, their dynamic interconnections—with one another and with his homosexuality. He began to understand that his hyperaggressiveness was a compensatory attempt not only to assert his manliness and ward off castration by the father but also to deny his dependency upon him. In essence he learned how the mechanisms we described earlier in our discussion of motivation applied specifically to him. He learned also that he need not look upon all men as his father, any more than he need look upon all women as his mother. Finally, he began to see that his ultimate answers lay neither in compensatory aggression with men nor in passive dependence nor in homosexuality, but in self-sufficiency, equality in relationships, and heterosexuality. Gradually, as he understood these things, he became less competitive with his father, with the therapist, and with other men, and his homosexual urges subsided.

He seemed to understand clearly the direction in which he had to move, but he was not quite ready to give up his dependency. The therapist, through his interpretations, had frustrated his attempts to be dependent on him. The patient thereupon took a step backwards and resumed the relationship with N., the girl who resembled his mother. He had not seen her for more than a year, but they quickly began to fight as though they had never been apart. He wondered why he had gotten reinvolved. Were there reasons beyond the unresolved dependency? He soon found his answer in a dream in which he saw his mother as a whore with red lights attached to her house. He felt that this dream was related to his mother's seductive behavior with him, which he had always found disgusting. At the same time, he recognized that he must have been attracted by it, or he would never have persisted so long with N. This recognition led into his Oedipal feelings toward his mother, which, in turn, revived the Oedipal rivalry with his father. He worked through both aspects of his Oedipus complex and again terminated the relationship with N., as his therapy settled down to many of the themes that had been previously dealt with.

The following year brought great changes in the patient's behavior. He became much less competitive at work and also much more successful. He began to date less hysterically. It was no longer important to date and to have intercourse with every attractive woman he met. A marked alleviation of his competitiveness occurred after the interpretation of a particularly revealing dream: *There was a man screaming in anger. He was outraged and frustrated and upset. He was the owner of the Chrysler Building. It was in the midst of construction, and he had just received word that a start had been made on the Empire State Building, which would be bigger. Even before his building was completed, it was going to be only second best.*

The patient recognized that this dream represented his extreme competitiveness, his aspiration always to be the number-one man, the biggest, and the best in any competition. As always, he used the penis and its size as the ultimate symbol of masculinity.

Shortly after this dream, the patient met L. and began an affair with her that eventually led to marriage. During the closing months of treatment, sexual relations with L. became extremely pleasurable, and his homosexual impulses abated almost completely. Therapy was terminated just before he married L., and the patient felt quite secure that homosexuality was a thing of the past for him. He was seen in follow-up four years later during a business crisis in which he felt his job was threatened. He had had a mild outbreak of both homosexual and pseudohomosexual fantasies, but he felt that he understood them, and he was certain that they would be transitory, which in fact they were. He was happy in his marriage, more relaxed, much less aggressive in his manner, and enormously successful vocationally. A year later all was still going well, and, in addition, he and his wife had a child.

Conclusion

I have described some psychodynamic formulations that I believe are useful in the treatment in heterosexual males of anxieties about being homosexual and in the treatment of homosexuality in homosexual males.[5] An understanding of the formulations is essential to any therapy of pseudohomosexuality and homosexuality that makes use of insight to help the patient resolve his conflicts.

REFERENCES

Kardiner, A., Karush, A., & Ovesey, L. A methodological study of Freudian theory: I. basic concepts. *J. nerv. ment. Dis.*, 1959, **129**, 11-19. (a)

Kardiner, A., Karush, A., & Ovesey, L. A methodological study of Freudian theory: II. the libido theory. *J. nerv. ment. Dis.*, 1959, **129**, 133-143. (b)

Kardiner, A., Karush, A., & Ovesey, L. A methodological study of Freudian theory: III. narcissism, bisexuality, and the dual instinct theory. *J. nerv. ment. Dis.*, 1959, **129**, 207-221.(c)

Kardiner, A., Karush, A., & Ovesey, L. A methodological study of Freudian theory: IV. the structural hypothesis, the problem of anxiety, and post-Freudian ego psychology. *J. nerv. ment. Dis.*, 1959, **129**, 341-356. (d)

Karush, A., & Ovesey, L. Unconscious mechanisms of magical repair. *Arch. gen. Psychiat.*, 1961, **5**, 55-69.

Ovesey, L. The homosexual conflict: an adaptational analysis. *Psychiat.*, 1954, **17**, 243-250.

Ovesey, L. The pseudohomosexual anxiety. *Psychiat.*, 1955, **18**, 17-25. (a)

Ovesey, L. Pseudohomosexuality, the paranoid mechanism, and paranoia: an adaptational revision of a classical Freudian theory. *Psychiat.*, 1955, **18**, 163-173. (b)

---

[5] The psychodynamic principles I have used in this article on men are equally applicable to problems of a similar nature in women (Ovesey, 1956).

Ovesey, L. Masculine aspirations in women: an adaptational analysis. *Psychiat.,* 1956, 19, 341-351.

Ovesey, L. Fear of vocational success: a phobic extension of the paranoid reaction. *Arch. gen. Psychiat.,* 1962, 7, 82-92.

Ovesey, L., Gaylin, W., & Hendin, H. Psychotherapy of male homosexuality: psychodynamic formulation. *Arch. gen. Psychiat.,* 1963, 9, 19-31.

13 | "Latent" Homosexuality

LEON SALZMAN

While the old saying "sticks and stones will break my bones, but names will never hurt me" is characteristic of children's play, in the adult world, unfortunately, names frequently do more damage than sticks and stones. In this connection, it is worth exploring certain psychoanalytic terms that not only have pejorative connotations but are also of doubtful validity either as descriptive or explanatory terms. The term "latent homosexuality," which has come into prominence since the contributions of Sigmund Freud, falls into this category. It grows directly out of the bisexual theory of sexual development, a theory that was prevalent during the late nineteenth and early twentieth centuries.

In recent years, biologists and sexologists have emphatically denied that this theory has any validity. In the face of this denial and the growing confusion about the definition and limitations of what constitutes overt homosexuality, it is essential that the concept be examined in a fresh light, free from preconceptions and prejudices. The necessity for such a re-examination has been underscored by recent proscriptive and primitive measures applied to homosexuals.

The difficulties of defining homosexuality make it even more imperative that the term "latent homosexuality" be defined with clarity and precision. Above all it is necessary to re-examine the prevalent assumption that everybody is latently homosexual in the sense that homosexual inclinations are present in all of us to greater or lesser degrees. Freud's authority, which grew out of his pioneering explorations in previously closed areas of human behavior, particularly in the area of sexuality, gave a sanctified and irrefutable aura to his views. For a long time they were accepted *in toto* as ultimate truths, even though some concepts like the libido theory and his theory of instincts have been under attack from the very beginnings of psychoanalysis. In recent years there has been considerable research in human sexual behavior by biologists, sexologists, physiologists, and psychologists, and many cherished dogmas about male and female sexual behavior have undergone marked revisions (Beach & Ford, 1951; Bieber, Dain, Dince, Drellich, Grand, Gundlach, Kremer, Rifkin, Wilbur, & Bieber, 1962; Horney, 1939; Kinsey, Pomeroy, Martin, & Gebhard, 1953; Lillie, 1939; Masters, 1960; Masters & Johnson, 1960; Salzman, 1954). Such revision has also taken place in the areas of homosexuality and other sexual deviations.

The concept of latent homosexuality especially needs re-evaluation, even though it may have played a useful role in the early development of personality theory. "Concepts that have proved useful in the constitution of an order of things readily win such an authority over us that we forget their earthly origins and take them to be changeless data" (Schilpp, 1955). It is thus no idle play or semantic juggling to review such concepts to determine on what grounds they have been erected and whether or not they are still valid.

It is useful to determine first the meaning of "latency," even though there is no clear notion of what constitutes homosexuality (Robbins, 1955). "Latency" implies either *dormancy*, that is, the presence of a fully developed and matured function in an inactive state (the hibernating bear and portions of our memory apparatus are examples of this latent state), or *potentiality*, that is, the possibility that some state of being or process may develop provided adequate stimuli and circumstances are provided (the acorn, which becomes an oak tree, is a clear example of latency as potentiality). The second use of the term is more consistent with both modern biology and psychology, neither of which views human development as a process in which all is preordained and merely awaits illumination. Modern psychological theory tends to be evolutionary. The potentialities inherent in the human are seen as influenced by environmental phenomena, and development is believed to be dependent on the stimuli and reactions that confront the developing organism. The only preordained state appears to be the potentiality for development. This concept of latency, however, is taken for granted, and the term is therefore never used in ordinary discourse. We do not speak of the "latent adult" or the "latent syphilitic" or the "latent heterosexual." These possibilities are all intrinsic in the developmental process, and an individual will become syphilitic, heterosexual, or adult if he receives the adequate and necessary stimuli or influences. In this sense, all humans are also potentially homosexual and may develop in that direction if certain conditions prevail and other necessary influences are absent. The term "latent homosexuality" was not originally used in this sense, however, nor is it currently applied in this way. It is used strictly in the sense of dormancy. As a dormancy concept, the term implies that the individual has, hidden inside himself, a fully grown and developed capacity to be homosexual that covertly influences his behavior and attitudes. It is presumed to be an aspect of everyone's personality structure, although more apparent in some people than in others.

Such a notion of dormancy, however, is highly questionable applied to the living, growing organism. Evidence for it is very rare, except in some inactive states in some lower organisms like spores or in states of hibernation in some more highly developed species. In hibernation, the entire organism is immobilized. The dormancy concept of latent homosexuality, however, which implies that homosexual needs and drives exist in fully developed form in the individual and are capable of being called into action under special circumstances by certain stimuli, is inconsistent and incongruent with current scientific theory.

What is the origin of this interesting idea, which has influenced psychoanalytic theory so profoundly? On what clinincal findings is it based? Does its existence tend to categorize many attitudes or behavior as latent homosexual trends that could be equally well understood under different rubrics? Does a tacit and un-questioned acceptance of its validity allow the collection of a whole variety of dissimilar phenomena into a "wastebasket" cate-gory that serves to impede the search for more definitive causes of such behavior? Does it tend to limit research into normal sexual development as well as into deviant sexual behavior? It is useful to examine these questions historically, as well as clinically.

The concept of latent homosexuality grew out of Freud's accept-ance of a biological hypothesis prevalent during the period in which he worked—the bisexual theory of sexual development. This theory was derived from mythological sources, comparative biological studies, and observation of certain histological rem-nants of the sexual *anlage* of both sexes in every individual. This conception of inborn bisexuality was the heritage of Freud's pred-ecessors and particularly of his friend Fliess, who found it useful in explaining many aspects of human sexual behavior. It implied that in the course of development the sexual potentialities for both sexes are present. In this respect, the theory is substantiated by embryological studies and accounts for the embryological rem-nants of the opposite in each individual (Ferenczi, 1938; Freud, 1933; Freud, 1962). The theory goes further, however, and insists that, even after physical sex has been determined and develop-ment of the sexual apparatus is proceeding toward maturation, there are present in each person not only physiological remnants *but also psychological remnants* of the other sex in a complete but dormant form (Rado, 1940). Consequently, a universal, normal, homoerotic development is postulated in which the homoerotic tendencies are held in check and lie dormant, to be aroused by both instinctual and experiential factors. Failures of repression or sublimation may allow emergence of these homosexual impulses, which may manifest themselves in a variety of ways. Such symp-toms are supposedly revealed in a host of data about maleness or femaleness based largely on passive-submissive attitudes in the male and active-aggressive attitudes in the female (Freud, 1933). Other manifestations are evident in expressed fears of homosex-uality or in the hidden content of dreams or other unconscious or conscious fantasies of homosexuality, homosexual panics, difficulties in adequate heterosexual functioning, and an endless list of activities or intimacies of a nonsexual nature between individuals of the same sex (Ovesey, 1954). It has long been believed that alcohol and other drugs that weaken repression may bring such latent tendencies into the open, revealing the hidden homosexual inclinations.

Although this concept had its origin in biological theory, modern biological theorists deny its validity (Lillie, 1939). One eminent biologist (Lillie, 1939), in summing up these objections, wrote, "Sex of the gametes and sex in bodily structure are two radically different things." Sandor Rado, in a review of the concept (1940), wrote, "Using the term bisexuality in the only sense in which it is biologically legitimate, there is no such thing as bisexuality either in man or in any other of the higher vertebrates." Biological sex activity cannot be partial—the depositing of sperm by a penile organ characterizes the male, and the presence of genital and related glandular apparatus to receive and nurture the ovum characterizes the female. The double embryological origin of the genital system does not speak for a physiological, let alone a psychological, duality of the biological function of sex and reproduction.

According to the bisexual theory, every individual, with his supposed heritage of so-called "masculine" and "feminine" traits, reveals latent homosexual trends if any of his attitudes or behavioral characteristics does not conform to the accepted qualities of maleness or femaleness. Where do these so-called qualities come from? The assumption of male aggressiveness and female passivity is metaphorically derived from the necessity for the male to penetrate and aggressively to overwhelm the female for the sex act to occur. The normal female is expected to be only the passive receiver, waiting to be invaded and to receive the sperm deposit, and her total psychology is presumed to be organized around the curious joke of nature that provides an "inside" warm and protected area for the development of the ovum. This picture, however, although superficially descriptive, does not even describe with accuracy the sexual behavior even of many animals, let alone of man. The male is certainly not always the aggressive member of all animal species—the human species included—even though the penis must still be inserted. This picture would not be accurate even for primitive man, who did have to immobilize the female. Without active cooperation and participation and unless the female was rendered incapable of resistance, sexual activity could not occur. The aggressiveness of the male varies from culture to culture in the nonsexual areas of behavior, but we might speculate that sexually the female is generally a willing participant in the drama and that force has only rarely been necessary.

What I have stated above is not a historical refutation of the "aggressiveness" of the male but rather a hasty review of the extraordinary complications that result from calling certain "masculine" characteristics "innate" and "implicit" because of the sexual role dictated by the sexual organs. While it is clear that the role of each sex in the culture is partly determined by the biological apparatus, psychological characteristics may be determined by many other aspects of life's experiences and cultural pressures. Recent studies of the actual behavior of each sex during courtship and intercourse throw serious doubt on the biological inevitability of male activity and female passivity (Beach & Ford, 1951; Kinsey *et al.*, 1953; Masters, 1960; Masters & Johnson, 1960).

In his *New Introductory Lectures* (1933), Freud stated:

> . . . [B]y masculine you mean as a rule "active"; and when you say feminine you mean "passive." Now it is quite true that there is such a correlation. The male sexual cell is active and mobile; it seeks out the female one while the latter, the ovum, is stationary and waits passively. The behavior of the elementary organism of sex is more or less a model of the behavior of the individuals of each sex in sexual intercourse (p. 156).

This formulation, which has produced untold mischief in the theories of female psychology as well as in the notions of latent homosexuality, has in recent years been completely negated by a most striking piece of research by Masters in St. Louis (Masters, 1960; Masters & Johnson, 1960). The notion of female passivity in sexual intercourse, which was extended to the psychological role as well, was shown by Masters, through visual biochemical and photographic evidence, to be quite fallacious. He clearly demonstrated not only that the sperm has motility but also that the contractions of the vagina and uterus act as a suction pump to facilitate and produce the passage of the sperm to the uterus. In addition, the active participation of the female in intercourse is made possible through the lubrication of the vagina, which actively promotes adequate insertion and ultimately total ejaculation through vaginal tumescence and contractions. Incidentally, these studies and others (Kinsey *et al.*, 1953; Marmor, 1954) do not support Freud's theory that "vaginal orgasm" is unrelated to clitoral sensitivity in the adult female. Most striking, however, was the evidence in these anatomical and physiological studies that Freud's views on sex, female sexuality, and bisexuality were hampered by inadequate evidence. His attribution of physiological roles to processes that we now know were falsely described raises valid doubts about his related psychological descriptions.

In Freudian theory, when an individual displays characteristics opposite to or deviant from the inherent characteristics of his biological sexuality, he is presumed to be displaying latent homosexual trends. The female thus betrays latent homosexual trends if she acts aggressively or becomes interested in such traditionally or conventionally male pursuits as physical labor, engineering, architecture, and so forth. It should be noted that, in the last fifty years, there has been a marked shift in the occupations that were previously reserved for males; many are now heavily populated by females. As far as the male is concerned, interest displayed in homemaking, beauty culture, and other areas traditionally associated with the female is regarded as evidence of latent homosexual trends. It is interesting to note in this connection that, when such behavior is observed in the male, it is regarded as evidence of latent homosexuality. If the female, on the other hand, shows so-called "masculine" interests, it is called "penis envy," or "masculine protest." The conception of latent homosexuality has come to be reserved largely to the male. Other evidences of latent homosexuality were once thought to include the expressed fear of homosexuality or the presence of homosexual fantasies, dreams, or ideas. If one reacted to these ideas or to homosexual advances with excessive fear, disgust, rage, or horror, this reaction would also be evidence of latent homosexual trends.

It should be noted that the term is not applied to the overt homosexual but to the heterosexual individual in whom homosexual tendencies and drives that might influence his behavior

and psychology lie dormant. It does not refer to repressed or dis-
sociated homosexual drives but is believed to be present in all individuals who are not overt homosexuals.

The term "latent homosexuality" is usually applied to those tendencies, attitudes, and behaviors that involve some difficulty
with mature sexuality and partake of some of the psychological
characteristics of the opposite sex. In therapy, the term is applied
to those elements in the patient's character structure that involve
personality traits not conventionally attributed to his sex. It does
not mean that he is actively engaged in homosexual activity. It is
not applied to the homosexual who has suppressed his homosexuality and tries to live a heterosexual existence, for his homosexuality is not latent. In the course of our development, we
must all achieve satisfactory relationships with individuals of the
same sex and must make our first real efforts at being social creatures before we can achieve similarly with the opposite sex. During adolescence, this effort becomes the main burden of our development. Some manage it successfully and have few problems
with the opposite sex. Such people may never experience even
fleeting notions of homosexuality. Others never manage it and
become overt, active homosexuals. Still others manage it with
difficulty yet never engage in homosexual activity; or they may
have only fleeting homosexual contacts; or they may, in varying
degrees, exhibit behavioral traits commonly attributed to the opposite sex. These individuals are those to whom the label "latent
homosexual" is applied, although latent homosexuality is presumed present in all people.

There is thus a tendency to characterize every withdrawal from
or difficulty with the opposite sex as either homosexual or arising out of latent homosexual drives. Every evidence in the male of
weakness, lack of aggressiveness, timidity, sensitivity, inclination toward nonmasculine pursuits, or interest in the arts becomes
evidence of homosexuality or latent homosexuality. The homosexual in our culture is symbolized as the weak, passive male
who is incompetent and incapable. Consequently, any traits or
attitudes that resemble or are derivatives of these unmasculine
tendencies are also considered evidence of latent homosexuality,
whether or not they have any relevance to sexual behavior or
interest. The term is also applied to those females who incline

toward such conventional male characteristics as aggressiveness, interest in outdoor activities or skills, and general pursuit of the so-called "masculine" concerns.

In therapy, so-called "latent" homosexual attitudes are often described as appearing in the course of psychoanalytic work. At these times, abortive attempts to relate to people of the same sex or to a therapist of the same sex are viewed as evidence of latent homosexuality. Such activity may actually be indicative of growing capacities and desires for more tender and intimate participation of a nonsexual nature. They may indicate only a need for expression of interest and affection from the therapist. The necessity for labeling this need "latent homosexuality" does not arise out of the nature of the phenomenon. Often the therapist's own difficulty in dealing with closeness or intimacy from a patient of the same sex can be acceptably rationalized by his labeling the patient's behavior "latently homosexual." The tendency to take homosexual fantasies or dreams (manifest content) at face value while searching for the latent content in other dreams often betrays this preconception. Too often the interpretation of behavior in terms of latent homosexuality loses sight of such other conflictual aspects of the problem as competitiveness, fear of aggression, or identification with the female figures who may play strong roles in the patient's current life.

The widespread prevalence of doubt about potency, particularly in the male, raises in the mind of the intellectually informed the possibility of homosexuality. The presence of these obsessive ruminations often serves as confirmation to the psychoanalyst of the existence of latent homosexuality. Yet these ruminations represent only one aspect of an individual's doubts and uncertainties about all aspects of his living. The strength of the Freudian impact on our culture is manifest in the way an individual turns these doubts into concerns over potency, which then means possible homosexuality. It is notable that, in the lower economic groups, as described in the Kinsey reports, this sequence does not occur nearly so frequently as in the middle and upper economic groups. In cultures in which Freudian psychoanlaysis has not taken hold as it has in the West (particularly the United States and Great Britain), the tendency to translate inadequacy into homosexuality is far less common (Weinstein, 1962).

At best, the term "latent homosexuality" can have meaning only if the definition of "homosexuality" is precise. Even this word, however, is markedly unspecific, and its usage is often rooted in the concept of latent homosexuality. The definition of one sexual deviation often rests on the imprecise and uncertain status of another deviation, and each draws support from the other, which weakens both structures (Bowman & Engle, 1956).

The term "homosexual" may be applied to anyone who has had contact with the same sex, no matter how fleeting or long ago, or it may refer only to those individuals whose sexual relations are limited to the same sex. Some psychiatrists label any closeness or intimacy with members of the same sex, whether it involves explicitly sexual activity or participation in poker games or attendance at beer joints, as "homosexual." Others refer to any sex activity with the opposite sex that does not involve the vagina as "homosexual." Still others apply the term to any individual who avoids the opposite sex, even though he has no intimate sex activities with members of the same sex. For still others, the term is synonymous with "effeminacy," and it is in this sense that it is most often used by the lay public. The term has no specificity or precision in a scientific sense. As a generalization it covers a multitude of behaviors derived from various sources and with various operational meanings. The need for more precision is essential. Perhaps it would be preferable to speak only of "homosexual behavior," rather than of "homosexuality." The first term would then take on an operational meaning, even though it would still be open to confusion about what constitutes homosexual behavior. From this framework, however, we could visualize a continuum between extreme or less extreme homosexual behavior. It would permit us the concept of occasional versus persistent homosexual behavior and would also leave room for the phenomenon of homosexual behavior as a situational problem. A definition in terms of behavior[1] is preferable, for homosexuality is a symptom of underly-

---

[1] In this connection, however, we must take into account the individual's view of his own sexual interests. That is, homosexuality cannot be defined exclusively on the basis of observable behavior patterns, for it is a subjective preference. This factor requires that we note the individual's preference, as well as his observed behavior. The definition of homosexuality should take this point into account.

ing personality distortion and not of a single integrated psychiatric syndrome. Such a broad definition would completely disregard the activities of the individual prior to the maturation of the sexual apparatus, on the theory that, before he is sexual in the adult sense, the label used for adult sexuality cannot be applied. It is clear that such a definition is not only difficult but inadequate. It might, however, suggest limits and encourage an operational framework within which to explore the phenomenon further. When we recognize the problems in defining homosexuality, we are struck by the looseness and limitlessness of the latent-homosexuality concept.

It is obvious that, although this concept may have served a useful purpose in the initial development of the psychology of sex behavior, its continued use is detrimental in a scientific and humanistic sense. While it supplied answers to much clinical material in Freud's and others' experience, it was based on anatomical and physiological fallacies that have been clarified during the past fifty years. Our knowledge of sex behavior, sexual anatomy, love, and intimacy has advanced our understanding beyond the mere biological or instinctual conception of sexual behavior. In this regard the existentialists and particularly M. Boss (1949) have been most influential in doing away with the conception of sex as a collection of "partial instincts" and seeing it as a total reaction of one human to another. Disturbances in its function are thus diseases of the total organism rather than of the sexual apparatus alone.

The role of sex in human behavior is a dual one: a biological function in terms of race survival and an extraprocreative or interpersonal role. The interpersonal aspect of the sex function is the role it plays in fulfilling man's need to avoid loneliness and to establish intimate and loving relationships with other human beings. Although this aspect of the sexual function is very intimately related to the biological aspects of sex, it is often extremely difficult to determine in a specific instance whether sexual activity is serving the purpose of procreation or of alleviating loneliness or anxiety or of proving one's manliness or of forcing some demand on one's partner. Because the procreative function of sex is so intimately (although not necessarily) involved in the extraprocreative function, they are often confused. Dr. Franz Alexander

(1956) expresses this idea in more general terms, stating that what distinguishes man as a personality is what he does with his faculties after he has secured his basic (biological) needs. "What makes man different from all other species is that he uses his creative forces not only for biological growth and propagation, but alloplastically for building different forms of culture which are not solely determined by survival needs. On the contrary, in his playful, nonutilitarian but libidinous exuberant exercise of his faculties, man makes discoveries, the utility of which is only later discovered" (p. 697).

For survival as integrated and functioning individuals some people are willing to give up the procreative aspects of sex. This surrender is characteristic of homosexual behavior. They still, however, actively use the dramatic integrating power of sex for establishing contact with other human beings, even of the same sex. The potentiality for the development of homosexuality is thus present in all of us. This potentiality can be fulfilled or by-passed. In adolescence the final choice must be made. If we accept the bisexual theory of sexual development and the libido theory, then everyone has latent homosexual tendencies. If we view the choice of the sexual object as psychologically deter-mined, then everyone has homosexual potentialities until the final heterosexual mode of sexual intimacy is accomplished. "Latent homosexuality" is a meaningless term in any new conception of homosexual behavior, for it always characterizes a possibility for behavior when heterosexual intimacy is interfered with—whether in early years by parental injunction or threats or in later years in prisons or under circumstances in which heterosexual behavior is impossible.

The conception of latent homosexuality can be given up only when we are prepared to accept finally the fact that sexual behav-ior, although dictated by biology, plays many roles in the human being's life. Homosexuality can then be visualized as a neurotic disorder characterized by readiness to relinquish the biological or procreative aspects of sex to fulfill a variety of individual needs.

Because the term "homosexuality" carries such derogatory con-notations and its application to an individual subjects him to serious social and occupational difficulties, it should be reserved for definite instances in which its presence is undoubted. The looseness of the term "latent homosexuality" and its abuse by professionals as well as by laymen demands that the validity of the concept be definitely demonstrated or the term completely abandoned.

REFERENCES

Alexander, F. Psychoanalysis in Western culture. *Amer. J. Psychiat.*, 1956, 112, 692-699.

Bieber, I., Dain, H. J., Dince, P. R., Drellich, M. G., Grand, H. G., Gundlach, R. H., Kremer, Malvina, W., Rifkin, A. R., Wilbur, Cornelia, B., & Bieber, Toby B. *Homosexuality*. New York: Basic Books, 1962.

Boss, M. *Meaning and content of sexual perversions*. New York: Grune & Stratton, 1949.

Bowman, K. M., & Engle, B. A psychiatric evaluation of laws of homosexuality. *Amer. J. Psychiat.*, 1956, 112, 577-583.

Ferenczi, S. Thalassa, a theory of genitality. *Psychoanal. Quart.*, 1938.

Ford, F. A., & Beach, C. S. *Patterns of sexual behavior*. New York: Harper, 1951.

Freud, S. The psychology of women. In *New introductory lectures in psychoanalysis*. New York: Norton, 1933.

Freud, S. In J. Strachey (Trans.), *Three essays on the theory of sexuality* (1905). New York: Basic Books, 1962.

Horney, Karen. *New ways in psychoanalysis*. New York: Norton, 1939.

Kinsey, S. C., Pomeroy, W. B., Martin C. E., & Gebhard, P. H. *Sexual behavior in the human female*. Philadelphia: Saunders, 1953.

Lillie, F. R. General biological introduction. In E. Allan (Ed.), *Sex and internal secretions*. (2nd ed.) Baltimore: Williams & Wilkins, 1939. Pp. 3-14.

Marmor, J. Some considerations concerning orgasm in the female. *Psychosom. Med.*, 1954, 16, 240-245.

Masters, W. H. The sexual response cycle of the human female: I. gross anatomical considerations. *West. J. Surg.*, 1960, 68, 52-72.

Masters, W. H., & Johnson, V. E. The human female, anatomy of sexual response. *Minn. Med.*, 1960, 43, 31-36.

Ovesey, L. The homosexual conflict. *Psychiat.*, 1954, **17**, 243-250.

Rado, S. A critical examination of the concept of bisexuality. *Psychosomat. Med.*, 1940, **2**, 459-467.

Robbins, B. S. The myth of latent emotions. *Psychother.*, 1955, **1** (1), 3-30.

Salzman, L. Premature ejaculation. *Int. J. Sexol.*, 1954, 69-76.

Schilpp, P. A. *Albert Einstein, philosopher-scientist.* New York: Tudor, 1955.

Weinstein, E. *Cultural aspects of delusion; a psychiatric study of the Virgin Islands.* Glencoe: Free Press, 1962.

14 Clinical Aspects of Male Homosexuality

IRVING BIEBER

Homosexuals differ from one another, as do all individuals. The phrase "the homosexual" is no more descriptive or identifying than is the term "the heterosexual." Yet, to paraphrase Kluckhohn's statement about man, we might say without overgeneralizing that every homosexual is like every other homosexual, like some other homosexual, and like no other homosexual. Homosexual behavior may be defined as erotic activity between two members of the same sex. This definition is operational, and I do not diagnose patients as homosexual unless they have engaged in overt homosexual behavior. Those who also engage in heterosexual activities are diagnosed as bisexual. An isolated experience may not warrant the diagnosis, but repetitive homosexual behavior in adulthood, whether sporadic or continuous, designates a homosexual.

Since the latter part of the nineteenth century, when Freud, Havelock Ellis, Krafft-Ebing, and others began their explorations of sex and personality, psychiatrists have pondered the determinants of homosexuality. Many explanations have been put forward, varying from the theory that homosexuality is an inborn, constitutionally fixed disorder to the theory that homosexuality comes about as a consequence of adverse life experience. Freud was one of the first to emphasize the experiential aspects, though he did not completely discard the idea that there were inborn tendencies, which he saw as part of a bisexual predisposition. Freud took issue with the prevailing theory of his time that male homosexuality was a degenerative disease. He advanced arguments in support of experiential determinants and against congenital etiology (1962). Yet he was unable to commit himself to either position. Instead, he elaborated the theory of an inborn bisexual predisposition directed toward masculinity or femininity, according to favorable or adverse influences of life experience on libidinal phases of development, and he included the possibility that constitutional factors might favor activity (masculinity) or passivity (femininity). Psychoanalytic clinical experience and research data accumulated since Freud's early explorations now permit a fuller understanding of the dynamics underlying the development, characteristics, and persistence of male homosexuality.

The investigation of male homosexuality by Bieber, Dain, Dince, Drellich, Grand, Gundlach, Kremer, Rifkin, Wilbur, & Bieber (1962) has documented the severely pathologic parent–child relationship revealed in the life histories of the homosexual patients studied.[1] The patterns of parent–child and interparental relationships are similar in the large majority of cases. These findings are in accord with a British study of homosexuals (Westwood, 1960), though this sample consisted of a nonpatient population and the socioeconomic status was lower. The results of both investigations strongly support the experiential hypothesis. In the American study, the extensive psychoanalytic material available illuminates the dynamic processes operant in the establishment of male homosexuality. The data reveal the homosexual to be the interactional focal point for extraordinary parental psychopathology.

Mothers relate to sons who become homosexuals in character-

---

[1] A research committee of the Society of Medical Psychoanalysts, New York City, over a nine-year period collected and subjected to clinical and statistical analysis a body of data assembled for a rigorous study of 106 homosexual males compared with 100 heterosexual males, all treated by members of the Society.

istic ways. The typical pattern is an overclose intimacy, posses-
siveness, domination, overprotectiveness, and demasculinization.
In families in which there are other children, the mother generally
favors the prehomosexual son, spends a great deal of time with
him, and demands undue attention and solicitude. She encourages
an alliance with this son against his father and frequently openly
prefers him to her husband. The son is often a confidant with
whom she shares intimacies. Masculine attitudes and behavior are
not encouraged and are even actively discouraged. The mother is
usually regarded as puritanical and sexually frigid. She interferes
with her son's heterosexual interests in childhood and adolescence, although she herself may be seductive with him. She babies him, is overly concerned about illness and physical injury,
and hinders his participation in the normal activities of boyhood,
presumably out of concern for his welfare. The prehomosexual
boy's salient attitudes to such a mother include submissiveness
and a tendency to worry about displeasing or hurting her. Yet,
fear of injury by the mother is infrequently noted. The prehomosexual son usually feels admired and accepted by his mother
whom he respects and considers to be an admirable person. On a
conscious level, few homosexuals hate or fear the mother, turning
to her for protection and siding with her in family quarrels. As a
wife, the homosexual's mother is almost always inadequate. In
most instances, she dominates her husband, whom she minimizes;
frequently, she is openly contemptuous of him. The husband is
usually detached, not openly affectionate, and tends to argue with
her.

The homosexual patient is seldom his father's favorite; in fact,
he is usually his least favored child and sometimes his scapegoat.
In the large majority of cases, the homosexual hates, fears, or lacks
respect or admiration for his father, who minimizes, humiliates,
and spends little time with him. Thus, the parental constellation
most likely to produce a homosexual son or a heterosexual one
with severe homosexual problems is a detached, hostile father and
a close-binding, intimate, seductive mother who is a dominating,
minimizing wife. In a few cases, the mother is seemingly detached, rejecting, and overtly hostile to her son, but the majority
of mothers form a possessive, controlling, inappropriately inti-

mate relationship with their sons. Sleeping arrangements with mother and son occupying the same bed far into the boy's adolescence and instances of the mother exhibitionistically exposing her nudity to her son are not uncommonly reported.

But, whether parents of homosexuals are possessive or rejecting, minimizing or overambitious, it is their sexual attitudes and disciplines that injure heterosexual development. Varying in neurotic motivation, both parents quite specifically direct themselves toward inhibiting manifestations of assertive, masculine behavior, and they unconsciously attempt to extinguish the son's heterosexuality. Evidences of heterosexual interest and clearly masculine role behavior evoke anxiety in homosexually inducive parents and, with it, suppressive behavior that is effectively castrating.

The homosexually inducive mother communicates a desire for singular and unusual closeness to her son and articulates her pathologic behavior with the child's natural need for maternal warmth and closeness. Between the third and fourth years of life, the wish for close contact with the mother becomes strongly reinforced by the developing capacity for heterosexual responsiveness that ushers in the Oedipus complex. At the same time, the mother has led her son to believe that he has a basis *in reality* for expecting gratification of wishes for exclusive rights, privileges, and possession of her. An adhesive tie between a mother and son promotes in the boy intensely rivalrous and murderous feelings toward the father; fear of retaliation gives rise to irrational fears of the father. Since most such sons have fathers who respond to a situation of this kind by acting out hostility or covertly expressing it through apparent disinterest and lack of involvement, a mutually competitive struggle between a young child and an adult enfolds. Clearly, the odds are stacked against the child who finds himself in the frightening situation of being faced with an opponent recognized as potentially overwhelming. The boy is not only deprived of realistic needs for paternal security and protection, but he is denied an admired, loved figure for masculine identification. When a father adequately fulfills the paternal role, that is, when he meets the realistic dependency needs of his son and encourages a masculine identification, the sexually determined competition is then neutralized or counteracted. The frustration of a son's need for his father only serves to intensify filial hostility and promotes even further pathologic dependency on the mother; at the same time, a yearning for paternal love endures.

A mother who is fearful of responding sexually to males will be particularly fearful of her son's sexuality. The homosexually inducive mother not infrequently unconsciously identifies her son with an incestuous object—father, brother, sometimes an uncle—and then attempts to control anxiety derived from incestuous fears by "castrating" the child who evokes her sexual feelings. Heterosexual immobilization of the son is also a paranoid maneuver oriented toward security against losing him to other females—hated rivals for the valued male. Because of an inadequate relatedness to adult males, the mother exploits her son in her pursuit of substitutive gratifications for the companionate and sexual life precluded by her inhibitions. The sexual gratifications are almost always experienced unconsciously, although the mother's behavior may be overtly seductive.

A morbid resolution of the Oedipus complex is determined by both the father and mother in a situation in which the son is overly attached to his mother and intensely hostile to his father. The dynamics of this triangular interaction illuminate the problem of the homosexual's persisting affectional tie to his exploitative, dominating, castrating mother and his enduring hatred and fear of a sexually destructive father, even when the paternal figure has been consciously viewed as weak and inadequate.

Although the central injury to personality development among homosexuals is *sexual*, other functions and areas of personality are affected, varying in characteristics, depth, and pervasiveness. By the time a child has reached the preadolescent period, personality difficulties will be reflected in grossly defective peer-group relatedness. The prehomosexual boy is not a member of a peer group; he avoids participation in competitive games; he tends to be an isolate, or he may form a strong attachment to a boy much like himself. The defective relatedness to peer groups deprives the prehomosexual of an opportunity to experience healthier attitudes and behavior in boyhood groups than he has found with his family and the chance to find support for the masculine identification that peer-mates provide for one another.

Biologically, homosexuals are normal males. There is a potential in all homosexuals for heterosexual excitatory response, which frequently occurs although awareness of it is usually repressed. The homosexual adaptation is a consequence of immobilizing fears surrounding heterosexual activity. Many homosexuals have a conscious awareness of their fears; many conceal fear under a veneer of apparent disinterest; others develop a reaction formation of repulsion toward heterosexual intercourse. The defensiveness of such attitudes is easily observable during psychoanalytic therapy, and heterosexual wishes become apparent sooner or later. Homosexual patients will remember such heterosexual events experienced in childhood as interest in girls, sexual play with them, and sexual excitement. Not uncommon is the recall of unusually harsh punishment when caught in heterosexual experimentation. The importance to homosexuals of relating to women is commonly manifested in their tendency to become restless and depressed should women be absent from the environment for any protracted period. It seems to be the specifically *sexually felt* element of the relationship that is frightening, and women who indicate sexual desire or availability are avoided. However, the sexually stimulating effects of social contact with women are reflected in dreams with heterosexual content that often occur following the contact; or there may be compulsive "cruising" as a defensive flight maneuver. It is self-evident that chronic apprehension of sexual contact with females derives from an awareness, at some level of consciousness, of a potential for heterosexual arousal.

Men who are exclusively homosexual sometimes reveal a history of one or many heterosexual affairs. Bisexual men may engage in and enjoy heterosexual intercourse although they cannot maintain a consistent, romantic, gratifying sexual relationship, and they escape into homosexuality—some permanently, others intermittently—with or without the rituals of homosexual romance. Sexual excitatory responses to other males cannot be demonstrated for the majority of heterosexual patients in either their current or past history. Contrary to classical psychoanalytic theory, the findings of the *Homosexuality* study (Bieber *et al.*, 1962) indicate that most men are not latent homosexuals; rather, all homosexuals are latent heterosexuals.

Homosexual patients usually express fear and aversion to female genitalia. This calls attention to the psychic basis of homosexuality and to the specifically sexual nature of the anxiety. Where in nature can a group of males be found with manifest *aversion* to the genitalia of the female of the species? In no other species in which reproduction depends on male–female sexual coupling have deviant types appeared that fear or abhor heterosexual matings and engage in homosexual behavior consistently, exclusively, and in highly organized patterns. Fear of and aversion to female genitalia, in themselves, demonstrate the pathology of the homosexual adaptation and the error of assuming that the homosexual deviation occurs within a biologically normal range. Colleagues who study our mammalian heritage are in a particularly favorable position to collect biological data relevant to inborn and patterned sexual traits. Such biologists as Kinsey (Kinsey, Pomeroy, Martin, & Gebhard, 1948) and Ford and Beach (1951) have, however, lent credence to concepts favoring the influence of a constitutional tendency toward homosexuality based on observations of sporadic sexual behavior between animals of the same sex, although heterosexual behavior in the same animals was also noted. Ignoring the complexities of human psychological interaction patterns, these authors generalize from animal observations to homosexuality in humans and postulate that homosexuality is a biologically rooted alternative.

Homosexuals do not *choose* homosexuality. The homosexual adaptation is a substitutive alternative brought about by the inhibiting fears accompanying heterosexuality. Thus, if interpersonal sexuality is to be experienced, homosexuality becomes the only alternative. It is a tribute to human adaptability that sexuality can be organized in such a way that arousal can occur in response to another male, particularly when one considers the extent of fear and hatred of other males that homosexuals develop during their early years.

In emphasizing the nonsexual aspects of homosexuality, the centrality of the sexual theme is sometimes neglected or deemphasized. Despite the distortions and elaborate projections of the adult homosexual partnership, one of its primary goals remains that of sexual gratification. Homosexuals tend to begin object-related sexuality earlier than do heterosexuals, and there is a tendency toward more frequent sexual relations. The early and frequent sexual activity may be a "riddance" phenomenon (Rado,

1956), involving a compulsive need to discharge in homosexual behavior the anxiety-laden sexual excitation evoked by the mother. The continued obsessive preoccupation with sexuality is evident in the concentration on sexual anatomy seen in the exhibitionistic and narcissistic presentation of genitals and buttocks by some homosexuals and the voyeuristic interest shown by others.

Homosexuals enter psychoanalytic therapy for diverse reasons, but, as a group, their presenting problems show a uniformity that is specifically related to the homosexual adaptation. The common occurrence of break-ups in relationships brings a substantial number of homosexuals into treatment. These men usually have been part of a complex, symbiotic, and pathologically dependent pairing. The threat surrounding the disruption of the relationship not infrequently precipitates an agitated depression in the abandoned partner; rage, vindictiveness, and vengefulness may be acted out. Some homosexuals become disillusioned after having had series of unsuccessful affairs. These liaisons run a stereotypic course. Passionate beginnings are followed by episodic phases of turbulence and fade into ennui before ending. In most cases, the presenting and most pressing problems are the symptomatic derivatives of emotional isolation and intolerable loneliness—the consequence of contradictions and defects inherent in the homosexual adaptation itself. Further, the fear of exposure, the risk of loss of employment, social censure, and isolation are sources of chronic tension, at least for most homosexuals who undergo psychotherapy. For the most part, social life is restricted to the company of other homosexuals and to superficial, guarded relationships with heterosexuals that are based in part on the fear of inevitable exposure and rejection. Older homosexuals often become dissatisfied and disenchanted with homosexual society, but the dread of isolation and emotional impoverishment leads them to feel hopeless about dissociating themselves from the homosexual coterie.

The pivotal psychoanalytic problem in the therapeutic management of homosexuals is that of delineating the many irrational beliefs underlying the fears of heterosexuality. Although such fears may include anticipation of sexual rejection, humiliation, and anger by women, the most disturbing and inhibiting fears are those linked to expectations of physical attack by other males should heterosexual wishes be translated into behavior. Such fears appear repetitively in dreams. Sometimes women even appear in "attack" dreams as protective figures, as illustrated in the dream of a patient who had been exclusively homosexual for many years. He dreamed that he was being pursued in a military camp by men who wished to kill him. Panic-stricken, he ran for cover to a barracks, where he was protected from his pursuers by a young, attractive woman. Some weeks later, the same patient dreamed that he was standing with a pretty woman of his acquaintance on a train platform. Two men who were threatening figures suddenly appeared. Sometimes dreams will open with a passage depicting the patient with a female, follow with scenes involving a threatening male, and conclude with the disappearance of the female. In one such dream, the patient was sitting with an attractive girl in the rear seat of a taxi while his father was in the jump seat. The father turned around angrily when he noticed that the young woman had soiled his sleeve with her nasal secretion (Westwood, 1960). In the next scene, the girl had gone and the patient was involved in homosexual activity. (The patient was exclusively homosexual at the beginning of treatment and has since become bisexual.)

My view of the basic psychodynamics of homosexuality, i.e., that the male is feared and hated and the woman is loved but avoided, is at variance with a widely held psychoanalytic view that the female is the centrally feared and hated figure. The admiration and love of the mother is interpreted as a screen hiding deeper hostile attitudes; homosexuality is considered a flight from the feared and hated castrating female. This conceptual difference is undoubtedly reflected in varying analytic interpretations and techniques. Although a background of a psychopathologic mother–son relationship is ubiquitous among the homosexuals I have studied or treated, and although their mothers played a determining role in the son's subsequent homosexual adaptation, and although many homosexuals are submissive to and fear displeasing their mothers, fears of mortal attack or injury by the mother or other women are conspicuously absent in dreams, free associations, and ideational content. Dominant attitudes are usually revealed on the death of a parent. When the mother dies, grief for the loss of a loved one may be observed, not the guilt-laden, depressive response associated with underlying hostility. On the other hand, reactions to the death of the father may range from apparent indifference to bitterness to depressive guilt feelings.

One may ask: If male homosexuals are so afraid of other men, why, then, are they chosen as love objects? First, if homosexuals are to experience human sexuality at all, there is obviously no alternative. Second, male homosexuals do not fear all men equally; they fear most those men who appear to be powerful, aggressive males. Patients have reported feeling especially uneasy with burly men in positions of authority—a transference from the father figure. In general, homosexuals do not have a concept of self as "a real man," nor do they view other homosexuals as completely masculine. They regard themselves as castrates and speak derisively of other homosexuals. Such epithets as "fag," "screamer," and the like are not infrequently used to describe an acquaintance. The society of other homosexuals is a haven, not only for the avoidance of sexual arousal by women, but for safety from the threat of aggressive, heterosexual males.

Psychological defenses to cope with and to minimize the basic fear of the threatening male find expression through sexual techniques in the homosexual act. During the sexual act, two functions are served: sexual gratification and the alleviation of anxiety through the defensive maneuvers of dominating or submitting to the feared male. The homosexual act symbolizes the heterosexual act in that one partner is perceived as feminine and the other as masculine. The heterosexual constellation is well defined in anal activity: the insertor is perceived as masculine; the insertee, as feminine; the anus is identified with the vagina by both partners. The domination–submission parameter is integrated with the heterosexual constellation and is associated with controlling or appeasing the feared male. Two roles are taken by each partner. The insertor acts as the dominating, powerful male who is subjugating the feared, hated, and threatening masculine object; he is also achieving sexual gratification by enacting a male role. The insertee acts as the submissive male in the defensive dominance–submission power constellation; he also takes a feminine role in the heterosexual dynamic. Thus, an attempt to achieve heterosexual fulfillment is acted out in sexual role play while simultaneously incorporating the defense of dominating the feared male or submitting to him. Similar psychodynamics are acted out in oral activity, although the psychologic roles are not so clearly delineated. The partner who performs fellatio, the insertee, may be perceived by the insertor as the submissive, placating male or, conversely, as the powerful, paternal figure beneficently granting sexual favors to a loved one. The orally active insertee may perceive himself to be a submissive male, or the act may symbolize the predatory incorporation of the magical, powerful penis; or fellatio may represent castration of the threatening male. The castration motif in fellatio was demonstrated by a patient who, after performing fellatio on a partner described as a masculine type, dreamed that he, the patient, had blood on his teeth. As in anal activity, fellatio is also identified with heterosexual activity by both partners in that the mouth symbolically displaces the vagina.

The assignment of great value to a large penis, commonly observed among male homosexuals, is symptomatic of serious reality distortion. The large penis represents the penis of the powerful, sexually aggressive father as he was perceived during the patient's Oedipal phase. Homosexuals who have this symptom act out a variety of highly irrational, defensive, and reparative maneuvers, including placating and submitting to the feared male; providing sexual gratification to win his love by evoking in him the excitement and interest thought to be evoked by females; providing sexual gratification to divert him from the valued, secretly desired female; castrating the feared male to eliminate him as a rival; and symbolically incorporating the envied penis as a way of repairing his own defective sexual functioning. Where such mechanisms are prominent, the diagnosis of schizophrenia should be considered.

The condensation of symbolic heterosexuality and symbolic defense against fears of aggressive males expressed in the homosexual act are also represented in the interpersonal transactions of the more permanent relationship. A love object is sought that may be unconsciously identified with the mother, sister, or other cardinal female figure in the life history. The homosexual in this regard resembles the heterosexual, though, despite the neurotic syndromes associated with unresolved Oedipal components, the latter's adaptation remains heterosexual for reasons attributable to early sexual patterning discussed fully in another publication (Bieber *et al.*, 1962). Jealousy of sexual rivals is usually more intense and more often characteristic of the homosexual than of the heterosexual. The derivative of homosexual jealousy is largely the unconscious association between homosexual love object and incestuous object. The instability of homosexual relationships may be attributable in part to sexually competitive attitudes toward perceived rivals, thus recapitulating the Oedipal dynamics of triangularity in a displacement to the homosexual partner as mother-figure and homosexual rival as father-figure. Overriding jealousy also reflects self-devaluation as well as distrust of others, particularly those whose love is valued. The disruptive behavior associated with jealousy frequently contributes to the dissolution of homosexual partnerships. The domination–submission parameter related to defensive operations against powerful males is always an element in these relationships; hence, the power conflict is another disruptive factor. Psychopathologically dependent attitudes further militate toward the transiency of homosexual couplings. Each seeks compensations from the other for inhibitions in emotional, sexual, and social areas. Each hopes, not only to preserve genital gratification, but to secure fulfillment of romantic longings. The frustration of unrealistic demands and dependency precipitates overtly hostile behavior. Though it may be concealed in reaction formations of overprotectiveness and idealization of the partner, hostility and mistrust are intrinsic to the homosexual relationship. The rage reactions of homosexuals, often seen in situations in which such responses seem disproportionate to the provocation, draw impetus from the wellsprings of chronically felt frustration and hostility.

The subject of transference is one that has been treated extensively, and it has become clear that transference varies with the personality and sex of the analyst. In my own analyses of homosexuals, transference phenomena toward me as a male are essentially those from father, older brother, or other influential males. In the early phases of treatment, transferential perception is usually that of a good father sought since childhood. The patient may attempt to evoke affection and personal interest through old techniques developed to achieve such ends, and he may avoid behavior that would threaten his aims. Hostility is usually not in evidence unless the patient feels that he is being thwarted. The genuineness and depth of analytic interest will be tested in subtle maneuvers. The attempt to gain special interest and affection is determined partly by affect hunger for paternal love and partly by the unconscious hope that paternal acceptance will restore heterosexuality. However, ambivalence about experiencing a positive interpersonal relationship is inevitable. The patient's competitive problems derived from the unresolved Oedipus complex sooner or later block the affectional aspects of analytic rapport. An irrational belief, persistent, destructive, and continuing into the adult life of the homosexual, is that heterosexuality for father and for son is mutually exclusive. Thus, the analyst as transferential father is thought to have the power to withhold heterosexuality for himself alone. Stated another way, if a patient believes that his homosexuality is a concession, a sacrifice, a submission to his father, straightforward feelings of affection to a male analyst are feared to be tantamount to a permanent renunciation of heterosexual aspirations. Heterosexual renunciation is accompanied by hostility to the father and to male transference objects, although unconsciously complete abandonment of a heterosexual goal probably never occurs. The belief that heterosexuality for both father and son is mutually exclusive continues to support ambivalent attitudes toward the analyst until this irrational belief is unlearned and the realistic situation understood. In the transference, the patient's homosexuality is perceived by him as a defense against attack for masculinity and heterosexual wishes; homosexuality is also felt to be a sacrifice to the analyst that deserves reward and affection. Understanding, acceptance, and so forth offer the patient reassurance, support, and comfort, but they present inherent pitfalls in treatment, since the patient's need to satisfy affect hunger also operates in the direction of perpetuating the homosexual adaptation. Heterosexuality is felt to be incompatible with receiving affection from a heterosexual male, and anxiety tends to be stimulated by positive analytic rapport. It only ceases to become threatening when the patient recognizes that he is not in competition with the analyst; when, in an appropriate situation, he has as much right to a heterosexual object as has the analyst (or other men); and when he is not in mortal danger if he does compete.

The increasing trend among psychoanalysts to orient patients to heterosexuality rather than to help them "adjust" to homosexuality is related to favorable therapeutic results, to changes in conceptions of the genesis of homosexuality, and to the increasing recognition that homosexuality is incompatible with a reasonably happy life. In the *Homosexuality* study (Bieber *et al.*, 1962), the majority undertook treatment with a conscious wish to shift; probably most, if not all, homosexuals would prefer to be heterosexual. As patients, however, they are fearful of change for the reasons that steered them into homosexuality in the first place. They react with mistrust and anxiety because they fear that the analyst will lead them into the "dangers" of heterosexuality, a situation that may be compared to the swimming student who is apprehensive that his instructor will push him into deep water while he is off guard and before he is ready to master the situation. Patients who enter therapy with the stated objective of remaining homosexual tend to be suspiciously alert to any analytic moves that may be interpreted as blocking homosexual activity and promoting heterosexuality. The analyst may be respected and envied for being "straight," but he is also perceived as a conformist who cannot apprehend the life style and problems of the homosexual. Moreover, the patient expects the analyst, as an authority figure, to disapprove of unconventional behavior, especially sexual deviance, and to require heterosexual compliance—an unpleasurable and frightening prospect. Such notions educe apprehension and resentment about giving up the gratifications of homosexuality; though, to please the analyst, particularly in the early phase of treatment, patients often are inclined to conceal doubts and fears. The early diminution in frequency of homosexual activity, the avoidance of reporting homosexual experiences, and precipitous heterosexual attempts should be cautiously evaluated as placatory gestures, the forerunners of resistance. Subtle probings of the analyst's toleration of homosexuality or direct questions about therapeutic goals are also indicators of apprehension. In this regard, I inform the patient that heterosexuality is desirable for many reasons to be elucidated as the analysis proceeds, but that he will neither be pushed nor tricked into it, that he will be the one to make sexual decisions, and that, as long as sexuality involves consenting adults, there is no judgmental bias or interest other than information necessary for the analytic work. Further, the curtailment of homosexual activity per se does not promote heterosexuality, but, as relevant problems and fears are resolved, the latent heterosexuality begins to emerge.

Homosexual patients who have sufficiently worked through underlying psychopathology may be quite successful in their initial heterosexual attempts. I have observed that such patients are potent and orgastic; the experiences are, in the main, unaccompanied by negative sequelae. Inroads into heterosexuality are reparative and prognostically favorable, even when the basic anxieties associated with the erroneous belief systems inherent in the homosexual adaptation are incompletely resolved. As patients proceed in psychoanalysis, the heterosexual adaptation becomes more firmly established through the continued uncovering and working through of irrational fears.

In view of the sensitive response of patient to therapist, it is of special interest that homosexuals often choose a woman analyst. Patients neither begin nor continue treatment with a therapist who is feared, distrusted, or disliked; yet these are attitudes toward women frequently claimed by homosexuals. In the *Homosexuality* study (Bieber *et al.*, 1962), the ratio of female to male analysts was equal. The proportionate representation of female analysts is inconsistent with the derogatory attitudes of homosexuals who elect to be treated by women. In referring patients seen in consultation, I routinely inquire about sex preference in choice of analyst. Some indicate strong preference; others are noncommittal. In one homosexual case when a female therapist was suggested, it was difficult to ascertain whether the proposal was being considered seriously, but he proceeded with the referral. Subsequently, the analyst reported that the patient was enthusiastic about working with her; that he had strongly preferred a woman —a choice he had been too fearful to expose to a male therapist; and that he was particularly gratified that she was attractive, having told her so after the first few sessions. Even following months of treatment, the patient sustained his positive feelings. Another case in point was the homosexual who expressed deprecatory feelings about women, whom he regarded as exploitative and castrating; yet his first analyst was a woman and, in the course of treatment, he suggested changing to a "sexy" female therapist who was treating a number of his homosexual friends.

The problem of variance in transference toward male and female analysts has yet to be systematically studied; however, the anecdotal data from female analysts indicate that transferences develop that do not appear in the analyses of male homosexuals with male analysts. The most obvious involves heterosexual transference with the illusion in some patients that they are participating in a romance even to the point of feeling more masculine and superior to other homosexuals. The protection of the therapeutic situation against genital acting out favors the establishment of such a transference, which can be advantageous in illuminating for the patient his latent heterosexual aims. Other transferential dissimilarities appear to be rooted in the qualitative difference between the homosexual's hostility to men and women.

In the course of psychoanalysis, heterosexual patients may raise questions about homosexual tendencies. Some patients may discuss such material without manifest disturbance; others become anxious and obsessively preoccupied whenever homosexual content appears. The intensity of anxiety is associated with the extent of injury anticipated from a stronger ipsosexual rival in a competitive situation. These situations may be related to such sexuality as a contemplated marriage or to activities and circumstances not directly related to sexuality, as when a pathologically dependent affiliation is threatened or disrupted. A homosexual panic may be precipitated when a "protective" business partner dies or leaves. Conversely, an intention to enter into a dependent relationship with a member of the same sex may trigger a homosexual conflict. Imminent success in a competitively charged endeavor may also set off anxiety associated with a homosexual trend. Such trends sometimes emerge in individuals who come into the power sphere of a dominant, authoritative, ipsosexual figure, as may occur in military life when a hostile, threatening officer is in command or in work situations when a supervisor or employer is feared. The psychodynamic kernel of the homosexual trend in both males and females is submissiveness or the fear of submitting to a member of the same sex who is perceived as powerful and threatening. Profound fear of an ipsosexual figure has its basic roots in the Oedipus complex, and, for this reason, patients who experience anxiety in seemingly nonsexual situations may respond with sexual obsessions.

The psychodynamics of homosexual trends and of homosexuality itself are similar in that each involves submissive renunciation of a goal believed to be attainable only through a rivalrous struggle, whether for sexual object, prestige, success, or so forth. The homosexual, however, actually renounces the heterosexual object, whereas the heterosexual with homosexual trends only veers in a renunciatory direction in situations evoking anxiety about competition. With rare exceptions, heterosexuals with homosexual problems do not react with sexual excitation to members of the same sex. Further, the homosexual lives in a subculture which patterns a life style foreign and discordant to heterosexuals.

The patient who is preoccupied with fears of homosexuality tends to accept readily the interpretation that his anxiety is unconnected with sexuality per se; that he is not a homosexual; that he has no homosexual proclivities. Reassurance of this type may temporarily relieve the patient, though he does not really believe it and though the homosexual obsession is easily reactivated. The therapeutic management of homosexual problems among heterosexuals may be pursued in accord with the same analytic technique and concepts used with homosexuals. Therapy should be directed toward the delineation and resolution of irrational beliefs connected with defenses against anticipated injury for heterosexual and other gratifications believed to be attainable only through competition.

Formulations to the effect that homosexuals are schizophrenics or that homosexuality is a defense against latent schizophrenia are well known. In the *Homosexuality* study (Bieber *et al.*, 1962), a psychiatric diagnosis was requested for each patient. Among the heterosexuals, one-fifth were designated as schizophrenics, about one-half were psychoneurotic, and the rest had character disorders; whereas in the homosexual sample one-fourth were schizophrenic, one third were psychoneurotic, and the rest had character disorders. Though there were more schizophrenics among the homosexuals, the difference was not statistically significant. The comparative data suggest that schizophrenia and homosexuality are independent psychopathologic conditions that may co-exist. The schizophrenic homosexuals were more like the schizophrenic heterosexuals than like the nonschizophrenic homosexuals, particularly in patterns of disturbed father–son relationships—a noteworthy finding in view of the emphasis usually placed on the mother's influence in the genesis of schizophrenia. However, the *sexual* adaptation of schizophrenic homosexuals was more like non-

schizophrenic homosexuals than like schizophrenic heterosexuals
—further indication that homosexuality is the outcome of specific
disturbances in sexual development and sexual functioning.

Inasmuch as a shift to heterosexuality is extremely rare among
homosexuals who have not had psychiatric treatment, two questions are pertinent: Why do not more homosexuals undertake psychoanalysis? If treatment is undertaken, what are the prognostic
aspects—favorable and unfavorable?

First, economic factors and the unavailability of competent psychotherapists may keep homosexuals from obtaining treatment in
remote areas, and the psychiatric facilities of smaller cities and
towns may not be adequate for the need; in large urban centers,
particularly New York, which tends to attract many homosexuals
from various parts of the country, psychoanalysis and psychoana-
lytically oriented psychotherapy are within the economic reach of
most people. In the main, the fears underlying homosexuality also
account for resistance to treatment. Unconscious fear of discovering heterosexual wishes and feelings, even greater fear of acting on
such feelings, fear of discovering the inevitable emotional bank-
ruptcy of homosexuality, and fear of an inability to shift to heterosexuality constitute the core *fear complex* around which a defensive
structure of denial and resistance is organized. Many homosexuals who would improve and change if treated are kept from
entering treatment by their own irrational ideas about psychoanalysis. A defense commonly noted is the denial of psychiatric
illness. Rather than accept homosexuality as pathologic but amenable to treatment, many homosexuals prefer to regard their condition as constitutionally determined; they more readily accept a
view of themselves as biological freaks. Others protest that homosexuality is deviant but not aberrant. This type of defensiveness is
further reinforced and institutionalized by homosexual social organizations. Such groups attempt to create a public image of homosexuals as people who differ in certain ways as other minorities
differ in other ways. The in-group pretense is that homosexuality
is superior to heterosexuality and that all men inwardly aspire to
inversion, but do not have the courage to take the step. A comparison with an organization such as Alchoholics Anonymous is striking in that members must recognize that alcoholism is an illness,
and this fact is consistently emphasized. In contrast, the homosex-

ual organization consolidates and more deeply entrenches the psychopathology of its members while offering the quick rewards of group acceptance and relief from isolation and loneliness. But, unless participation is aimed at converting such groups into institutes for the prevention and cure of homosexuality, these organizations only intensify anxieties about heterosexuality and encourage a habituation to homosexual mores. Resistance to therapy is lowered when the homosexual becomes aware of the true nature of his illness, of the optimistic prognosis for change, of the fact that treatment does not convert him into a sexless or sexually inactive person.

Second, with the possible exception of effeminate transvestites, one cannot say of any homosexual that he cannot shift to heterosexuality. His own motivation to change is in his favor, though no single factor carries with it absolute prognostic certainty. Homosexuals who express no overt wish to do so may shift to heterosexuality, whereas others who say they wish to give up homosexuality may have great difficulty and may not succeed. A history of having had conscious heterosexual interests, having made at least some heterosexual attempt in the past, or having had dreams with erotic heterosexual themes promises a more favorable outcome than one in which the sexual background is devoid of conscious heterosexual interests or attempts. Effeminacy of voice and gesture is an unfavorable indicator, whereas a history of response to stress and threat with overt rage is prognostically favorable. The patient's age at the beginning of psychotherapy has more bearing on the results of treatment among homosexuals than among heterosexuals, the potential for change being greater in younger than in older homosexuals, though age as a single factor is not determining. In general, the longer the commitment to homosexuality—not only in terms of sexual behavior, but in homosexual socializing patterns, techniques, and interpersonal relationships—the greater the difficulty in separating from this life and adapting to heterosexual society.

Ideally, psychotherapy should be started as soon as disturbances suggesting homosexual tendencies or patterns of development are noted. Homosexuals who are motivated to change and remain in treatment long enough to effect a stable change have a favorable prognosis for a shift to heterosexuality.

REFERENCES

Bieber, I., Dain, H. J. Dince, P. R., Drellich, M. G., Grand, H. G., Gundlach, R. H., Kremer, Malvina, W., Rifkin, A. H., Wilbur, Cornelia B., and Bieber, Toby B. *Homosexuality*. New York: Basic Books, 1962.

Bieber, I. Olfaction in sexual development and adult sexual organization. *Am. J. Psychother.*, 1959, 13, 851-859.

Ford, C. S., & Beach, F. A. *Patterns of sexual behavior*. New York: Harper, 1951.

Freud, S. In J. Strachey (Trans.), *Three essays on the theory of sexuality* (1905). New York: Basic Books, 1962.

Kinsey, A. C., Pomeroy, W. B., Martin, C. E., & Gebhard, P. H. *Sexual behavior in the human male*. Vol. 1. New York: Grune & Stratton, 1956.

Rado, S. *Psychodynamics of behavior*. Vol. 1. New York: Grune & Stratton, 1956.

Westwood, G. *A minority*. London: Longmans, Green, 1960.

15 | Clinical Aspects of Female Homosexuality

CORNELIA B. WILBUR

The concluding chapter of a study of male homosexuality published in 1962 by the Research Committee of the Society of Medical Psychoanalysis (Bieber, Dain, Dince, Drellich, Grand, Gundlach, Kremer, Rifkin, Wilbur, & Bieber, 1962), of which this author was a member, stated, "The capacity to adapt homosexually is, in a sense, a tribute to man's bio-social resources in the face of thwarted heterosexual goal achievement. Sexual gratification is not renounced; instead, fears and inhibitions associated with heterosexuality are circumvented and sexual responsivity with pleasure and excitement to a member of the same sex develops as a pathological alternative" (p. 303). This conclusion supports Rado's (1949) suggestion that male homosexual adaptation is a result of "hidden but incapacitating fears of the opposite sex." Furthermore, the authors of the research study wrote, "We assume that heterosexuality is a biologic norm and that unless interfered with all individuals are heterosexual. Homosexuals do not by-pass heterosexual developmental phases and all remain potentially heterosexual." It seems reasonable to suggest that these conclusions about male homosexuality may also apply to female homosexuality; in order to determine whether or not they do, a parallel study of female homosexuality has been undertaken by the same research committee, although with some changes in personnel. It is altogether possible that, within the next three years and as a result of this long-term research, some of the statements in this chapter may have to be modified.

Causes of Female Homosexuality

For a comprehensive review of the historical development of traditional theoretical and clinical concepts of overt female homosexuality, the reader may refer to the article by Socarides (1963). A great variety of such concepts has been put forward in the literature:

(1) Father "fixation" and mother "fixation" have both been postulated as causes of female homosexuality. "Fixation" usually refers to an attachment developed in infancy or early childhood that persists in an immature or neurotic form, with an associated inability to form normal attachments with other persons or objects. Sexual deviations and the Oedipus complex are explained on this basis by many psychoanalysts. The "fixation point" marks the level of development at which the fixation has occurred. Fixation thus suggests a cessation of growth. As homosexuality is more probably a deviation of growth than a cessation, the concept of fixation does not adequately explain female homosexuality.

(2) Seduction in childhood, real or imagined, by an individual of the same sex has also been postulated as a cause of homosexuality. Some authors have suggested that childhood seduction by an individual of the opposite sex can foster homosexuality by leading to feelings of revulsion against the opposite sex. In adolescence, seduction by an older female has been considered one cause of female homosexuality. The information available from the research study on males and from female case histories does not support any of these theories. Some homosexuals, it is true, report fantasies of homostimulation very early. In many of these instances, however, the acquiescence of the child or adolescent to a seduction by an individual of the same sex appears to be the result of an

early sexual interest in the same sex, rather than a cause of such an interest.

(3) "Penis envy" recurs in the literature as a suggested reason for female homosexuality. The fantasy of possessing and using the penis, commonly reported by the "aggressive" homosexual woman, tends to favor this interpretation. Some of these women conceive of the penis as a threatening weapon, usurpation of which reduces anxiety. This fantasy is, however, less common in "passive" homosexual women.

(4) The presence of a "seductive" father in early childhood is often mentioned as influential, as is the possibility that the father was a "mothering person." A seductive father in early childhood might intensify the Oedipus complex, with an increase in anxiety and a more severe repression of heterosexual interest, especially in the presence of a hostile or competitive mother.

(5) Another suggested dynamic is that the female patient renounces the father at puberty, especially if this renunciation is in response to the patient's feeling that her father has rejected her. This rejection alone, however, does not appear sufficient to account for a turning away from heterosexuality, especially as pubertal and early adolescent responses occur late in sexual development. A rejection of the father suggests rather an already formed prepubertal mechanism of rejection of the male figure.

(6) Prolonged absence of the mother (for any reason) has been considered a factor in the development of female homosexuality, especially if the patient suffers guilt about hostile feelings toward the mother because of her absence. A resultant longing for the mother in which the homosexual behavior is conceptualized as "searching for a mother" has been suggested. Making sexual advances then becomes an attempt to obtain affection from a mother-surrogate.

(7) The "primal scene" has also been mentioned as a factor in the development of female homosexuality. As primal-scene material, however, occurs in the analyses of many patients, both heterosexual and homosexual, it cannot be specific for homosexuality.

(8) Freud (1959) believed the birth of a sibling during puberty to be a specific factor in the case he reported. He pointed out, however, that the patient's father was tender-hearted yet enraged

at his daughter's homosexuality, displaying a strongly ambivalent attitude. Furthermore, the mother was "decidedly harsh towards her daughter and over-indulgent to her three sons" (p. 205) and "saw in her rapidly developing daughter an inconvenient competitor; she favoured the sons at her expense, limited her independence as much as possible, and kept an *especially strict watch against any close relation between the girl and the father*" [Italics mine—C.W.] (p. 214). In the discussion of the case, Freud also reported "these presages of later homosexuality had *always* occupied her conscious life . . ." [Italics mine—C.W.] (p. 227), referring to the patient's early interest in women—her schoolmistress and other young women—which suggests that her homosexuality was established *before* the birth of the last male sibling.

(9) The continuation of a childhood "bisexual" phase or a fixation at or regression to an earlier adolescent stage of psychosexual development also has been offered as a cause of homosexuality. The dubiousness of the concept of "bisexuality" has, however, been ably documented by Rado (see Chapter 10), and we have already discussed the inadequacy of the concept of fixation.

(10) The presence of "tomboy behavior" in early childhood and concentration on athletics in adolescence have been postulated as early signs of a tendency toward female homosexuality. The analyses of women, however, reveal many who were "tomboys" and who nevertheless developed heterosexually. Such behavior would in any case be symptomatic rather than genetic.

(11) Several other kinds of family relationship have been pointed out as having genetic significance: a weak, ineffectual father and strong, domineering mother; either or both parents' preference for a child of the opposite sex; hatred of the mother; the mother's unconscious wishes to be a prostitute perceived and "carried out" by the patient or reacted to with revulsion resulting in homosexual behavior; reaction to a mother who is consciously or unconsciously antiheterosexual.

(12) Problems of identification have also been considered in relation to female homosexuality: Does the patient identify with a father who is cruel and domineering? Is the patient seeking revenge on the father for disappointment at his weak and ineffectual or cruel and domineering behavior? Does the patient identify with a "latent homosexual" mother? Or is she unable to

identify with her mother for reasons of hostility and competitiveness?

(13) A variety of fears also has been thought to have genetic significance. Such fears include fear of castration, of pregnancy, of venereal disease, of penetration, of injury, of the penis, and of heterosexuality (as a reaction to heterosexual trauma or heterosexual disappointment).

(14) Masturbation, with a resulting clitoral fixation, has also been suggested as a cause. It is highly questionable that such a universal experience could be a specific causative factor in homosexuality.

(15) Social factors have also been suggested as determining the onset or maintenance of a homosexual orientation. The existence of heterosexual taboos in current society; the existence of such unisexual groups and group activities as separate girls' and boys' playgrounds, girls' and boys' schools, girls' and boys' camps, and so forth; and the possibility that children and adolescents will have their first sexual experiences with persons of the same sex have been postulated as causative. We must also consider the indirect conditioning effect of social codes on an individual's decision to accept or reject either a heterosexual or a homosexual orientation.

(16) Physical factors have been discussed as possibilities by many writers, and there is still considerable argument about the significance of genetic determinants, endocrine predisposition, and constitutional or congenital traits or tendencies toward homosexuality. There is no convincing evidence, however, that female homosexuality arises from a genetic predisposition. The female homosexuals that have been studied and reported in the literature do not come from families in which there have been significant numbers of other homosexual individuals. Endocrine imbalance has not been discovered in female homosexuals, and their endocrine development seems to parallel that of heterosexual females to the extent that the beginning of menses occurs at the usual time and menstrual histories are relatively normal. What is known of female homosexuality to date suggests strongly that it is the result of psychodynamic factors rather than of physiological ones.

Role Behavior of Female Homosexuals

There are shifting roles in female homosexuality, as well as "types." There is a spectrum ranging from "feminine" homosexuals to "dykes," with frequent polarization at either end. What accounts for the differences between these individuals? The "dyke" is considered the "aggressive" individual, the woman who takes over the role of a man and may even talk as female homosexuals imagine that males talk in sexual situations. The aggressive female homosexual pretends that she has a penis. The "feminine" homosexual acts the role of a female. The question immediately arises: If she is able to act the female role in the homosexual situation, what prevents her from acting similarly in a heterosexual situation? What determines the role that the female homosexual takes in her homosexual practices? Because the female is not dependent on physiological function (the capacity to have an erection) to act as a sexual partner in any situation, it is not uncommon for the female homosexual to have had heterosexual experience. Is there, then, a latent heterosexual drive in every female homosexual? In the final analysis, what is the basic psychodynamic difference between the "aggressive" or "feminine" homosexual woman and the "aggressive" or "feminine" heterosexual woman?

There are many other questions that can be asked about female homosexuality. For example, what about homosexuality and the child-bearing function of women? Every physician who has treated female homosexuality or who has seen a number of female homosexuals has had the opportunity to observe that female homosexuals often express desires for children and sometimes have them with or without benefit of marriage. In the author's experience, there have been several female homosexuals who have had children out of wedlock and have insisted on keeping and raising them. This observation suggests that the female homosexual, in spite of her aversion to heterosexuality, has not lost or sacrificed her biological reproductive function or the emotional values associated with it.

Early Family Relationships and Experiences

The statement has been made that homosexuality is a pathological alternative that develops in the face of fears and inhibitions associated with heterosexuality. What kinds of experience lead to such intense fears and inhibitions of heterosexuality that homosexuality can be the only outcome? In histories of many female homosexuals the fact that heterosexuality has been taboo is evident. Female homosexuals frequently talk about their homosexuality with some freedom. In discussing masturbation, their attitudes range from "it is not very nice" to excessive guilt reactions. Although many female homosexuals do admit to masturbation, there seems to be enormous guilt and shame associated with it, so that it is more difficult for them to talk about masturbation than about homosexuality. Toward heterosexuality the female homosexual often shows more embarrassment, self-consciousness, unease, distaste, and revulsion than do inhibited heterosexual individuals.

Statements from female homosexuals about sexual training at home show a wide range of distortions. The treatment of heterosexuality as completely taboo, behavior of the family as if there were no such thing as heterosexuality, and both overt and covert parental reactions suggesting that heterosexuality is something very bad have all been reported.

In addition, female homosexuals often point out that, although their often obvious behavior ought to have aroused suspicion of homosexual problems, their parents seem to have remained blind to it for long periods of time. Indeed, even when it is brought to their attention, either forcibly or accidentally, these parents often tend to deny any knowledge of the homosexuality. The homosexual patient is thus led to feel that there is more tolerance for homosexual behavior than there would be for heterosexual behavior. One example is that of the patient who stated, "My mother was upset when she found me in bed in a compromising position with my homosexual girl friend, but she was not as distressed by this as she had been when she saw me necking with a boy."

One other aspect of parental attitudes toward heterosexuality has been pointed out regularly to this author by female homosexuals. They state that, at the beginning of puberty and dating, they have been cautioned, warned, and even threatened by their mothers or other adult females in the family about the sexual dangers implicit in the boy–girl relationship. Conversely, never a word is spoken about any sexual dangers implicit in a girl–girl relationship. Female homosexuals often use this fact defensively in discussing their problems and even carry it over into their assumptions about the rest of society.

There are many families, however, in which the heterosexual taboo is present, sexual education is absent, and implied and overt warnings about heterosexuality are expressed to girls at puberty and adolescence, yet only some of these girls become homosexuals. Consequently the factors of the mother's or father's antiheterosexuality cannot be the only dynamic in the production of the homosexual maladaptation. One parent can make a statement over and over again, yet it does not necessarily influence the child; on the other hand, another parent may make a statement on one or two occasions and so deeply impress the child that she never forgets it. Clearly, the dynamics of female homosexuality must also depend on the *kinds* of individual the parents are.

There has already been some preliminary agreement among the members of the Research Committee studying female homosexuality about the nature of the "typical" mother and the "typical" father of these patients. The "typical" mother seems to be an overbearing individual who is dominant in the family and excessively controlling of the girl who is destined to become the homosexual. The relationship between the mother and the female homosexual is usually a very active one; there is a "chronic struggle" between them, in which the child is the loser. There are innumerable attempts by the mother to dominate, conquer, and control. The commonest techniques are rejection or threats of rejection, depreciation, and guilt induction. The female child destined to be a homosexual looks upon her mother with hostility and rebellion. She is in conflict, however, because of the concomitant presence of great longing for affection and approval from her mother. Identification with the mother is impaired by her own hostility.

The "typical" father is apparently a detached, "submerged" individual. He can be concerned and overanxious about his daughter. On occasion, his behavior toward the child is designated as "maternal." Next to the hostile, rejecting, controlling, and guilt-inducing techniques of the mother, the father seems a very pallid figure. Actually he is often quiet, withdrawn, and unassertive. He may remain apart from emotional involvement in the family and may even absent himself, using the pressure of work as a rationalization. He does not present a strong masculine ideal toward which the daughter may relate positively. Freud describes the father of his patient as earnest, worthy, and basically very tender-hearted, but he had to some extent estranged his children by his sternness. In two instances in which this author had opportunities to interview the fathers of female homosexuals, both fathers expressed feelings that they had "failed" their daughters. They were both quiet, reserved persons dominated by their wives. Both daughters saw them as "nice people" but ineffectual and weak.

In summary, then, in the triangular constellation of the father–mother–homosexual daughter we generally find a father who tends to be passive, unassertive, gentle, and detached; a mother who is dominant, domineering, guilt-inducing, and hostile; and a daughter who is hostile toward her mother, who cannot turn to her father because of what she perceives as his weakness, and who suffers from severe feelings of rejection and longing.

Little is known about sibling problems as they may relate to homosexuality. Of four patients whom this author has studied rather extensively, one was an only child, two were only daughters with single male siblings of whom they were extremely jealous, and the fourth had an older brother and a much older sister. This patient preferred her older sister to her mother. None of these patients related well to their siblings.

The female homosexual finds loneliness and isolation within her family, in relation to her siblings as well as to her mother and father. With the onset of overt homosexual behavior and a consistent tendency to conceal her activity, the isolation from her family is intensified.

Relationships to Peers

Whether or not isolation within the family contributes to the female homosexual's inability to relate to her peers is not clear. Experiential factors alone might account for some difficulty. Fragmentary information is available that suggests that female homosexuals have some hostility toward peers of the same sex. They tend to play by themselves and to be "lone wolves" in childhood. Some patients are "tomboys" and indulge in competitive relationships with peers of the opposite sex, but neither of these adaptations permits affectional relationships with peer individuals.

From what is known of the preadolescent life of the female homosexual, it appears that she differs fundamentally in childhood from females who develop heterosexually. Isolation, the inability to make affectional peer relationships, and play behavior that is predominantly "tomboy" appear distinguishing factors for the homosexual group. Perhaps no single factor is critical. Evidence of early sexual tension is probably also a distinguishing characteristic of female homosexuals.

Patterns of Sexual Object-Choice

The varied sexual adaptations of the female homosexual have never been studied extensively or comparatively. Articles on female homosexuality, of which there is a dearth, do not include detailed descriptions of the sexual adaptation of the female homosexual. As a consequence, a listing of the varieties of sexual adaptations must await a broader study of female homosexuality. Certain characteristics, however, seem prominent. Female homosexual patients who have been studied do not seem averse to the company of males. Although they look with some contempt on male homosexuals, female homosexuals often associate with them. There may be two reasons why. One is the desirability of male escorts in social situations; the other is the desire for male company without the danger of possible sexual contact. There is evidence of overt heterosexual interest. In fact, some female homosexuals use such arguments as "society demands it" or "it is because of curiosity" or "I would like to have a child" as excuses for indulging in heterosexual activity. Evidence of covert heterosexual interest is revealed in dreams and daydreams. The female homosexual is conflicted, however, in her choice of a heterosexual partner. She desires masculine men and looks on unmasculine men with contempt, but her greatest sexual fear is of the masculine man, and her contempt does not encourage her to sexual activity with the unmasculine man.

Some homosexual females seek "masculine" qualities in their female partners, but only study of a large number of female homosexuals can reveal the incidence of such partner choices, the reasons for them, and whether or not they are related to transference or identification with father or brother and mother or sister.

Observation of attitudes toward partners' physiques reveals that female homosexuals are frequently involved with those whom they consider to have beautiful faces or beautiful bodies. There is also a preoccupation with breast development in both themselves and their partners.

Patterns of Sexual Behavior

In the variety of female homosexual acts, there are frequent shifts in the roles of the partners. Either may act as the masculine or feminine partner. The definition of role then lies in the preference or the usual mode of behavior.

The partner who customarily plays the aggressive role and is considered the "masculine" partner tends to insert her tongue, her fingers, or a priapus into the "feminine" partner either orally or genitally. She indulges in fantasies, often verbalized to the partner, that she possesses a penis and states or threatens that she is about to or is using the fantasied penis. The "masculine" partner's words indicate that the release of hostility is an important part of the homosexual act for her. The preferentially "feminine" partner usually states that she prefers being touched to touching and prefers being stimulated by insertion. She may express some aversion to performing cunnilingus on her partner; to her the affectional aspects are apparently as important as the sexual release.

Female homosexual patients are usually compulsively preoccupied with sexuality in general and with sexual practices in particular. In addition to providing sexual release and gratification, the homosexual relationship appears to serve a range of irrational defenses and reparative needs.

Although some homosexual relationships may appear stable, continuity is unusual. In some apparently stable female homosexual relationships, either or both partners secretly indulge in homosexual relationships on the side. Discovery of such "infidelity" often results in a break between the partners. Within the relationship itself, there are a great many tensions and a tendency toward hostile eruptions that may lead to a break in the relationship. Extreme ambivalence in both partners leads to impermanence in homosexual partnerships. The frequency of verbal or physical fighting between homosexual partners and among homosexuals in groups suggests that there is much in homosexual relationships that is destructive. There is certainly a longing to develop and maintain meaningful relationships. Frequent attempts to relate are frustrated by chronic ambivalence, hostility, and anxiety.

Treatment of Female Homosexuality

Psychoanalysts usually report that it is difficult to keep female homosexuals in treatment. It is not known whether or not as many female homosexuals as male homosexuals apply for treatment. Among the psychoanalysts who provided the research committee with more than 100 male homosexual protocols for study (Bieber *et al.*, 1962), less than half as many female homosexuals are in treatment and available for study. The "dyke" rarely seeks treatment; female homosexuals in treatment are usually of the "feminine" type. Some psychoanalysts have reported privately that they interview more female homosexuals than they treat, as these patients are less likely to enter upon extended treatment. We can only speculate on the reasons for this reluctance: The female homosexual is presumably not in so difficult a situation socially as is the male homosexual; the existence of female homosexuality is not so readily recognized in our society as is the existence of male homosexuality; the necessity for treatment of the female homosexual and the hope for a favorable outcome in treatment are not well known in society as a whole.

Treatment has been carried out successfully on a once-a-week basis, but two to four times a week are preferable and should be considered necessary. Patients should be told that they will need to remain in treatment three to four years or perhaps longer. Neurotic, characterological, and even psychotic symptoms may improve before change in the sexual adaptation begins. Treatment orientation should be toward heterosexuality. Treatment of female homosexuals may result in reversion to exclusive heterosexual behavior and, in some instances, to the loss of the recognition of the female as a primary sexual object.

Summary

It can only be assumed at this time that all psychiatric diagnoses would be represented in a large group of homosexual women. Female homosexuality can be associated with schizophrenia, psychoneuroses, and character disorders.

The homosexual pattern seems to be associated with specific types of family constellation, the commonest of which probably includes a domineering, hostile, antiheterosexual mother and a weak, unassertive, detached, and pallid father. The ambivalence and hostility of the female homosexual's mother may tend to intensify the Oedipal problems with the father. The father is not perceived as hostile. The daughter may turn to her father for affection, and her incestuous wishes toward the father may thus become augmented. What affection is displayed and accepted tends to come from the father, and this affection further intensifies the Oedipal complex. The daughter may then adopt homosexuality as a defense against the powerful Oedipal problem and against maternal hostility, or she may succumb to the mother's antiheterosexual attitudes and give up her own heterosexual wishes. At the same time, she removes herself from competitiveness with the mother.

Failure to establish herself in the peer group seems only to intensify her homosexual adaptation. It is possible that peer-group acceptance, particularly by other females, would promote heterosexuality. In addition, there is no doubt that identification with a homosexual group adds disturbing elements to the already seriously disturbed psychopathology of the female homosexual.

Female homosexual relationships are characterized by great

ambivalence, by great longing for love, by intense elements of hostility, and by the presence of chronic anxiety. These relationships are unstable and often transient. They do not contribute to the individual's need for stability and love.

With adequate motivation and cooperation, successful psychotherapy resulting in reversion to exclusive heterosexual behavior is possible.

REFERENCES

Bieber, I., Dain, H. J., Dince, P. R., Drellich, M. G., Grand, H. G., Gundlach, R. H., Kremer, Malvina W., Rifkin, A. R., Wilbur, Cornelia B., & Bieber, Toby B. *Homosexuality.* New York: Basic Books, 1962.

Freud, S. The psychogenesis of a case of homosexuality in a woman (1920). In *Collected papers of.* . . . Vol. 2. New York: Basic Books, 1959. Pp. 202-231.

Rado, S. An adaptational view of sexual behavior. In P. Hoch & J. Zubin (Eds.), *Psychosexual development in health and disease.* New York: Grune & Stratton, 1949. Pp. 186-213.

Socarides, C. W. The historical development of theoretical and clinical concepts of overt female homosexuality. *J. Amer. psychoanal. Assn.,* 1963, **2**, 386-414.

16

Sexuality and Homosexuality in Women

MAY E. ROMM

Practically every article written about female homosexuality notes the fact that, in comparison with the voluminous literature on male homosexuality, female homosexuality is a neglected subject. In trying to evaluate the reason for this neglect, several ideas come to mind. As most writers on psychoanalytic and psychiatric subjects are men, it is possible that the idea that women may libidinally prefer members of their own sex may be unacceptable to them. It could also be that, because society is not so alert in discovering and censoring the sexual preferences of homosexual women, such women have less anxiety about their inversion and therefore seek psychiatric help less frequently than do male homosexuals. Or perhaps authors are still under the impression that sexual expression is not so important to women as it is to men and that a woman who is not married and has no heterosexual life can relax in her celibacy and completely sublimate her sexuality. Our culture is not too far from the Victorian era, when it was considered unfeminine for a woman to acknowledge or display sexual feelings of any kind, even in the conjugal relationship. The implication was and perhaps to a certain extent still is that, for men, sexuality is mandatory and that, for women, it is optional. Caprio (1954), in his book *Female Homosexuality,* expresses the view that man's unconscious refusal to acknowledge woman's ability to have sexual pleasure without his participation may account for the absence of specific statutes against female homosexuality—laws, by and large, being made by men.

Can homosexuality be labeled an illness, or is it more correctly classified as an arrested psychosexual development at the pre-puberty level? In the pregenital stage, the individual is completely polymorphous perverse. From the time that the infant develops muscle coordination and is able to detect genital areas, which on contact produce erotic sensations, he reaches out to induce this pleasurable feeling through contact with parts of his own body or with animate or inanimate objects in the outside world. He is neither heterosexual nor homosexual. He is purely sensual. It is only later, when he establishes object relationships and is, of necessity, somewhat erotized in the process of receiving physical care, that he reaches out on all counts to be ministered to by mother or a mother surrogate. This phase can be categorized as a fusion of generalized sensuality with the beginning of sexual feelings. It is at the Oedipal stage, when the child is approximately between three and four years of age, that he normally develops an emotional or sexual reaction toward the parent of the opposite sex. The intensity of this involvement, both emotional and sexual, varies considerably with many factors. It can be either increased or decreased by the reaction of his parents, especially the one of the opposite sex. A child brought up by one parent, by relatives, or by the state in a foster home or orphanage may also have difficulty in accepting a surrogate for a parent who would love and accept him and whom he could in turn accept and with whom he could identify. The psychosexual phase in such a child may not develop to adequate maturity, as the formative years greatly influence the individual's developmental path.

The latency period gives the child a respite from the intensity of the emotional and psychosexual feelings present in the Oedipal phase. Herding with peers of his own sex and not only ignoring but frequently even denigrating members of the opposite sex usually lead to relative equanimity toward the latter. Puberty, however, with its surge of sexuality, confronts the adolescent with the need to choose unequivocally his psychosexual path.

Allowing for the differences in the psychosexual development of men and women, the essential dynamic factors causing homosexuality are in many respects similar in both sexes. "Castration anxiety" connected with the surrender of the body to union in the sexual act can prevent heterosexuality in either sex. The man may react with impotence or premature emissions; the woman may express her anxiety through vaginismus or total frigidity. Many individuals who later become overt homosexuals protect themselves from such untoward reactions by avoiding completely any experimentation involving bodily contact with the opposite sex. We know that an insufficiently resolved Oedipal phase carrying with it the incest taboo can be a focal deterrent to heterosexuality. When the potential love object represents a parent, a sibling, or an individual who is identified with an incestuous object, the sexual act becomes imbued with anxiety and frequently cannot be consummated.

An individual should be considered homosexual only when erotic activity with the same sex is practiced repeatedly and preferentially after adolescence. When interrogated, individuals suffering from this deviant psychosexual pattern as a rule do not know the reasons for their inversion. Many of their fears and conceptions of danger associated with heterosexuality are frequently if not invariably repressed from consciousness. Allowing for the similarities in emotional reactions of human beings but also keeping in mind the uniqueness of each person, we must explore the dynamic and genetic factors of every homosexual under observation without preconception, in order to determine the causal factors in the problem.

It is generally assumed that the male homosexual fears intercourse with a woman because of the incest taboo and that he therefore chooses a love object with external genitals like his own who cannot confront him with the body of a female, which would arouse his castration-anxiety. How then can we explain female homosexuality? What are the similarities and the differences between the causations of male and female homosexuality? Does the adult woman react to the sight of a nude male with a feeling of horror, fear, envy, rage, inferiority, indifference and lack of sexual desire toward him?

Freud (1962) theorized that the little girl who discovered at the approximate age of three the genital difference between the sexes reacted to her lack of a penis with a lasting feeling of inferiority. He believed that this discovery was so traumatic to the female child that it not only laid the foundation for her later neurosis but also had a decisive effect on her character, creating in her a superego that could not adequately compare with that of the man. He based this theory on his idea that the little girl, feeling herself already castrated, lacked sufficient reason to repress her Oedipal complex and therefore allowed herself more overt ego-alien feelings and wishes than would a boy who had more to protect and who would therefore repress his incestuous drive much more actively and more completely.

There is little doubt that young female children on first becoming aware that males have organs that they themselves do not possess are puzzled, confused, and desirous of what they do not have. We can speculate that the female child's reaction to the discovery of the penis depends on several factors: her age at the time of the discovery, the age of the possessor of the male organ, the circumstances under which the discovery occurs, the state of her affect at that time, and the environmental climate. If she makes the discovery in a relaxed state, if the possessor of the penis is an infant or is close to her own age, and if her self-esteem is satisfactory and the environment unthreatening and tolerant, she may weather this experience with little or no anxiety. She may react with curiosity and interest. She may be intrigued by this foreign phenomenon. She may seek clarification. She may verbalize freely to her elders without shame and without guilt at her interest. If her questions are handled with respect, honesty, and proper concern for enlightenment, she may count this experience as simply another new discovery. If she sees the penis of an adult, however, it may be a frightening experience for her, or, if she is shamed, threatened, or punished because of her interest, it may prove highly traumatic for her.

Nor do all female children suffer for the rest of their lives from a penis envy so intense that it influences their futures, their characters, their goals, their aspirations, their accomplishments, and their sexual development. The emotional climates that surround them when they discover this genital difference play an important role in whether or not they develop pathological fixations, as the following case demonstrates.

A three-year-old girl was prepared by her parents for the birth of a sibling. The mother planned with her the happy times they would have when the new baby arrived. After the mother came home from the hospital with the male infant she invited her daughter to help her bathe the baby. The little girl joyfully accepted the invitation. When the infant was put in the bathinette the little girl's eyes became glued to his genitals. Almost immediately there followed a distinct change in her reaction to her mother. She refused to be fed by her, she became irritable, listless, and apathetic. The pediatrician could find no organic cause for her illness. She was referred for psychotherapy. After she established a relationship with her therapist, she confided in her that she was very angry at her mother because the latter did not give her the "trimmings" which her brother possessed. Her recovery was rapid after the therapist evaluated with her not only the disadvantages but the advantages of being a female, and peace was re-established in the family.

Do all little girls react in such dramatic fashion to the recognition of sex differences, or was this one unique? Had she not had therapy would she have developed a severe neurosis, or would she have become homosexual later in life? We cannot answer these questions. We can only state that three-year-old children's reactions and desires are not necessarily the same as those of adult women.

Fenichel, in his book *The Psychoanalytic Theory of Neurosis* (1945), stated that in female homosexuality two etiological factors must be considered: the repulsion from heterosexuality originating in the castration complex and the attraction through early fixation on the mother. He also believes that the factors that make normal heterosexuality repulsive to female and male homosexuals are analogous.

Many other etiological factors have from time to time been suggested for female homosexuality. For example, unresolved Oedipal feelings with consequent identification of each eligible man as a father figure may create an insurmountable incest taboo, or rejection by the father during puberty may cause the girl to identify with him and to seek a love object representing her mother (in this way the young woman takes over the sexual feelings of both parents). Freud described a case (the case of Dora) in which the important precipitating factor in the development of female homosexuality was the disappointment in the father when the patient was an adolescent (Freud, 1959b).

According to many authors, the roots of homosexuality, especially in the female, lie in a very early phase of life. In the process of regression, there may be revived memory traces of the primitive tie to the mother (Fenichel, 1934). This point is understandable as, in order to make a heterosexual adjustment, the female must give up her infantile homosexual love object, the mother, yet she must identify with this very person in order to be able to accept her psychosexual feminine role. Disturbance in the relationship with the mother, whom the girl may see as rejecting, as a dominating and controlling figure toward a beloved father, or as a masochistic, compliant, long-suffering creature at the mercy of the males in the household, may produce in the girl intense ambivalence in her feminine identification and in her reactions to men. All of these factors may create in her a barrier against the final and active step toward postadolescent heterosexuality. The mother becomes a symbol of identification that is fraught with anxiety. There may be fear either of destroying the male in self-preservation or of being destroyed by him. It may appear safer to deal with the mother—with a woman—than to risk the vicissitudes of heterosexuality that seem to confront the mother and therefore all women. It may be more desirable to identify with the father or with some other important male on the horizon and to accept a female as a love object. It is also quite possible that, if the girl at the height of her Oedipal phase feels thoroughly frustrated in her attempts to reach out and be accepted by her father and the rejection is repeated later in life, she may relinquish all hope of ever being accepted by any man, and she may seek freedom from unbearable anxiety in a psychosexual relationship with a woman. In "Psychogenesis of a Case of Homosexuality

in a Woman," Freud (1959a) explained homosexuality in his patient as withdrawal from men in order to remove one cause of her
mother's hostility. Such withdrawal may be an element in the
etiology of female homosexuality, especially if the mother is envi-
ous of her daughter, hostile to her own mate, and verbally pessi-
mistic about the girl's future in a sexual relationship with a man.

Ernest Jones (1927) questions the full validity of what he considers the "unduly phallo-centric" view that male analysts have
expressed in their writings about the development of female sexuality. He believes that, in the evaluation of the sexual development of woman, the importance of female organs has been under-
estimated. He considers inordinate intensity of orality and sadism
to be the core of later development of homosexuality in the woman.
It seems to me, however, that we cannot pinpoint one developmental phase as the main source of any neurotic reaction, be it
abnormal psychosexuality or any other psychic or somatic symptom. The human being in the process of growth tests his strength,
psychic and somatic, in the struggle to reach maturity and its rewards. One of the cardinal requisites for maturity is heterosexual
mating and the creation of a family. The capacity to make the
transition from childhood to adulthood depends on the ego
strength of the individual. The development of the ego, in turn,
is dependent on the following factors: the biological endowment
of the organism; the environmental situations, which may be pro-
pitious, overwhelming, or lacking sufficient challenge (overpro-
tection) in the formative years; and the interplay between the
individual and the environmental situations. There are many persons who, in their formative years, are able to withstand stress that
might lead to homosexuality or psychotic breaks in others not so
strong. Here is an illustration of this point:

A bright, talented young woman of nineteen had a brother four
years her senior with whom she had practiced mutual masturbation from early childhood. Six months before she came for treatment, she and her brother had indulged in sex activities stopping
short of intercourse. When she was five years of age, her father
had seduced her into masturbating him to the state of orgasm,
and he in turn masturbated her. Her mother, who was the bread-
winner of the family, was oblivious to what was going on between

the patient and the two males in the family. Nevertheless, the patient reacted with hostility and guilt toward her mother and with an intense fear of being discovered in her incestuous sex activities. She developed the interesting symptom of being unable to urinate away from home or even at home when a male guest or worker was in the house. It became clear from her dreams and associations that her distended bladder represented to her both an introjected penis and a baby. Obviously she was ashamed of not possessing a penis, which she had seen so frequently throughout her early years in her dealings with her father and her brother. She claimed that she had never seen her mother's body in the nude. She verbalized her resentment of what her father and her brother had done to her, but she quickly became aware of the part that she had played as the compliant seductress. How can we explain that, in spite of these inordinate traumatic occurrences of prolonged and frequent duration, this young woman subsequently sought marriage and motherhood and succeeded in both? It may be of interest to report that, although she married a man who was in physical appearance the antithesis of her father, she, like her mother, became the principal provider for the family.

In contrast to this case, here is an illustration of a woman who did not succeed in overcoming the obstacles in her situation.

This twenty-year-old girl stated in the first interview that she had always been emotionally involved with girls and that her sexual drive had been toward females as far back as she could remember. She was at this time in the throes of an intense romance with a girl several years younger than herself. She reacted with depression when her parents became aware of her "abnormal" involvement and when her father threatened her with dire consequences if she did not give up her homosexual relationship and "return to her senses." In evaluating the family constellation, she revealed that her father was an austere, autocratic person who ruled the household with an iron hand and who not only had intimidated the patient and her younger sister but also had beaten down his wife to a state of compliant subservience to all his demands. The patient had feared her father from her earliest memory. He ordered about the three women in his home as if he were a top sergeant. There had been complete rejection of this girl by her father whenever she had attempted to establish a tender relationship with him during and after her Oedipal phase. Identification with her mother was too painful and unthinkable. As all men appeared to her in the image of her father, as tyrants and monsters who relegated women to the position of slaves, the patient identified with the aggressor—the father—and wooed and sought a sexual partner in the image of the mother, soft and compliant. So far the case holds tight. Her sixteen-year-old sister, however, who had been brought up in the same environment, was a feminine person whose erotic interests were entirely heterosexual. Can we speculate that the traumatic experience of the sister's birth when the patient was four years old, combined with the untenable relationship with her father, had so crippled her ego that she could not make the transition to heterosexuality? Her sister, on the other hand, not having had the painful experience of having to cope with a younger rival, was perhaps therefore able to weather the difficult environment more successfully.

Both Clara Thompson (Green, 1964) and Karen Horney (1939) have emphasized that cultural factors can explain the tendencies of women to feel inferior about their sex and, as a result, to envy men. If we accept this explanation, which certainly appears reasonable, then we should use the term "penis envy" in a symbolic sense, and we must admit that those possessing penes are realistically endowed in our culture with more power than are women and actually are favored in our society. When a woman feels the discomfort associated with this inferior status, her reaction frequently consists of anger and hostility toward the individual in a more fortunate position.

These ego-alien drives can be sublimated, however, through successful achievement on a productive basis. This sublimation can open up avenues of sufficient satisfaction to the woman not only to neutralize her envy of men but also to raise her self-esteem to a point at which she feels complete and satisfied with her lot. Some of the factors contributing to this desirable state range from gratification at being a wife and a helpmate, running a home adequately, and bearing and rearing children to social, business, or professional success, including success in various sports or forms of artistic expression.

All these factors, however, whether singly or in harmonious combination, complete a woman only if she is also capable of forming a compatible psychosexual relationship with a mate. Sexuality cannot be sublimated *in toto*. When there is overwhelming anxiety associated with feelings of inferiority, then hostility, envy, guilt, incest taboo, fear of destruction, and fear of injury or of injuring others may take over. As a result, the woman may escape into neurosis or psychosis, or she may turn away from threatening relationships with men and form a sexual relationship with another female.

Homosexuals occasionally marry in the hopeless attempt to conform with what they think society expects of them. Invariably their homosexual drives take over, and the marriages are usually dissolved unless they are marriages of convenience entered by homosexuals of opposite sexes with amicable understanding that each partner may pursue his sexual preference.

Homosexuals of both sexes are human beings who have given up hope of ever being accepted by their parents and by the society in which they live. They are basically unhappy because normal family life with the fulfillment in having children can never be within their reach. The label "gay" behind which they hide is a defense mechanism against the emptiness, the coldness, and the futility of their lives. Their claim that homosexuality is a way of life for persons who are more artistic, more sensitive, more creative than those who are heterosexual is a denial of their inability to test life on a responsible and mature psychophysiological level.

Much research has been done on the assumption that homosexuality may have an endocrine basis. So far this assumption has not been proved, nor does the evidence suggest that there exists in either sex an endocrine or congenital factor responsible for or influencing this psychosexual abnormality. In 1934, Henry and Galbraith tried to examine constitutional factors in homosexuals in conjunction with their psychosexual histories. Among the 105 female homosexuals evaluated, they found the following characteristics: fine adipose tissue, deficient fat on shoulders and abdomen, excess bodily and facial hair with a tendency to masculine distribution, a small uterus, over- and under-development of the external genitalia, underdevelopment of the breasts, and a low-pitched voice. What they did not bring out was that many women exhibiting these characteristics are definitely heterosexual! For example, one woman in her early thirties not only had a number of these secondary male characteristics, but she also had a growth of facial hair that required shaving several times a week. Yet she was happily married, orgastically potent, and the mother of three children.

It is important to bear in mind that every individual reacts in a specific manner to each situation. What may be traumatic to one individual in the formative years may make only a slight impression on another person of similar age. The threshold of tolerance may be different in different persons, in respect not only to the intensity of the stress but also to the type of stress and to the chronological age of the individual. Even in the same individual, similar stresses may affect him in different degrees depending on his emotional states when they occur. If stress takes place when his self-esteem is high, he may weather it successfully. If he is suffering from a sense of guilt, shame, or need for punishment, for whatever reason, stress may result in a fixating traumatic experience.

The first love object of the infant of either sex is the mother. In order to be able to become involved heterosexually after puberty, the girl must transfer her libidinal interest in her mother or mother-surrogate to a heterosexual object. Whether or not this transfer occurs in her Oedipal phase, in her latency period, or more gradually between the Oedipal stage and adolescence, is not yet clear. Girls of three or four have been known to have intense interest in boys. Occasionally some have become enamored as young children of males much older than themselves and continue through latency and puberty to prefer investing their emotions in males. We have no clear-cut answers or conclusions about when during psychosexual development the roots of later homosexuality take hold.

It is relatively easy to demonstrate and even to pinpoint what we consider to be the etiological factors in the development of a particular case of homosexuality. We must not, however, be deluded into accepting the specific experiences that occurred in these particular patients as axiomatically the causative factors in all homosexuals. Many similar or even more drastic traumatic occurrences befall individuals in the same culture, yet they go on to live adequate heterosexual lives. To demonstrate the unique psychosexual reactions that different individuals may display, let us consider two short case histories.

A woman of twenty-eight, the middle of three sisters, came to therapy because of depressions, a sense of futility, and many somatic symptoms among which were gastrointestinal discomfort, persistent morning vomiting, insomnia, and general weakness and lack of energy. She admitted in the first interview that she was homosexual and had recently interrupted a relationship with an exploitative woman who had treated her sadistically. Her history included a childhood barren of love from both parents, who were themselves unhappy, were constantly quarreling, and were later divorced. According to her, she never received any praise from either parent but was frequently and consistently criticized for inadequacy in learning, in social graces, and in her relationships with her sisters and her peers. Her father took no interest in her except, on occasion, to tickle her and make superficial sexual passes at her girl friends when she was an adolescent. She was under the impression that her parents, especially her father, had reacted to her birth with disappointment because they had wished for a son. She tried desperately to fight her sexual feelings toward women. She confided her problem to one of her cousins, who advised her that she needed sex with men. In desperation, she tried on several occasions to cohabit with men but reacted to their sexual advances with intense vaginismus, so that penetration was impossible.

In the transference, she identified me with a good mother who would accept her as a child in need of love, encouragement, and food and who would supply them to her through tolerance, understanding, and acceptance of her and her sexual pattern. She related to women as in a mother–child relationship, her preference being to be treated as a child by her love object, who would do to her and for her in the sex relationship. For such treatment she was willing to be generous monetarily and to serve her lover in many

other ways. She frequently dreamed of the therapist cradling her
in her arms. Other dreams had as their locale what she thought
was the therapist's domicile, where she would be accepted as a
member of the family. According to the patient, she desperately
wanted affection and approbation from her parents, but neither of them had any time for her or had showed any interest in
her. She was, in her turn, hostile to both parents. She expressed
her shame at being what she considered abnormal and felt that
she had disgraced not only herself but her parents and that she
had short-changed them by not being married and by failing to
provide them with grandchildren.

We have here a woman who has not been given an opportunity
to develop the Oedipal complex. As she claimed that she had not
received love from either parent, why did she choose homosexuality? Can we explain it by her disclosure that her interests were
similar to those of her father? It appeared from her associations
that she identified with her father—in essence, she became the
father and sought the love of a woman as she felt her father
did. She constantly stressed that she must follow in the footsteps
of her father professionally, in order to prove to him that she was
worthy of his respect for her.

Another patient, a woman aged thirty-eight, came for treatment because of insomnia of many years duration and vertigo for
which no organic basis could be found. She, like the first patient, suffered feelings of despair. Her history disclosed a mother
who had been an invalid most of her life and who had died
when the patient was an adolescent. Her father was a ne'er-do-
well alcoholic who, when he got into difficulties during his alcoholic binges, imposed both monetary demands and embarrassment upon the patient. Her associations and particularly her
dreams indicated hostility toward both parents—toward her
mother who, through illness and death, had deprived her of love
and protection and toward her father who, because of his alcoholic addiction and psychopathy, not only had not contributed to
her welfare when she was a child, but had also been a thorn in her
side for many years. In one of her outstanding and repetitive

dreams, she was lying in bed and suddenly realized that her body ended at her umbilicus. Her associations brought out clearly that, because she thought herself so much better than her derelict father and other men in her background, she felt that she should have been a man. She felt that she would then have had a better professional break in our patriarchal culture. In the dream, she accepted her breasts, of which she was proud, but she did not wish to see the depreciated genitals with which nature had endowed her, and she therefore eliminated them. This dream can certainly be labeled a "castration dream." Yet this woman did not become homosexual. She was professionally successful and effectively aggressive. She was married, had three children, and could be generally evaluated as a feminine person—in spite of the fact that in therapy she disclosed intense envy of what she considered the unearned privileges of men in our culture. This patient enjoyed being a woman, a wife, and a mother, but she was bitter about the patronizing attitude that men expressed toward women's accomplishments.

In my opinion, it is unfortunate that many psychoanalysts still concur with Freud's (1962) thesis that the elimination of clitoridal sexuality is a necessary precondition for the development of femininity. Some authors of scientific papers on female sexuality still frequently label the clitoris a "vestigial" organ the erogenicity of which must be eliminated if the woman is to attain mature heterosexuality. This attitude persists in spite of the fact that it has been anatomically and neurologically demonstrated that the clitoris is endowed with as many, if not more, nerve endings as the glans penis (Marmor, 1954). The erroneous belief that clitoral participation must be given up by the woman if she is to qualify as a genitally mature sexual partner may be a hostile fantasy of the male who may unconsciously be threatened by the woman's active participation in the sexual act. It is significant because it is a reflection of the general reaction of many men in our culture who displace their depreciation of the female genitals to the women who possess them. Actually the role of the clitoris is most important in triggering the sexual drive in the woman. If it is sufficiently stimulated in the sexual

foreplay, then the sexual impulses fan out from it during intercourse into the vagina, cervix, and pelvis and, during the orgastic
release, involve the entire psychosomatic system.

There is a history of depreciation of the woman's sexual role by
men. Less than 100 years ago an English surgeon named Acton
(Ellis, 1953) wrote a book that was for many decades the standard authority on sexual questions. In this book, he stated that to
attribute sexual feelings to women was a "vile aspersion" on
the women. In another standard medical work of the same period
(Ellis, 1953), it was pointed out that only "lascivious women"
showed signs of physical pleasure in the embraces of their husbands. Clearly, according to the views of many men not so long
ago, a woman was expected to submit to sex for masculine
pleasure but was not herself supposed to indicate or feel in
any way desirous of sexual pleasure and orgastic release.

Granted that, because of its connection with maternity, the sex
act has weightier consequences for a woman than it has for a man,
this fact merely suggests that the woman is and perhaps should be
more sensitive and discriminating in her choice of a heterosexual
partner. The sexual act per se can and should, however, be a
gratifying and fulfilling experience for her as well as for her
partner.

When the female is rejected in her formative years by her parents; when she feels unloved, depreciated, and demeaned; when
a male sibling is preferred to her; when she feels that her sex is a
disappointment to her parents; or when she becomes convinced,
justifiably or not, that males in our society are the favored sex, she
may react with feelings of inferiority and hostility toward men.
She may then take refuge in psychosexual identification with the
male and may assume a masculine role in a homosexual relationship; or, in a reaction formation, she may become the helpless
passive ultrafeminine partner in a homosexual relationship in
which a "masculine" and strong mother-father representative
loves only her and does for her and to her what she sought from
one or both parents earlier in life. Frequently the partners in a
homosexual relationship exchange roles in mother–child and
child–mother relations.

Many other factors may also enter into the choice of female
homosexuality: fear of growing up and assuming adult responsi-

bilities; fear of dominance and destruction through bodily penetration; fear of mutilation and destruction by pregnancy and childbirth; defiance of parents and society; and desire to conquer and possess the mother by identifying her with the female lover. At times, the homosexual involvement may represent an attempt, not always successful, to obviate a schizophrenic episode by acknowledging and complying with a homosexual urge that breaks through from the unconscious. Perhaps because homosexuals are, at all times, more at odds with themselves than are most heterosexuals, their reactions to their love partners are frequently supercharged. Jealousy among homosexuals is frequently violent, with paranoid coloring. Depressions also seem to be frequent among them. They tend to feel comfortable only among groups composed of homosexuals of either or both sexes. They coin words to indicate their own uniqueness. They try desperately, through clubs, magazines, and cliques, to acquire some semblance of safety and security by clinging to each other in the face of a society that does not trust them and frequently considers them a menace and a threat. Female homosexuals often defend themselves by blaming their lot on the fact that their sex is looked down on, denigrated, and exploited by men. They envy the male his physical endowment and the social preferences that they think are meted out to him in our culture.

Many authors, including Freud (1962), Helene Deutsch (1930), and Sandor Rado (1933), stress that masochism is basic in feminine mental life. Freud claimed that the repression of aggression imposed on women by their constitutions and by society favors the development of strong masochistic impulses in them. Masochism, according to his thinking, is therefore truly feminine. He added that, when men display masochistic tendencies, they must be labeled as displaying obvious feminine traits of character. Helene Deutsch argues that what women ultimately want in intercourse is to be raped, violated, and humiliated by men. Rado, in 1933, wrote that his female patients persistently and recurrently demonstrated in their dreams and fantasies themes of horror, bloody injuries, and frightful mutilations. Analysis revealed that these ideas stemmed from their reactions to the onset of menstruation. He agreed with Helene Deutsch that the woman wishes to be violated in sex. He added that the woman reacts masochistically to impending childbirth with the belief that a part of her body will be torn away. As a reaction to the above dangers the woman, according to Rado, may take flight into homosexuality, finding her way to clitoral pleasure. She thus avoids the "dangerous man," realizes her own masculinity in equating her clitoris to a penis, and neutralizes her genital masochism. Interestingly enough, in 1940 Rado stated that some of these fantasies of his women patients drew their content from experience and therefore to a large extent reflected environmental influences. He added that the behavior of some homosexuals is in no way related to the behavior pattern of the opposite sex and claimed that any altered scheme of sexual stimulation is an attempt at a "reparative adjustment."

Regardless of the way in which masochism expresses itself, it is essential to recognize that it is not an inherent biological reaction to life. We cannot, in all truth, state that an infant reaches out for pain. Masochism must therefore be a reaction to frustration, in which the individual repetitively reaches out for pleasure or satisfaction and is continually blocked in his goal or punished for his attempts. In desperation, he may then erotize pain in an unsuccessful attempt to cure himself through suffering. This process may lead to psychopathology of various degrees, from neurosis to psychosis, from mild acting out to criminal behavior, and from sexual perversion to inversion.

The tendency in most writings on female sexuality has been to confuse the ideation, thinking, feeling, and behavior of emotionally disturbed individuals with those of relatively normal women who do not react with permanent psychopathology to the discovery of the anatomical differences between the sexes. These women accept and even welcome menstruation. They do not dread mating. They look forward to it, and they react to intercourse with pleasurable anticipation and orgastic joy. They also consider pregnancy, childbirth, and nursing as creative, miraculous, and happy privileges.

Female homosexuality is a psychosexual aberration. It is an unfortunate result of the early impact of a stressful environment upon an individual who, for reasons not yet fully understood, is unable to handle the ensuing anxiety connected with heterosexuality. As a compromise, such a person may take refuge in an erotic relationship with a member of her own sex.

In the therapy of a homosexual, whether male or female, each patient must be carefully studied and evaluated, with attention to his or her specific difficulty. The genetic and dynamic factors involved must be taken into consideration. The objective of the therapist should be to help the patient to free himself or herself from pain, whether psychic or somatic. As a great deal of the anxiety associated with homosexuality is based on or is a reaction to early developmental factors that have been repressed and on conscious fears of exposure, ostracism, shame, sadness, and loneliness, psychoanalysis can offer a possibility of considerable benefit. This possibility does not necessarily mean that, even with extensive treatment, the patient will invariably change her psychosexual pattern to heterosexuality. As a matter of fact, the therapist has no right to set such personal goals for his patient and should certainly not stress his desire to plan to remake her into a heterosexual individual. His aim should be to treat the patient with dignity and with interest in her problems whatever they may be and to help her to work through and to face and understand the vicissitudes of her past as they have influenced her present life, in the hope that she will develop enough insight and become capable of applying it so that her life will become more productive and satisfying to herself and to others. This goal can be accomplished only if the patient becomes capable of exchanging her anxiety-ridden masochistic points of view for more realistic ones. She must raise her ego strength and her self-esteem to the point at which she can neutralize the demands and commands of her punitive superego. If it is possible for her through therapy to dissolve her castration fears and to alter her pathologically determined psychosexual patterns, she may orient her erotic drive toward heterosexuality. She will then recognize that a woman is a person endowed with adequate genital organs constructed to fit and fuse with the male sexual organs in love-making. She will become capable of enjoying intercourse and orgastic potency. She will welcome her fulfillment through pregnancy and maternity, a process of creativity that, in the healthy woman, transcends all other satisfactions in life. In addition, she will acquire an evaluation of herself as a worthwhile member of society who is expected to contribute to others in whatever fashion she may be capable. On the other hand, if she is incapable of making the transition to heterosexuality, she should gain enough benefit from treatment to lead a productive life relatively free from anxiety and to reconcile herself to her homosexual pattern with adequate self-esteem and dignity. She should free enough energy from her narcissistic fixations for satisfactory investment in productive functioning with benefit to herself, to her chosen love object, and to the society in which she lives.

REFERENCES

Caprio, F. *Female homosexuality*. New York: Citadel, 1954.

Deutsch, Helene. The significance of masochism in the mental life of women. *Int. J. Psychoanal.*, 1930, **11**, pp. 48-60.

Ellis, H. The sexual impulse and the art of love (1933). In A. M. Krich (Ed.), *Women: the variety and meaning of their sexual experience*. New York: Dell, 1953.

Fenichel, O. Outline of clinical psychoanalysis. New York: Norton, 1934.

Fenichel, O. The psychoanalytic theory of neurosis. New York: Norton, 1945.

Freud, S. The psychogenesis of a case of homosexuality in a woman (1920). In *Collected papers.* . . . Vol. 2. New York: Basic Books, 1959. Pp. 202-231. (a)

Freud, S. Fragment of an analysis of a case of hysteria (1905). In *Collected papers of.* . . . Vol. 3. New York: Basic Books, 1959. Pp. 13-146 (b)

Freud, S. In J. Strachey (Trans.), *Three essays on the theory of sexuality* (1905). New York: Basic Books, 1962.

Green, M. R. (Ed.) *Interpersonal analysis: the selected papers of Clara M. Thompson*. New York: Basic Books, 1964.

Henry, G. W., & Galbraith, H. M. Constitutional factors in homosexuality. *Amer. J. Psychiat.*, 1934, **91**, 1249-1270.

Horney, Karen. *New ways in psychoanalysis*. New York: Norton, 1939.

Jones, E. The early development of female sexuality. *Int. J. Psychoanal.*, 1927, 8, 459-472.

Marmor, J. Some considerations concerning orgasm in the female. *Psychosom. Med.*, 1954, 16, 240-245.

Rado, S. Fear of castration in women. *Psychoanal. Quart.*, 1933, 2, 425-475.

Rado, S. The concept of bisexuality. *Psychosom. Med.*, 1940, 2, 459-467.

17

Psychotherapy of Homosexuals: A Follow-up Study of Nineteen Cases

PETER MAYERSON

HAROLD I. LIEF

It is only within the past two decades that psychiatrists have considered that patients with homosexual problems could be successfully treated by psychotherapy. Although the early concepts of physical bisexuality formulated by Krafft-Ebing (1892) were significantly revised by Freud (1962), the latter's thesis of psychological bisexuality and his emphasis on the constitutional basis of homosexual behavior still left little hope for therapeutic remission of homosexual behavior. In 1940, Rado re-examined these theories, and his refutation of many of their basic tenets laid the foundation for an adaptational view of aberrant sexual behavior. Rado argued that, in general, the chief causal factor of aberrant sexual behavior is anxiety, which inhibits the standard pattern of reactivity and brings about a reparative and substitutive pattern of altered reactivity.

Many recent investigators (Ellis, 1956; Poe, 1952; Rubinstein,

1958; and Thompson [Green, 1964]) have adopted Rado's views, emphasizing the anxiety- and conflict-producing factors of family, society, and accidental circumstance in the explanation of homosexual behavior. Most important, they have considered homosexual fantasies and activities not as separate entities but rather as partial manifestations of more basic underlying adaptational disorders (conflicts dealing with competition, dependency, and power). Considered in adaptational terms, the potential reversibility of homosexual orientation and behavior varies with the characteristics of the underlying disorder. Adaptationally oriented investigators have found that the best results are obtained when therapy is directed toward treatment of the patient's problems as a whole; overemphasis on the homosexual aspects of his adaptive defects usually leads to therapeutic failure.

Despite this potentially optimistic point of view, a review of the literature shows too few reports of treatment of series of homosexual patients, although there are a number of individual case reports discussing treatment and various criteria for successful prognosis (Fenichel, 1945; Monroe & Enelow, 1960; Poe, 1952; Rubinstein, 1958; Thompson [Green, 1964]). The exceptions include a series by Ellis (1956) in which he reports the results of his treatment of forty-one homosexuals, Woodward's (1956) notations on the treatment of homosexual offenders, and the recent comprehensive cooperative study of male homosexuality reported by Bieber, Dain, Dince, Drellich, Grand, Gundlach, Kremer, Rifkin, Wilbur, & Bieber (1962), which includes a section on results of treatment. The only follow-up study of the subject is a brief analysis by Curran and Parr (1957). It was therefore considered that a thorough retrospective analysis of not only the immediate results but also the long-range, post-treatment endurance of the psychotherapeutic effects on patients with homosexual problems would be of significant value. A follow-up study was conducted of nineteen homosexual patients (fourteen males, five females) who had been treated in the Hutchinson Memorial Psychiatric Clinic of the Tulane University Department of Psychiatry and Neurology (hereafter referred to as H.M.P.C.).

Method of Study

Throughout the psychiatric literature in recent years there has been a plea for more objective evaluation of the results of psychotherapy. The inherent difficulties of accurately assessing such extremely subjective methods and materials, thoroughly described by Stevenson (1959), Zubin (1953), Oberndorf (1942, 1948), Rosenbaum, Friedlander, and Kaplan (1956), and others (Herzog, 1959; Löfgren, 1960), have, however, limited the number of such studies. Miles and his colleagues (Miles, Barrabee, & Finesinger, 1951) summarized the major follow-up studies of psychotherapeutic effectiveness conducted up to 1951 and concluded that the studies generally were not "comparable to one another, largely due to lack of sufficiently detailed clinical data and precisely defined criteria." In his evaluation of psychotherapy, Miles attempted to remedy these deficits. The method used in the present study was modeled after that of Miles, employing his approach of evaluating the individual patient from the point of view of psychodynamics as well as of descriptive behavioral changes and analyzing holistic character modifications rather than concentrating exclusively on changes in one area of a patient's personality.

Details of the method are outlined in Appendix A (see p. 333). As a general guideline, a protocol form was devised, which included a dynamic evaluation of each patient's presenting illness and a profile of each patient's adjustment in the areas of psychic and psychosomatic symptoms, social relationships, sexual relationships, and depth of insight. The charts were reviewed separately by two psychiatrists, and the pre- and post-treatment profiles were compiled. Joint follow-up interviews were then conducted, and separate evaluations were made of each patient at this stage. Patients who had moved out of town were sent detailed questionnaires covering the same general topics as were discussed in the interviews, and the questionnaires were again separately evaluated. The results were thus based primarily on a comparison of the pretherapy, post-therapy, and follow-up profiles.

As the population studied consisted of patients formerly treated in the H.M.P.C., the sample does not represent a random group of homosexuals. All the patients had voluntarily applied for psychiatric aid, had been screened through several intake interviews, and had been accepted for treatment only because they seemed to be reasonable candidates for psychotherapy.

A detailed breakdown of the population is included in Appendix A. It included fourteen males and five females. At the commencement of therapy, most of the patients had completed college, and their mean age was 27.7 years. At follow-up, social-class distribution was predominantly upper middle class. Four and one-half years was the mean interim between end of therapy and follow-up.

Results and Discussion

As stated in the introduction, the follow-up evaluation was organized around a holistic approach; the patient's homosexual orientation was considered an important part, but only a part, of his total character structure and psychopathology. The evaluation of the over-all change reflected this point of view and is presented in Table 17–1. The cases in classes 1 through 3 (73 per cent) at follow-up are regarded as having had a satisfactory psychothera-

Table 17–1.

Over-all evaluation[1] of patient improvement since beginning of therapy.

	At end of therapy		At follow-up	
	no. of cases	% cases	no. of cases	% cases
Class 1. Apparently recovered	0	0	1	5.3
Class 2. Much improved	3	15.8	8	42.0
Class 3. Improved	7	36.8	5	26.3
Class 4. Slightly improved	7	36.8	1	5.3
Class 5. Unimproved	1	5.3	3	15.8
Class 6. Worse	1	5.3	1	5.3
Totals	19	100.0	19	100.0

[1] See Appendix B, Section 2-E, for description of classification criteria.

peutic outcome, and the cases in classes 4 through 6 (26 per cent) are considered essentially unchanged or worse. Although, as Miles points out, it is difficult to compare results of different studies because of the variations in defining the criteria for improvement and in the composition of the samples, our over-all results of treatment are almost identical to Miles's findings in his compendium of thirty-one different follow-up reports, showing improvement in an average of 75 per cent of patients with psychoneuroses after some form of psychotherapy.

Three definite conclusions may be drawn from the results reported in Table 17–1. First, homosexual patients treated in our clinic show excellent over-all improvement with psychotherapy. Second, improvement in over-all status tends to increase after conclusion of therapy. Third, to be accurate, an evaluation of the efficacy of psychotherapy should be performed after a follow-up interval rather than immediately on completion of therapy.

Specific Areas of Change

Because of the small number of cases, the various categories of change from the end of therapy to follow-up listed in Table 17–1 are condensed into three groups for further analysis:

Group A—cases much improved
 (includes "apparently recovered" and "much improved" classes of Table 17–1)
Group B—cases improved
 (includes only "improved class")
Group C—cases considered essentially unchanged or worse
 (includes "slightly improved," "unimproved," and "worse" classes)

For convenience, these groups will be referred to as groups A, B, and C.

Comparisons are first made in terms of change in the patients' status at the beginning of therapy and at the time of follow-up in various areas of social, symptomatic, and sexual adjustment and depth of insight (defined in Section 5 of Appendix B, see page 339).

The data are graphically presented in Figure 17–1. It is evident that the greatest difference between the group profiles is in the area of sexual adjustment. Seven out of nine Group A patients achieved a "much improved" sexual status, whereas none of the Group C patients showed even slight improvement in the sexual area. Although sexual orientation is but a symptom of the patients' total psychopathology, it is the most difficult area in which to achieve psychotherapeutic change, as demonstrated by Bieber and as postulated by many other investigators. Of the four sub-groupings analyzed here (sexual, social, symptoms, and insight), improvement in heterosexual orientation is thus probably the best guideline for judging the degree of therapeutic success.

Table 17–2 shows the marital-adjustment component of the sexual evaluation. Eight of nine Group A patients (three females and five males) were unmarried at the beginning of treatment; one married toward the end of therapy, and five married within one year after the conclusion of therapy. Their marriages seemed directly attributable to attitudinal changes occurring in therapy. Of the two Group A patients who remained single (one male and one

Table **17–2.**

Marital status of patients at start of therapy and at time of follow-up.

Scale evaluation classification[2]	Status at start of therapy			Status at follow-up		
	no. of patients in group			no. of patients in group		
	A	B	C	A	B	C
5 Excellent marital adjustment	–	–	–	2	–	–
4 Good marital adjustment	–	–	–	3	1	–
3 Fair marital adjustment	1	–	–	–	–	–
2 Poor marital adjustment	–	1	–	1	–	–
1 Divorced or separated	–	–	–	1	2	–
0 Never married	8	4	5	2	2	5

[2] See Appendix B, Section 5-D-2, for criteria used in classification.

female), the man had been living with a female mistress since a year after conclusion of therapy but was not willing to assume the responsibilities of marriage; the woman was heterosexually oriented but had no permanent sexual relationships. One of the Group A patients, who had subsequently married, later separated because of personality conflicts in extrasexual areas. The patient in Group B who was married (unhappily) before treatment divorced his wife and resumed exclusive homosexual activities during therapy. One other has adjusted fairly well, although he still has homosexual fantasies; a third separated from his wife partially because of sexual conflicts. At the time of the follow-up, no Group C patients had married.

In the area of social adjustment (which includes changes in occupational adjustment and interpersonal relationships), Figure 17–1 shows a negligible difference between the graphic profiles of groups A and B, and even 40 per cent of Group C patients show definite improvement. Even though psychotherapy may not significantly affect the patient's sexual orientation, it can be of definite value in improving his adjustment in other spheres of behavior.

Similarly, the profiles of change in symptoms are comparable for groups A and B, although it is noted that fewer than 45 per cent of the patients in each of these groups fell in the "much improved category." These data may be a true reflection of a lag in symptomatic, as opposed to sexual and social, progress; they may also show an artifact due to the empirical numerical grading system used for symptomatic evaluation, as opposed to the more subjective criteria used in the other evaluations.

The "insight" profiles seem to demonstrate that improvement in insight, although following the general trend in other areas, is a poor criterion by which to judge over-all improvement. Although a patient may come to understand his problems and his psychodynamics during therapy, the strength of his defenses and his ability to cope with his problems may not be significantly improved. Considering these results, it is interesting that 58 per cent of all the patients (representing a cross-section of the three groups) said that their most significant gains in therapy had been increased insights.

There are 22 per cent more patients classified in groups A and

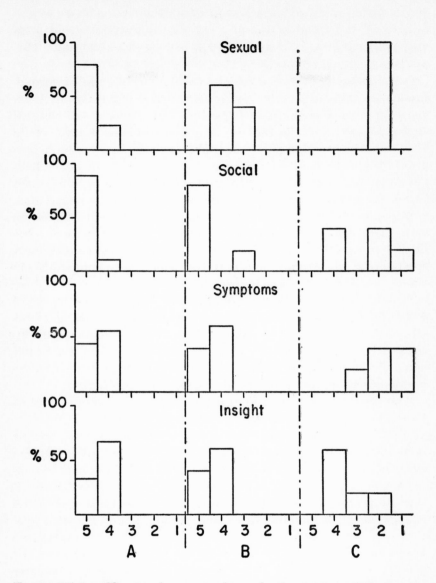

FIGURE 17–1. Changes by group from the beginning of therapy to follow-up: 5 = much improved; 4 = improved; 3 = slightly improved; 2 = unchanged; 1 = worse.

B at follow-up than at the end of treatment. An analysis of the specific areas of improvement in the post-treatment period is an important factor in assessing the efficacy of psychotherapy. This analysis is presented in Figure 17–2.

A comparison of these profiles for "social" and "sexual" improvement since termination of therapy demonstrates that Group A patients had made equal gains in both areas, Group B patients had improved principally in the area of social adjustment, and Group C patients had tended to remain stable sexually but to decompensate socially. These "socially worse" patients had all been diagnosed as probable schizophrenics. Their problems in adjustment evidently were more centered in the social than in the sexual area.

Figure 17–2 demonstrates that the post-therapeutic losses in symptomatic adjustment of these psychotic Group C patients paralleled the social profiles. Groups A and B showed similar post-treatment gains in symptomatic status, which were comparable to their over-all symptomatic improvement.

It is encouraging that psychotherapy benefited so many of groups A and B patients not only by broadening their insights during treatment but also by enabling them later to enhance their introspective analysis on their own. Figure 17–2 shows that 44 per cent of Group A and 60 per cent of Group B patients had increased their depths of insight since completion of therapy.

The "over-all" profile in Figure 17–2 reveals that 80 per cent of Group C patients had lost many of the gains achieved during therapy, and it is probable that their status in most areas will continue downhill, eventually reaching or exceeding pretherapy levels. On the other hand, we should expect groups A and B patients to continue increasing their gains. It is quite difficult, however, to separate gains directly attributable to therapy from those caused by change in environmental stress and situation. For example, one Group B patient was converted from exclusively homosexual behavior to exclusively heterosexual behavior while in therapy. Shortly after leaving therapy, he married a woman who later turned out to be similar to his "castrating" mother. Although maintaining many gains in other areas, he had reverted to exclusively homosexual activities. If he had married a different type of woman, he might still be married, might have consolidated more therapeutic gains, and might now be classed in Group A. But per-

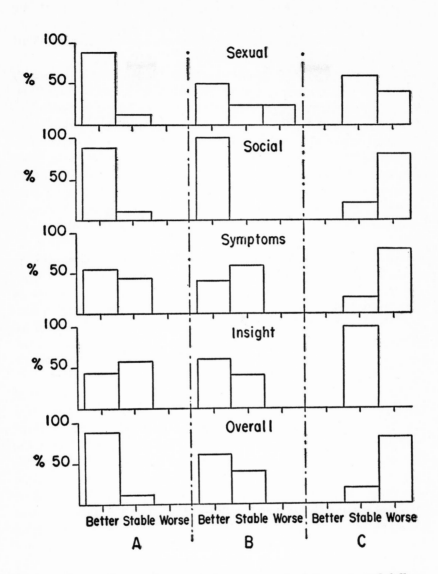

FIGURE 17–2.   Changes by group between end of therapy and follow-up.

haps his maladaptation to married life was due more to the limited psychodynamic change achieved during therapy, which also would account for his poor choice of mate. The stability and improvement, in the past few years, of another patient, a "power-type pseudohomosexual" classed in Group A, have been largely caused by his changing occupations two years after leaving therapy and by his present position of prestige in business. But would he have changed his occupational outlook at all without psychotherapy? The use of control groups as employed by Bieber provides only a partial answer to the dilemma of whether to attribute changes to therapy or to environment, for it is impossible to set up experimental and control groups that are psychodynamically comparable in this regard.

In order to compare our results with those of other investigators, we have organized our data to reveal the absolute changes between beginning of treatment and follow-up status in sexual dynamics and behavior, as shown in Table 17–3.

Using these computations, 47 per cent of our patients were found at follow-up to be "heterosexual." These patients comprised 22 per cent of those who had been exclusively homosexual, 57 per cent of those who had been mostly homosexual, and 100 per cent of those who had been bisexual at the beginning of therapy. Section B of Table 17–3, which excludes the five women in the study, shows that the data for the male group are not significantly different from those of the total group.

These statistics can be compared to those of Bieber *et al.* (1962), who report that an over-all 27 per cent of their pretreatment homosexuals were found to be exclusively heterosexual during or at the end of therapy. Nineteen per cent of their exclusively homosexual patients and 50 per cent of their bisexual patients had converted to exclusive heterosexuality. In a pretreatment–post-treatment comparison study, Ellis (1956, p. 194) reports that 39 per cent of his homosexual male patients and 66⅔ per cent of his homosexual female patients were "considerably improved" in "achieving satisfactory sex-love relations with members of the other sex." Using Kinsey's scale of sexual orientation (Kinsey, Pomeroy, & Martin, 1948) in their follow-up study of fifty patients treated in private practice, Curran and Parr (1957) found that only 4 per cent of their pretherapeutic "exclusively homosexual"

Table **17–3.**

Change in sexual orientation between start of therapy and time of follow-up.

Classification at start of therapy[3]	Total no. of patients	Classification at follow-up[3]		
		Homosexual (classes 1 and 2)	Bisexual (class 3)	Heterosexual (classes 4 and 5)
A TOTAL GROUP				
Exclusively homosexual (Class 1)	9	7 (78%)	0	2 (22%)
Mostly homosexual (Class 2)	7	1 (14%)	2 (29%)	4 (57%)
Bisexual (Class 3)	3	0	0	3 (100%)
Totals	19	8 (42%)	2 (11%)	9 (47%)
B MALE PATIENTS ONLY				
Class 1	7	5 (71%)	0	2 (29%)
Class 2	4	1 (25%)	1 (25%)	2 (50%)
Class 3	3	0	0	3 (100%)
Totals	14	6 (43%)	1 (7%)	7 (50%)

group, 14 per cent of their "predominantly homosexual" patients, and 43 per cent of their "bisexual" patients had "less intense homosexual feelings" or increased capacity for "heterosexual arousal" at time of follow-up. Woodward (1956) reports that only seven of eighty-one cases referred by courts and other agencies to the Portman Clinic in London achieved "satisfactory results" of "no homosexual impulses, increased heterosexual interest" through psychotherapy, and none of these patients was initially "exclusively homosexual." In Knight's composite report of statistics from several large clinics (1941), of eight "homosexuals" treated by psychoanalysis for longer than six months, two were "apparently

---

[3] Numerals refer to classifications in Appendix B, Section 5-D-1. Group titles are worded to coincide with terminology used by other investigators.

cured," none was "much improved," five were "improved," and one was "not changed or worse."

As previously stated, such interstudy comparisons are extremely tenuous because of variations in the composition of the populations studied and in the criteria of evaluation. Rather than drawing any conclusions from these comparisons, we re-emphasize the concept that eclectic evaluation of an individual's progress is a much more valid way to judge the success or failure of psychotherapy than is evaluation of the absolute changes in only one major aspect of personality. One Group B patient illustrates these points. Although he is married, has produced three children, and has had no homosexual experiences since shortly after completing therapy, he still has occasional homosexual fantasies and dreams related to his dependency needs, which treatment had modified only slightly. On a descriptive behavioral basis, he would be described as "exclusively heterosexual" but on a purely dynamic basis as "bisexual." Using our five-point scale for heterosexual adjustment, we rated him as "4." But more important, we felt that the changes in sexual combined with nonsexual areas rated only an over-all classification of "improved"—a rating of "4" on a six-point scale.

The question arose whether or not it might be possible from the available information to determine some of the factors associated with improvement or failure to improve. Certain factors were found to be either relatively constant for the group, too poorly distributed, or extraneous to the question and have therefore not been analyzed. These factors include religion, occupation, age of the therapist (fourteen of the nineteen therapists were under the age of thirty-four), professional experience of the therapist (all were second- or third-year residents in psychiatry at the beginning of therapy), sex of the therapist (eighteen of nineteen were male), and subsequent psychiatric treatment (none of the patients had returned to formal psychotherapy or had been hospitalized for psychiatric reasons after concluding treatment begun with the clinic therapist).

The analysis of potentially variable factors is divided into three areas: the factors concerning the therapeutic situation, various aspects of the patient's status at the beginning of therapy, and the patient's background history.

The first area includes the comparisons shown in Table 17–4. Reparative therapy is the usual method employed in the residents' clinic; the data show that many patients with homosexual problems can be significantly helped by this type of therapy. No comparison between reparative and reconstructive (analytic) therapy is possible in this study, as there are only three cases in the latter group. There was no significant correlation of duration of treatment and the number of therapy sessions with over-all patient improvement. The tendency toward longer duration of treatment

Table 17–4.

Variable factors in the therapeutic situation.

	Group Classification			
	A	B	C	
	No. of patients in each group			
	9	5	5	
	No. of patients in each category			Total
Type of therapy				
reparative	8	3	5	16
reconstructive	1	2	0	3
Duration of therapy (in years)				
range	0.2–3.1	0.2–3.8	0.5–5.0	
mean	1.4	1.9	2.2	
No. of therapy sessions				
range	13–420	14–410	18–270	
mean	154	180	123	
Cause for end of therapy				
external reasons	4	3	0	7
discontinuation by patient	2	1	5	8
conclusion by therapist that patient improved	3	1	0	4
Interim between end of therapy and follow-up (in years)				
range	1.5–8.7	1.3–9.0	0.6–5.8	
mean	5.6	4.7	2.5	

and fewer over-all total sessions for the patients in Group C is consistent with the usual therapeutic arrangements in the psychotherapy of schizophrenics.

The interim period of approximately five years for patients in groups A and B supports the belief that their improvements are valid and stable. Unfortunately, inspection of the individual interview records of Group C patients leaves little hope that their statuses would be improved by environmental support during the next few years. They are all definitely therapeutic failures.

Variation in reasons for ending therapy did not distinguish Group A from Group B patients. The preponderance of Group C patients in one category might be interpreted as showing that most patients who themselves decide to end psychotherapy make few if any gains after leaving treatment. But perhaps this statement is putting the cart before the horse, as it is most probable that those patients showing least improvement (generally the "sicker" ones) are most likely to terminate therapy of their own accord. Many of the patients and all the therapists were still completing their formal education at the commencement of therapy. Professional opportunities subsequently required many of them to move away from New Orleans before therapy was ideally concluded, thus accounting for the large number of patients in the "concluded due to external reasons" category.

Evaluation of the patients' statuses at the beginning of therapy, as presented in Table 17–5, proves to be of more prognostic value than does analysis of the therapeutic situation.

Rubinstein (1958) states that homosexuals between the ages of twenty and thirty, or possibly up to age forty if the individuals' patterns are still flexible, are most amenable to therapy. Bieber *et al.* (1962) report increased heterosexual adaptability in patients below the age of thirty-five. Sixteen of our nineteen patients were between the ages of twenty and thirty-five at the start of therapy. There was no correlation between the narrow age range of the group studied and the success of treatment.

Ellis (1956) reports that he has had significantly more success in treating female than male homosexuals. In comparing the male and female homosexual he finds that it is easier for females to relate to the male therapist; that it is easier for the female to consumate coitus once she is so determined; that prior to therapy more

Table 17–5.

Various aspects of patient status.

	Group Classification			
	A	**B**	**C**	
	No. of patients in each category			
	9	5	5	
	No. of patients in each category			**Total**
Age at start of therapy (in years)				
range	20–40	26–32	18–36	
mean	28.2	27.0	27.5	
Sex				
male	6	5	3	14
female	3	0	2	5
Social class position at follow-up				
Class I	4	1	0	5
Class II	5	4	1	10
Class III	0	0	3	3
Class IV	0	0	1	1
Class V	0	0	0	0
Total years of education at follow-up				
range	18–20	18–20	11–18	
mean	19	19	15	
Mannerisms of the opposite sex at initial presentation				
yes	1	2	1	4
no	8	3	4	15
Primary diagnosis made during therapy				
personality pattern or trait disturbance	6	1	1	8
psychoneurosis	3	3	0	6
schizophrenia	0	1	4	5
Therapeutic motivation				
strong	8	2	0	10
moderate	1	3	3	7
weak	0	0	2	2

females had had heterosexual experiences; and that therapeutic motivation is greater in females. Although our data support the last two points, they show no significant difference in over-all improvement between females and males. Nor did we find that active female homosexuals are "more disturbed" than their male counterparts, as Ellis claims. The only significant difference we found between the tabular analyses of male and female patterns was in the stability of homosexual pairs, a point to be discussed later.

The data do show that there was a definite trend toward lower socioeconomic levels and fewer total years of education among Group C patients. Ellis notes a similar trend in educational level in his patients who showed little or no improvement with psychotherapy. The importance of these trends, if any, would apply to the common observation that a better rapport is often achieved if the therapist and patient are of similar socioeconomic and intelligence levels (Hunt, 1960).

Hemphill, Leitch, & Stuart (1958) explored the popular concept that the male homosexual is effeminate and found that, in a prison population of sixty-four men convicted for homosexual offenses, only about 5 per cent showed overt feminine mannerisms. Most males who flagrantly exhibit effeminate mannerisms (and their female counterparts with strong masculine mannerisms) have strong exhibitionistic drives (and, obviously, severe problems of sexual identification) complicating the therapeutic problem. It is not surprising that only three of the fourteen males and two of the five females in our group exhibited overt mannerisms of the opposite sex. We did find, however, that there was a significantly greater incidence of these mannerisms in groups B and C than in Group A patients. The absence of overt cross-sexual mannerisms therefore probably indicates a better chance for good therapeutic results.

Bieber found no correlation between diagnosis and heterosexual reorientation in the psychoanalytic treatment of patients with homosexual problems. In sharp contrast, our results indicate that, at least with our generally less intensive treatment methods, there is a relationship to diagnosis. Patients with primary diagnoses of personality-pattern or trait disturbances showed greater improvement than did patients with psychoneuroses, who in turn showed greater improvement than did patients with schizophrenia. This improvement included heterosexual improvement. This result is not surprising, as we should expect that patients with less severe psychiatric illnesses would show better responses.

The degree of therapeutic motivation is listed by most investigators as one of the paramount factors in determining the success of treatment. Our results corroborate this view. The degree of motivation was one of the areas of most significant group differences in our study.

Factors concerning patients' patterns of sexual behavior and types of homosexual conflict are presented in Table 17–6.

Rado (1956) states that reparative patterns (of modified sexual behavior) are ushered in by the inhibition of standard performance through sexual fears and repressed yet overflowing rage. These patterns arise from unconscious processes of repair, marked by a high degree of inflexibility; the individual depends on them for full orgastic gratification and, though he may force himself to go through the motions of standard performance, he does not obtain full gratification except through reparative and substitutive patterns.

Seventeen of our nineteen patients fell into this reparative pat-

Table 17–6.

Patterns of sexual behavior and types of homosexual conflict.

	No. of patients in each category			Group classification		
				A	B	C
	Male	Female	Total	$N=9$	$N=5$	$N=5$
Etiology of behavior pattern						
reparative, organ replacement	12	5	17	7	5	5
incidental	1	0	1	1	0	0
situational	1	0	1	1	0	0
Type of homosexual conflict						
dependency component prominent	8	3	11	4	4	3
power component prominent	6	2	8	5	1	2

tern of behavior. Although these patients all showed various degrees of sexual inhibition, twelve of the seventeen (71 per cent) were classified in groups A and B at follow-up, indicating that, since the beginning of psychotherapy, marked modifications had been made in these previously inflexible patterns.

Rado goes on to note that "most if not all the motor features seen in the reparative patterns reappear in the situational and variational patterns as well" (p. 200). But, as these patterns are more the products of conscious deliberation than of unconscious processes, they are more "flexible and show a marked tendency toward combination." Two of our male patients fit best into these categories. Both are members of Group A. The more conscious and flexible nature of their patterns probably explains their marked over-all improvement at follow-up.

There is no need to review Ovesey's (1954, 1955a, 1955b) concepts in detail in this chapter, but our psychodynamic orientation is basically the same as his. According to this view, the true homosexual seeks sexual gratification as the motivational goal, while the "pseudohomosexual" seeks nonsexual goals related to conflicts over power and dependency but makes use of the genitalia to symbolize and achieve these goals. Ovesey has emphasized that these pseudohomosexual components usually exist in the true homosexual as well, modifying and often determining the pattern of the reparative behavior. The two men classified in Table 17–6 under "incidental" and "situational" patterns exhibited primarily the psychodynamics of the pseudohomosexual, although each acted out his conflicts in a brief, transient, orgastic homosexual relationship. Nevertheless, sexual gratification was not the primary motivational goal. Through psychotherapy both came to understand the origins of their homosexual fantasies and transient experiences. Although at follow-up remnants of their power and dependency conflicts were still evident in other areas of behavior, both men were completely heterosexual in thought and behavior.

The seventeen patients classified as exhibiting reparative patterns of homosexual behavior were considered to be true homosexuals according to Ovesey's definitions. Elements of dependency or power conflicts were found in varying degrees in all their sexual patterns. The majority of Group A patients were true homosexuals with dominant power components; the preponderance of groups

B and C patients were dependent-component homosexuals. This differentiation, however, does not in any clear-cut statistical fashion aid prognostic evaluations.

Of the five psychotic patients in the sample, all were true homosexuals exhibiting reparative patterns of sexual behavior; none could be classified under a heading of "confused" or "chaotic" sexuality, terms occasionally applied to aberrant sexual behavior in schizophrenics. The two paranoid schizophrenics fell into the category in which power conflicts were prominent. Of the three in the dependent category, two were of the schizo-affective type and one a chronic schizophrenic.

Monroe and Enelow (1960) maintain that strong therapeutic motivation is the most important factor in successful psychotherapy of homosexuals. In the seven cases they reported, only when there was separation between an orgastic love object and an alimentary love object did sufficient conflict arise to promote strong therapeutic motivation. Although many of our male patients had backgrounds of excessive dependence on feeding but castrating mothers, only three men patients exhibited patterns involving separate love objects. All three relied on homosexual contacts for orgastic gratification and on one or more older women for dependency gratification. Therapeutic motivation was equally distributed between strong to slight in these patients, and none was in Class A at follow-up.

At the beginning of therapy, two other male patients were exclusively involved in heterosexual relationships with dominating, aggressive women and were suffering from acute conflicts between the dependency attractions and simultaneously sexually threatening aspects of the partners. Therapeutic motivation was strong in one patient; at follow-up he had married the partner but had still not completely resolved his basic conflict. The other man, whose motivation was judged moderate, solved the conflict by returning to a stable homosexual relationship with a feeding, nonthreatening male. He had improved in many ways, but adjustment still did not closely coincide with ideal results. Both these patients were classified in Group B.

Clearly, although our results support Monroe and Enelow's initial premise that therapeutic motivation is a paramount factor in the psychotherapeutic improvement, we have been unable to support their isolation of the separation of love objects as an important source of motivation.

The most striking difference we found between males and females was in the stability of homogeneous pairs, a point that is also emphasized in Kinsey's studies (Kinsey, Pomeroy, Martin, & Gebhard, 1953). Whereas all our female patients had had stable homosexual relationships (relationships lasting longer than two years), only one of twelve paired males had had such a stable relationship. The women generally seemed much less dissatisfied with their homosexual lives than did the men. The female relationships seemed to be primarily vehicles for expression of dependent or passive needs; dynamically they seemed to be mother–daughter relationships in which actual or symbolic sexual gratification assumed far less importance than in the male pairs. Two of the women were strongly motivated toward therapy because of conflicts between alimentary ties to female partners and dependent relationships with nonthreatening males that had arisen shortly before application for treatment. Through therapy these new ties were strengthened, and both women later achieved orgastic sexual relations with male partners without significant conflict. At follow-up both women had greatly improved in all fields and were classed in Group A.

We modeled our investigation of background historical factors on the criteria used by Bieber *et al.*, but soon found that we had embarked on a difficult task. Bieber's group obtained its results by sending detailed questionnaires to psychoanalysts currently treating homosexual patients. It was impossible to obtain from the clinic charts uniform accurate profiles of the interrelationships among the patients' families and home environments and the patients' own attitudes during childhood and adolescence with anywhere near the degree of accuracy possible in Bieber's study. We tried to place the patients according to Bieber's proposed classifications—"close-binding intimate" mother, "detached-hostile" mother or father, and so forth—and to classify the type and degree of sibling rivalry, but our results were so thinly distributed that the small numbers in each subclass had no statistical or clinical value. We also believe that in most of our cases the classifications were based on insufficient evidence. Limited by our methods, we can therefore neither confirm, deny, or extend the results in those areas reported by Bieber to be of various levels of prognostic significance.

The background information we felt we could determine with reasonable accuracy is reported in Table 17–7. In general, the Group A patients had had their first homosexual contacts later, were less likely to have had them before age sixteen, tended to have had their first homosexual relationships after age sixteen, and had had their first repeated homosexual experiences with the same partners at older ages than had the patients in groups B and C. The duration of active homosexuality prior to therapy was also somewhat less than for the patients in groups B and C. Table 17–7 also reveals that the patients in Group C had had heterosexual experiences significantly earlier than the more improved patients. There is thus a suggested correlation between a later age of onset of overt homosexual and heterosexual activity and increased improvement in psychotherapy.

As 74 per cent of the total patient sample had achieved heterosexual coitus at least once before therapy, the data reveal no significant group differences. The results indicate, however, that, as Group A had the lowest percentage of patients who had had pretherapy coital experience, actual heterosexual performance is not so important a prognostic factor as is psychological heterosexual orientation. This suggestion is supported by the presence of heterosexual dreams or fantasies at the beginning of treatment in Group A patients and their relative absence in groups B and C patients. The contrast between performance and fantasy again emphasizes that analysis of dynamic orientation is a much better criterion for evaluating psychotherapy than is description of behavior.

In contrast to our findings, Bieber and his group reported that heterosexual contact before the age of sixteen suggested a greater likelihood that a patient would remain in analysis and be converted to heterosexuality but that homosexual experiences before the age of sixteen are of no prognostic significance. Bieber's results and ours are, however, in agreement that the presence of manifest erotic heterosexual content in dreams is directly correlated with heterosexual improvement.

Table 17–7.

Variable factors in sexual history.

	Group Classification			
	A	B	C	
	No. of patients in each group			
	9	5	5	
	No. of patients in each category			Total
Homosexual contacts				
Age of first homosexual experience involving physical contact (in years)	16.4	14.2	9.4	
First homosexual contact before age sixteen	2	2	4	8
First homosexual *relationship* before age sixteen	2	1	3	6
Mean age of first homosexual relationship involving three or more repeated homosexual contact experiences with same partner	18.6	16.6	15.6	
Mean duration of active homosexuality prior to therapy (in years)	9.5	10.4	12.0	
Heterosexual contacts				
Mean age of first heterosexual experience involving physical contact	18.3	18.0	13.3	
First heterosexual contact before age sixteen	2	2	3	7
Mean age of first voluntary attempt at heterosexual coitus	23.6	21.4	20.7	
First heterosexual coitus at age twenty-one or younger	4	2	3	9
First heterosexual coitus before therapy	6	4	4	14
Erotic heterosexual dreams prior to therapy	6	0	1	7

Illustrative Case Histories

For purposes of illustration, four cases typical of the three groups of therapeutic evaluation at follow-up are presented. Included are two successful cases in Group A, one moderately successful case in Group B, and one failure in Group C.

The first case provides an example of a highly successful therapeutic outcome in a "true" female homosexual. Paradoxically, Miss A first sought treatment at the age of thirty-eight in a period of acute depression precipitated by her male lover's threat of desertion.

Her mother had died when she was six years old; her father, a cold and rejecting figure, had been alcoholic and an economic failure. The patient had been raised by rather indifferent relatives. In her youth she had had few friends and was constantly searching for a strong mother figure. But, as a helpless child, she had also sought her father's love; he, however, had rejected her, and she felt a great deal of rage and fear toward him, which were later displaced to other male figures. The patient had had no sexual experiences, other than mild petting with one boy in college, until she was 29, when she had been seduced by an older, dominating, aggressive woman, with whom she began an active homosexual relationship. The patient was the more passive in sexual play, her partner fulfilling her dependency needs, but as time went on the patient felt more and more shame at the sexual relationship. She had stopped living with this woman two years before she began therapy but continued to see her periodically. During these two years, she had become attracted to two unaggressive and weak males who "reminded me of my father." Sex was difficult and the infrequent coitus nonorgastic and less pleasurable than homosexual relations, yet the relationship with the second man provided satisfactory dependency support. Relations with her female partner became progressively strained, and the strain was accentuated by discussions of homosexual psychopathology in a social work course the patient was attending when she started treatment.

When first seen in therapy, the patient was severely disturbed, with a confused self-image but a strong desire to get well. She usually dressed plainly but had no masculine affectations. The diagnosis was depressive psychoneurotic reaction. (In our evaluation, the patient's heterosexual adjustment was graded as "2" on a five-point scale.) Treatment consisted of reassurance and dynamically oriented reparative therapy during seventy-two sessions over a nine-month period. Therapy was largely directed toward increasing her ego strength and insight into her maladaptive patterns. Toward the end of therapy, the patient broke off homosexual relationships and married her lover. Treatment was terminated by the patient with the therapist's approval. All symptoms of acute anxiety had been resolved, but prognosis was guarded, dependent upon the success of the marriage.

The follow-up came 8.7 years after termination of therapy. The patient was by then a well-dressed, quite feminine middle-aged woman. She was still married and had a young son. She had been troubled by homosexual fantasies during the first year of her marriage but since then had enjoyed frequent orgastic coitus. Her relationship with her husband had developed into one of mutual dependency with complete rejection of her old homosexual partner. She had become increasingly active and aggressive in her social work, successfully directing several important projects. Socially and professionally she felt increasingly secure and confident in dealings with men. This patient was rated as "much improved" in all categories.

Mr. B is an example of a "pseudohomosexual" who was also considered to be "much improved" at follow-up. This patient applied for treatment at age twenty-nine while he was working toward an M.S.W. degree.

As a child the patient had never adequately identified with his father, a retiring, distant, henpecked man. The principle male figure in the family had been an older brother, an athletic and aggressive person who had developed infectious encephalitis at age eighteen, followed by a psychotic break and eventual death in a mental hospital. This brother had been sexually promiscuous before his illness, but these traits had later been accentuated and had included homosexual advances toward the patient. Mr. B had become terrified of aggressive sexuality and of assertive activities in general; this fear had been reinforced by maternal infantilization and by a quite seductive but castrating older sister. The patient's character was marked by feelings of inferiority, passivity, and low self-esteem. In the patient's mind, indecision = inferiority = passivity = feminization = homosexuality.

The patient had had several unsuccessful heterosexual experiences as a youth and fearfully avoided the excessive homosexual practices prevalent in his prisoner-of-war camp during World War II. His sole homosexual experience had consisted of mutual masturbation with a crippled buddy in the POW camp. Most pretherapy heterosexual experiences had been with aggressive females who had "seduced me"; these experiences had been marked by premature ejaculation and fear of penetration.

At the beginning of therapy, he had appeared acutely disturbed and was suffering from numerous, almost incapacitating, symptoms, mostly arising from his fears of social, occupational, and sexual inadequacy. He was masculine in appearance. Primary diagnosis was psychoneurotic anxiety reaction with depressive overtones. (He was rated at stage 2 in all spheres of adjustment.)

Treatment consisted of 239 reparative psychotherapeutic sessions, held two or three times a week over one and one-half years. Definite but not marked improvement was noted by the time the therapist concluded treatment. The principle achievement was an increase in insight, gained through an understanding of pseudohomosexual dynamics and leading to somewhat more assertive sexual and social behavior.

At follow-up nine years after conclusion of therapy, the patient appeared much improved. He had left social work and was doing well in a responsible position as manager of a large suburban branch of a retail store. Shortly after therapy he had married a woman whom the original therapist had described as "severely emotionally disturbed" and who at the time of follow-up appeared to be a severely phobic psychoneurotic. The patient, however, showed remarkable ability to control and to solve realistically his many marital problems and was completely oriented heterosexually.

Mr. C is an example of a merely fair long-term therapeutic result in a chronic homosexual. He was considered much improved (Class A) at termination of therapy but only moderately improved (Class B) at follow-up. When accepted for treatment he was twenty-three and employed as a graduate social worker. His primary motivation for treatment was to alleviate severe anxiety symptoms.

During Mr. C's childhood, his father had been away from home most of the time and, even when home, had showered all his affection on one of the patient's younger brothers. His mother was the punitive authority figure in the family, and the patient was her favorite. He was sheltered and overprotected by his mother, who, while occasionally seductive, was usually harsh and extremely denigrating both physically and psychologically. His intense fear of women in later life was interpreted as the result of equating women with mother, who represented authority and castration. His behavioral pattern exhibited fear of social or sexual aggressiveness. He had had only scattered platonic heterosexual relationships up to the beginning of therapy, but his first overt homosexual contact had occurred at age sixteen. By the end of his first year in college, the patient had become an active homosexual, his activities including mutual masturbation and fellatio, in which he was usually the insertee. He preferred younger, effeminate partners in these activities, probably reflecting his search for feeding dependence and concomitant defeat of his younger sibling.

His anxiety symptoms had been acutely intensified when he was placed in a responsible position upon graduation from social-work school, and they had prompted his application for psychiatric aid. Diagnosis was passive-dependent personality trait disturbance plus acute anxiety neurosis. The patient seemed moderately well motivated for therapy and desirous of achieving heterosexual adjustment, although he was uncertain whether or not it would be possible. Although he dressed in a masculine manner, he exhibited several effeminate mannerisms.

He was seen three to four times a week for a total of more than 400 reconstructive sessions during a period of 3.8 years, and he was thought much improved in all areas at the end of therapy. He had achieved significant insight into his own psychodynamics, most of his anxiety symptoms had abated, and he had gained new self-assurance and aggressiveness in interpersonal relationships and occupational activities. He moved from passive homosexual acts to being the insertor in anal intercourse to confidence with women and finally to heterosexual coitus, albeit with continuing occasional homosexual fantasies and affairs. Treatment was discontinued because of the therapist's move to another city. Further therapy was advised, but the patient did not seek further help.

At follow-up, 4.7 years later, the patient had further consolidated his gains in social and occupational adjustment, insight, emotional stability, and ego strength. He had married shortly after the conclusion of therapy, and sexual relations with his wife had been initially satisfying; she had immediately become pregnant. The patient's security was, however, threatened by his mate's dominant, aggressive behavior and deprecating attitudes. Within five to six months after marriage, the patient began to return to homosexual outlets, and his marriage accordingly deteriorated. He eventually obtained a divorce and for a year before follow-up had been living with another homosexual male. He exhibited considerable insight into his sexual dynamics and the disintegration of his marriage, however. His homosexual activities were no longer promiscuous or compulsive, as they had been before therapy, and he was sexually "more satisfied than ever before."

Miss D presents a complete therapeutic failure. She was twenty-four when she began therapy. She had left school after the eleventh grade and had worked as a clerk-typist. Her presenting problem was severe depression with suicidal impulses.

The patient had a chaotic family background. She was born two days after her parents' marriage and raised by a maternal grandmother and aunt and uncle. The grandmother was an extremely rigid and punitive religious fanatic, who preached that sex was a cardinal sin. The aunt was probably psychotic; she was emotionally unstable and continuously ambivalent toward the patient. The uncle was a completely passive man and was frightened by any display of emotion or affection. The mother lived a sexually promiscuous life and entirely rejected any relationship with the patient. Also in Miss D's family constellation was an older (five years) mentally defective cousin, who subjected the patient to various forms of psychic and physical violence, including forced coitus, when the patient was between the ages of six and eleven. The patient began to drink and date when she was about twelve, and she engaged in regular, nonorgastic coitus with an older male youth between the ages of thirteen and eighteen.

She associated heterosexual coitus with filth and depravity. Overt homosexual activity was begun in play at about the age of six and continued intermittently until the age of seventeen or eighteen, when the patient formed the first of several semipermanent relationships with older homosexual women. The patient exhibited tremendous guilt about her homosexual relations, although she regarded homosexuality as free of filth and violence and consequently usually quite pleasurable. She always adopted the passive homosexual role and finally had seemed to gain some sense of love and security while living with an older woman for two years before therapy.

At the start of treatment, the patient was an attractive young woman who dressed with a masculine flair and affected masculine mannerisms. She was severely depressed and hysterical with an almost complete lack of identity. Therapeutic motivation was marked by magical expectations. Diagnosis was chronic undifferentiated schizophrenia. Supportive and beginning reparative therapy was attempted for about 120 sessions, once a week, for 2.3 years. The patient showed superficial improvement in mood, ego strength, psychosomatic symptoms, and social relationships, and her fear of men began to diminish, although she never reached the point of accepting dates with men. The patient eventually deserted therapy, and she and her homosexual partner moved to another state. On the over-all rating, she was considered "slightly improved" at the end of therapy.

The follow-up took place eight months after the termination of therapy. Having lost the support of her doctor, the patient had decompensated on all levels and presented essentially the same clinical picture as at the beginning of therapy.

Summary and Conclusions

To estimate the success of psychotherapy in homosexuality and the factors associated with therapeutic success or failure, a follow-up study of nineteen patients (fourteen males and five females) with homosexual problems was conducted. The mean duration of therapy was 1.7 years, and the mean interval between end of therapy and the follow-up was 4.5 years.

In the over-all evaluation at the time of follow-up, 47.3 per cent of patients were found to be "apparently recovered" or "much improved," and 26.3 per cent of patients were "improved" in comparison to their statuses at the beginning of therapy. In the majority of patients, the follow-up revealed progress in all behavioral areas since the end of treatment.

For a comparison of patient change from beginning of therapy to follow-up, the sample population was divided according to the over-all evaluations into three groups: Group A patients were "apparently recovered" or "much improved"; Group B patients were "improved"; Group C patients were "slightly improved," "unimproved," or "worse." The following conclusions are based on the data:

A. Factors in our study not amenable to differential analysis
   1. patients' religions
   2. patients' occupations
   3. age and sex of therapists
   4. professional experience of therapists
B. Factors definitely not correlated with the patient change
   1. patients' ages at start of therapy
   2. patients' sexes
C. Equivocal factors
   1. lower frequency of therapy sessions for Group C patients
   2. reparative therapy perhaps more successful than reconstructive therapy (note that there were only three cases treated by psychoanalysis)
   3. lower educational and socioeconomic level in Group C patients than in groups A and B
   4. a suggestive direct correlation between increased age at the beginning of overt homosexual and heterosexual activity and increased improvement during and after psychotherapy; Group C patients definitely had been more active sexually at more precocious ages
D. Factors of definite prognostic value
   1. abandoning psychotherapy usually indicative of therapeutic failure
   2. the more severe the psychopathology, the less the chance for improvement

3. the degree of patients' therapeutic motivation directly correlated with the degree of therapeutic success
4. better responses in "pseudohomosexuals" than in "true" homosexuals (note that only two of our nineteen cases were "pseudohomosexuals")
5. patients who had had erotic heterosexual dreams prior to therapy generally most improved at follow-up
6. initial degree of heterosexual orientation (psychodynamically) directly correlated with the degree of heterosexual improvement at follow-up
7. presence of overt cross-sexual mannerisms usually indicative of poor prognosis.

Although the sample in this study was too small to produce data of definite statistical significance, it is hoped that the trends indicated by the results will be of value to those interested in the psychotherapy of homosexuality and that the therapeutic concepts proposed and the therapeutic successes achieved will help to refute certain defeatist points of view like that implied in the recent report of the British Committee on Homosexual Offenses and Prostitution (1957): "We were struck by the fact that none of our medical witnesses were able, when we saw them, to provide any reference in medical literature to a complete change. . . . our evidence leads us to the conclusion that a total reorientation from a complete homosexual to a complete heterosexual is very unlikely indeed."

As Bieber (Bieber *et al.*, 1962) reported that 19 per cent of his group's cases changed from "complete homosexuality to complete heterosexuality," and as we now can report that 22 per cent of our patients made such sexual reversals, therapists should take hope that this change is possible. And there is, accordingly, still greater hope for those patients who, while still primarily homosexual, retain important remnants of heterosexual behavior or fantasies. If the developmental sexual fears, guilty fears, and miscarried attempts to reduce these fears while searching for some degree of sexual pleasure, however inappropriate, have not completely extinguished heterosexual strivings, there is an even chance that psychotherapy can effect significant changes in the patients' sexual lives, as in other spheres of behavior.

We also urge that, both diagnostically and therapeutically, homosexual orientation and behavior not be regarded as separate nosologic entities but as partial manifestations of more basic adaptational disorders.

APPENDIX A

Methodology

Four procedures were involved in the study: selecting the cases, reviewing the charts, conducting follow-up interviews, and conducting follow-up Rorschach testing.

Selection of cases was performed by reviewing charts of all H.M.P.C. patients who had been recorded on the McBee Clinic Keysort Card (Lief, Lief, Warren, & Heath, 1961) as having "homosexual personality disturbance" as part of their diagnoses.

From a review of the charts, a profile of each patient was compiled and recorded in a protocol form, which is reproduced in Appendix B (see p. 336). Section 2-B on pattern of sexual behavior was based on Rado's classification (1956). The diagnosis of true homosexual versus pseudohomosexual conflict in Section 2-C was applied in accordance with Ovesey's concepts (1954; 1955a; 1955b). Sections 2-D and 2-E on family constellation and sexual history were adapted from Bieber (Bieber *et al.*, 1962). Sections 2-F, 2-G, 3-A, and 4-B were modified from an evaluation system proposed by Malan (1959). The patients' statuses at the beginning and at the end of treatment were rated according to the scales in sections 5-B, 5-C, and 5-D. These five-point rating scales were adapted and modified from those of Miles *et al.* (1951). In several charts no mention was made of change in structured symptoms. The symptomatic evaluation was therefore supplemented by having each patient complete a Cornell Medical Index (Broadman, Deutschberger, Erdmann, Lorge, & Wolff, 1954; Broadman, Erdmann, Lorge, Gershenson, & Wolff, 1952a; Broadman *et al.*, 1952; Broadman, Erdmann, Lorge, & Wolff, 1954), hereafter referred to as CMI, which was modified to include a self-evaluation of the presence and the degree of severity of the patients' somatic and psychological symptoms at the beginning of therapy, at the end of therapy, and at follow-up. The parts of the CMI analyzed included areas M through

R in which all questions relate to mood and feeling patterns and those symptoms in other areas of the CMI thought relevant. It was impossible to rate this evaluation on the scale, so, again according to Miles's method, the symptoms from the CMI and the chart were scored on three degrees of severity, as indicated in Section 5-A of Appendix B. Symptomatic status was summarized by adding the total scores.

For follow-up, the patients who still lived in New Orleans were contacted and asked to come in for joint interviews, with two psychiatrists, lasting about one hour each. The interviews were loosely structured within the limits of covering as thoroughly as possible the topics of occupational, marital, and sexual adjustments, interpersonal relationships, and degree of insight. The CMI that each patient had completed was reviewed with him, and any newly discovered symptom changes were noted.

The patients who had moved out of town were sent CMIs and detailed questionnaires covering the same general topics as were discussed in the interviews.

Immediately following the interview, or on receipt of a questionnaire, each interviewer separately evaluated the patient's follow-up status according to the criteria listed in the five-point rating scales described in Appendix B. Generally the interviewers' evaluations concurred; the occasional minor disagreements never involved rating differences of more than one level of the scale and were resolved by joint reviews of the interview material.

Using the patients' pretreatment statuses as baselines, summaries were then made of changes in status at both the end of treatment and at the follow-up time according to the categories listed in sections 6-A through 6-D. An over-all evaluation was then made, based on the criteria listed in Section 6-E. This appraisal was subjective and based partly on the numerical rating but chiefly determined by the interviewers' discussion of the clinic chart and the interview. Although less easily defined in explicit terms, such an over-all appraisal seemed to give a more sensitive and representative picture of the patient.

The Rorschach tests were administered to the patients still residing in New Orleans during subsequent appointments with the staff psychologist. As far as possible, the responses were analyzed with the same protocol employed for the interview material, the current card responses being compared to the individual card responses recorded during the initial Rorschach. Although some investigators have found that psychological tests are of questionable significance in evaluating the results of psychotherapy (Barron, 1953; Carr, 1949), others have found that the Rorschach and TAT tests are valid indices in determining homosexual orientation (Davids, Joelson, & McArthur, 1956). As most of the patients in the study group had been given Rorschach tests just before or soon after the commencement of therapy, we thought it would be of interest to correlate the findings from the follow-up Rorschach tests with the evaluations made through the follow-up interviews. This phase of the study is not yet complete and will be reported at a later date.

Description of the Population Studied

Of the forty patients eligible for the follow-up study, three had died since the completion of therapy, and six could not be located. Of the thirty-one remaining, sixteen were still living in the New Orleans area, and of these thirteen or 81 per cent agreed to follow-up interviews. When contacted by telephone, one who refused, a woman who had discontinued therapy after only five interviews, stated that she "got nothing out of psychotherapy." Another patient stated that he was "much improved" since terminating therapy but repeatedly resisted making a definite interview appointment. A third declined to answer any questions over the telephone or in writing. The fifteen patients living outside the New Orleans area were sent questionnaires; six or 40 per cent responded. As these six cases were fairly evenly distributed throughout the range of over-all follow-up evaluation categories, they were considered a representative sample of the total group and were therefore included.

The group of nineteen cases studied exhibited the following characteristics:

Sex distribution (fourteen males and five females). When this factor is compared with the almost 1:1 ratio among all patients seen in the H.M.P.C., it is in keeping with Kinsey's (Kinsey *et al.*, 1953) report that homosexual males outnumber females by almost two to one and our clinical findings that male homosexuals more frequently apply for treatment.

Age of commencement of therapy (range eighteen to forty years; mean 27.7 years). Over half the group was within the twenty-to-thirty-year age span, suggesting that patients with homosexual problems who seek psychiatric aid usually apply as young adults.

Religion and race (nine Protestants, five Roman Catholics, two Jews, three unaffiliated). All patients were white.

Educational level. One patient had completed only the eleventh grade in high school; one had had two years of university education; two were university graduates, and fourteen (74 per cent) were either in graduate school or had graduate degrees when they began treatment ment. This distribution partially reflects the high educational level of the general patient population in our clinic (13 per cent of whom are college graduates only, while an additional 40 per cent have done some graduate work (Lief *et al.*, 1961); the increase above the mean clinic level possibly supports Kinsey's observations (Kinsey *et al.*, 1948; Kinsey *et al.*, 1953) that the incidence of homosexuality increases with the level of education.

Social class at follow-up. The (two-factor index) system Hollingshead and Redlich (1958) devised to combine educational and occupational levels to determine social position was applied to the homosexual group. Psychotherapy did not seem to effect length of schooling or occupation significantly, and, as so many patients were students during the therapy period, the group was classified according to status at the time of follow-up. According to the Hollingshead-Redlich scale, the social-class distribution was Class I, five patients; Class II, ten patients; Class III, three patients; Class IV, one patient. As was true of educational level alone, this distribution is slightly higher than that reported for the Resident Clinic as a whole (Lief *et al.*, 1961). Occupations at time of follow-up ranged from a stock room clerk to several college teachers, a physician, and a clergyman and included eight practicing social workers. Fourteen of the fifteen patients in classes I and II were in professional fields, and all the lower-class patients were white collar workers.

Follow-up interim. The range of duration between the end of psychiatric treatment and the follow-up interview or questionnaire was 0.5–9.0 years; mean interim was 4.5 years. Zubin (1953) has reported that a five-year follow-up is the ideal interval for a psychiatric study, as there is usually little change in a patient's status in the five-to-fifteen-year post-treatment interval.

APPENDIX B

Protocol Form Used in the Study

1. *Identifying and vital data:* name, clinic number, address, age, race, sex, religion, occupation, socioeconomic level, educational level
2. *Outline of original illness and treatment*

A. Chief complaint:
B. Pattern of sexual behavior:
    1. situational homosexuality
    2. variational or incidental homosexuality
    3. reparative homosexuality
        a. organ replacement
        b. sexual pain dependence
            1. sadistic
            2. masochistic
    4. contact avoidance
        a. self-exposure
        b. voyeur
    5. solitary gratification
        a. fetishistic
        b. transvestite
        c. orgastic dream or daydream in illusory twosome
            1. heterosexual type
            2. homosexual type
        d. blank orgastic self-stimulation
            1. physical masturbation
            2. mental masturbation
        e. surprise orgasm
    6. homogeneous pairs
        a. stable
        b. fickle
    7. adult–child pairs
    8. human–animal pairs
    9. pattern involving two or more mates
        a. dignified mate versus degraded mate
        b. alimentary love objects versus orgastic love objects
        c. other
C. Homosexual conflict:
    1. true homosexual conflict
        a. dependency prominent
        b. power prominent
    2. pseudohomosexual conflict
        a. dependency
        b. power
D. Family constellation:
    1. mother: close-binding intimate; controlling dominating; detached-hostile; not-detached, hostile; mother surrogate; unclassifiable mother; detached, poorly related

2. father: detached-ambivalent; detached-hostile; detached-in-
   different; not detached, ambivalent; not detached, hostile; not
   detached, overprotective; absent; detached-dominating-ex-
   ploitative; unclassified
3. sibling rivalry: with brothers; with sisters; outcome; no siblings; siblings, but no rivalry, detached

E. Sexual history:
   1. heterosexual contacts: age first heterosexual experience in-
      volving physical contact; age first attempted heterosexual
      coitus; first heterosexual coitus before, during, or after ther-
      apy; erotic heterosexual dreams prior to therapy
   2. homosexual contacts: age first homosexual experience involv-
      ing physical contact; age first sustained homosexual relation-
      ship; duration active homosexuality prior to therapy
   3. attitude toward homosexuality

F. Brief outline of disturbances in patient's life
G. Minimum psychodynamic hypothesis required to explain pattern
   of behavior
H. Diagnosis (APA classification)
I. Aim and ideal result of treatment

3. *Outline of psychotherapy*
   A. Aim and ideal result of treatment
   B. Motivation for therapy: strong; moderate; slight; unmotivated
   C. Therapist: name; age; sex; training and experience
   D. Type of psychotherapy: ventilation without interruptions by the
      therapist; reassurance; explanation of symptoms on simple physi-
      ologic level; situational manipulation; suggestion; insight therapy
      dynamically oriented:
      1. reconstructive
      2. reparative
   E. Therapy details: inclusive dates; number of sessions; frequency
      of sessions; age of patient at start of therapy; treatment con-
      cluded due to:
      1. external reasons
      2. patient decided to discontinue therapy
      3. therapist decided treatment was completed
      4. hospitalization, psychiatric

4. *Interim history*
   A. Duration of interim:
      1. date treatment concluded
      2. dates and details of subsequent psychiatric treatment
      3. date of follow-up interview questionnaire

B. Life situation since treatment:
  1. change in environmental situation: residence; employment; education; marriage
  2. change in environmental stress

5. *Evaluation ratings* (at beginning and end of treatment)

A. Psychic and psychosomatic symptoms:
  1. rating: 1 = mild or occasional symptoms
              2 = moderate in intensity or frequently present
              3 = severe or almost constant
  2. list of symptoms from old chart
  3. patient's description of symptoms
  4. list of symptoms from Cornell Medical Index
  5. summary (additive weights of all symptoms)

B. Social adjustment:
  1. occupational adjustment
    1 = unable to work because of the mental illness
    2 = unable to work more than 50 per cent of the time, which might include long periods of continuous inability to work, running into weeks or months; or frequent short absences from work, such as days or weeks
    3 = able to work most of the time, with only short periods of inability to work, such as occasional days or weeks off
    4 = able to work steadily, but because of psychiatric problems, there is definitely impaired efficiency
  2. interpersonal relationships
    1 = unable to make and maintain adequate human relationships
    2 = unable to make and maintain more than a few adequate relationships; marked ambivalence toward most of the people in the social orbit, or able to maintain relationships only with perpetuation of neurotic symptoms
    3 = able to make and maintain adequate relationships with most people, most of the time, but may have marked ambivalence toward a few specific figures in the social orbit
    4 = able to make and maintain smooth and consistent relationships with only minor conflicts
    5 = no apparent disturbances in interpersonal relationships

C. Depth of insight:
    1 = does not consciously admit psychogenic factors in the illness
    2 = admits psychic nature of illness, but constructs vague

rationalizations such as "nervous breakdown" "hormone imbalance," etc.

3 = admits the relationship of emotional difficulties to the illness, but insight is mainly intellectual; a tendency to blame others for inner conflicts persists

4 = realizes the significance and personal origin of past emotional conflicts, but rejects insight that would occasion severe narcissistic trauma

5 = deeper insight into ambivalence and inner conflicts, including those arising from erotic urges and aggressive drives previously repressed

D. Sexual adjustment:

1. heterosexual adjustment

1 = unable to tolerate heterosexual genital relations; complete impotence, cannot permit intercourse (women); able to utilize only perverse methods of gratification; homosexual relations with marked guilt or anxiety; adults who are restricted to masturbation because of neurotic conflicts

2 = marked difficulties in heterosexual relations; disgust, anxiety, disturbing fantasies, or symptoms which inhibit genital activity; partial impotence, premature ejaculations most of the time, frigidity which permits rare or occasional intercourse without pleasure or orgasm; frequent reliance upon perverse activity as an adjunct to genital relationship

3 = able to perform heterosexually, but without consistent pleasure or potency; some premature ejaculations, partial frigidity; satisfaction restricted in various ways by guilt, fears of pregnancy, fears of infection, etc.

4 = able to derive pleasure and satisfaction in intercourse most of the time, with only minor difficulties or dissatisfaction

5 = able to enjoy mature, consistently satisfactory heterosexual adjustment without significant conflicts

2. marital adjustment

1 = completely unsatisfactory marriage; patient and spouse separated because of neurotic conflicts (separations because of realistic factors are not included here)

2 = difficulties in many areas of the marriage; finances, common interests, personal habits, friends, inlaws, religion, sexual relations, children, etc.

    3 = difficulties in a few areas of the marriage

    4 = marriage mutually satisfactory to patient and spouse except for minor problems, or the marriage was satisfactory in all areas except sexual

    5 = marriage consistently satisfactory and harmonious for patient and spouse

6. *Evaluation summaries* (In comparison to status at beginning of therapy, separate ratings were made for status at the end of therapy and at follow-up.)

A. Symptomatic evaluation:

    1 = worse; total additive weights exceeds pretherapy total by more than one-eighth

    2 = unimproved; same number as pretherapy total, plus or minus one-eighth

    3 = slightly improved; retained two-thirds to seven-eighths of pretherapy total

    4 = improved; retained one-fourth to two-thirds of pretherapy total

B. Social evaluation:

    1 = worse; total social adjustment is less adequate than at the beginning of therapy

    2 = unimproved; no change in total social adjustment

    3 = slightly improved; total social adjustment shows less than one level of improvement

    4 = improved; total social adjustment has improved by one level in the rating scales

    5 = much improved; total social adjustment has improved by more than one level in the rating scales

C. Insight evaluation (same scale as used in 6-B):

D. Sexual evaluation (same scale as used in social evaluation): (6B)

E. Over-all evaluation:

    1 = worse; a decline in all phases of adjustment, with an increase in number and degree of symptoms

    2 = unimproved; some improvement in the fields of social adjustment and/or depth of insight, and symptoms, but no improvement in sexual adjustment

    3 = slightly improved; slight or variable improvement in symptomatic, social and/or sexual adjustment or apparently more marked improvement is actually due to superficial changes in environmental stresses or situation

    4 = improved; definite improvement in sexual adjustment,

with some associated gain in the social, symptomatic and depth of insight fields. Several elements of the original dynamic patterns still persist, however, and the total adjustment does not closely coincide with the expected ideal results.

5 = much improved; basic reorientation in sexual areas and marked improvement in symptoms, sexual adjustment and depth of insight. Under severe stress a transient exacerbation of the original drives and patterns might occur.

6 = apparently recovered; recovery from symptoms (except possibly for one or two complaints) and marked improvement in depth of insight, social and especially sexual adjustment, with no return to original patterns even under severe stress. This implies a complete and stable recovery.

7. Diagnosis at follow-up interview

8. General comments, including: an appraisal of the accuracy and completeness of the old chart; the resistance of the patient to coming for interview or returning the questionnaire; the general appearance and behavior of the patient at the interview; comments on points in each area not adequately covered by the rating scales

REFERENCES

Barron, F. Some test correlates of response to psychotherapy. *J. consult. Psychol.*, 1953, **17**, 235-241.

Bieber, I., Dain, H. J., Dince, P. R., Drellich, M. G., Grand, H. G., Gundlach, R. H., Kremer, Malvina W., Rifkin, A. H., Wilbur, Cornelia B., & Bieber, Toby B. *Homosexuality: a psychoanalytic study of male homosexuals.* New York: Basic Books, 1962.

Broadman, K., Deutschberger, J., Erdmann, A. J., Jr., Lorge, I., & Wolff, H. G. Prediction of adequacy for military service. *U.S. armed force med. J.*, 1954, **5**, 1802-1808.

Broadman, K., Erdmann, A. J., Jr., Lorge, I., Gershenson, C., & Wolff, H. G. The Cornell medical index-health questionnaire III. the evaluation of emotional disturbances. *J. clin. Psychol.*, 1952, 8, 119-124.

Broadman, K., Erdmann, A. J., Jr., Lorge, I., Gershenson, C., & Wolff, H. G. The recognition of emotional disturbances in a general hospital. *J. clin. Psychol.*, 1952, 8, 289-293.

Broadman, K., Erdmann, A. J., Jr., Lorge, I., & Wolff, H. G. The Cornell medical index-health questionnaire II. as a diagnostic instrument. *J. Amer. med. Ass.*, 1951, **145**, 152-157.

Carr, A. C. An evaluation of nine nondirective psychotherapy cases by means of the Rorschach. *J. consult. Psychol.*, 1949, **13**, 196-205.

Curran, D., & Parr, D. Homosexuality: an analysis of 100 male cases seen in private practice. *Brit. Med. J.*, 1957, **1**, 797-801.

Davids, J., Joelson, M., & McArthur, C. Rorschach and TAT indices of homosexuality in overt homosexuals, neurotics and normal males. *J. abnorm. Psychol.*, 1956, **53**, 161-172.

Ellis, A. The effectiveness of psychotherapy with individuals who have severe homosexual problems. *J. consult. Psychol.*, 1956, **20**, 191-195.

Fenichel, O. *The psychoanalytic theory of neurosis.* (2nd ed.) New York: Norton, 1945.

Freud, S. In J. Strachey (Trans.), *Three essays on the theory of sexuality.* New York: Basic Books, 1962.

Green, M. R. (Ed.). *Interpersonal analysis: the selected papers of Clara M. Thompson.* New York: Basic Books, 1964.

Hemphill, R. E., Leitch, A., & Stuart, J. R. A factual study of male homosexuality. *Brit. Med. J.*, 1958, **1**, 1317-1323.

Herzog, E. Some guide lines for evaluative research. U.S. Dept. of Health, Education and Welfare, Soc. Security Admin., Children's Bureau, Washington, D.C., 1959.

Hollingshead, A. B., & Redlich, F. C. *Social class and mental illness.* New York: Wiley, 1958.

Hunt, R. G. Social class in mental illness: some implications for clinical theory and practice. *Amer. J. Psychiat.*, 1960, **116**, 1065-1069.

Kinsey, A. C., Pomeroy, W. B., & Martin, C. E. *Sexual behavior in the human male.* New York: Saunders, 1948.

Kinsey, A. C., Pomeroy, W. B., Martin, C. E., & Gebhard, P. H. *Sexual behavior in the human female.* New York: Saunders, 1953.

Knight, R. P. Evaluation of the results of psychoanalytic therapy. *Amer. J. Psychiat.*, 1941, **98**, 434-446.

Krafft-Ebing, R. von. *Psychopathia sexualis.* Philadelphia: Davis, 1892.

Lief, H. I., Lief, V. F., Warren, C. O., & Heath, R. G. Low dropout rate in a psychiatric clinic. *Arch. gen. Psychiat.*, 1961, **5**, 200-211.

Löfgren, L. B. Difficulties and ambiguities in using "results" as an evaluating norm in psychiatry. *Brit. J. med. Psychol.*, 1960, **33**, 95-103.

Malan, D. On assessing the results of psychotherapy. *Brit. J. med. Psychol.*, 1959, **32**, 86-105.

Miles, H. H. W., Barrabee, E. L., & Finesinger, J. E. Evaluation of psychotherapy. *Psychosom. Med.*, 1951, **13**, 82-105.

Monroe, R. R., & Enelow, M. L. The therapeutic motivation in male homosexuals. *Amer. J. Psychother.*, 1960, **14**, 474-490.

Oberndorf, C. P. Consideration of results with psychoanalytic therapy. *Amer. J. Psychiat.*, 1942, **99**, 374-381.

Oberndorf, C. P., Greenacre, P., & Kubie, L. Symposium on the evaluation of therapeutic results. *Int. J. Psychoanal.*, 1948, **29**, 7-33.

Ovesey, L. The homosexual conflict. *Psychiat.*, 1954, **17**, 243-250.

Ovesey, L. Pseudohomosexual anxiety. *Psychiat.*, 1955a, **18**, 17-25.

Ovesey, L. Pseudohomosexuality, the paranoid mechanism and paranoia. *Psychiat.*, 1955b, **18**, 163-173.

Poe, J. S. The successful treatment of a 40-year-old passive homosexual based on an adaptational view of sexual behavior. *Psychoanal. Rev.*, 1952, **39**, 23-33.

Rado, S. A critical examination of the concept of bisexuality. *Psychosom. Med.*, 1940, **2**, 459-467.

Rado, S. An adaptational view of sexual behavior. In *Psychoanalysis of Behavior*. New York: Grune & Stratton, 1956. Pp. 186-213.

Report of the Committee on Homosexual Offences and Prostitution (*Wolfenden Report*.) London: Her Majesty's Stationery Office, 1957.

Rosenbaum, M., Friedlander, J., & Kaplan, S. M. Evaluation of the results of psychotherapy. *Psychosom. Med.*, 1956, **18**, 113-132.

Rubinstein, L. H. Psychotherapeutic aspects of male homosexuality. *Brit. J. med. Psychol.*, 1958, **31**, 14-18.

Stevenson, I. The challenge of results in psychotherapy. *Amer. J. Psychiat.*, 1959, **116**, 120-123.

Woodward, M. The diagnosis and treatment of homosexual offenders. *Brit. J. Delinq.*, 1956, **9**, 44-59.

Zubin, J. Evaluation of therapeutic outcome in mental disorders. *J. nerv. ment. Dis.*, 1953, **117**, 95-111.

These cases were taken from the Department of Psychiatry and Neurology, Tulane University School of Medicine, New Orleans, Louisiana.

We should like to express our appreciation of the help rendered by Thomas Fulmer, M.D., who aided in the interviewing of patients and the analysis of data, and by James Alan Long, Ph.D., who did the psychological testing. Henry H. W. Miles, M.D., and Morton Enelow, M.D., made some helpful editorial suggestions.

INDEX

Abraham, Karl, 203
Achilles, 159
Acta Sanctorum, 160
acting out, 258, 320
Adam and Eve, 158, 162
adaptability, learning and, 10
adaptive responses, 220, 268
Adon, 149
Adonis, 154
adultery, in ancient world, 147; and
    Hebrew religion, 150
advertising, 134, 223
Aeschylus and Athens (Thomson), 168 n.
age limits, in "gay" bars, 100
agenesis, ovarian, 51
aggression, defined, 28; fear of, 256-
    258, 326-328; of male, 238-239, 256-
    258, 273; in mother, 5, 276, 287;
    sexual mannerisms and, 58-61; thera-
    peutic motivation and, 321; in
    women, 5, 273, 276, 287, 297, 327
alcohol, 238, 329
Alcoholics Anonymous, 265
alcoholism, 265, 294, 325, 329
Alcuin, 144
Alexander, Franz, 244-245
Allan, E., 179
Allee, W. C., 36
Allport, Gordon W., 103-104
alpha-estradiol, 50, 53
Amazons, 159
ambisexuality, 11; in animals, 27-42;
    defined, 28; *see also* bisexuality
amenorrhea, 50, 53
American Indians, 13, 63, 116, 119-120
amplexus, in frogs, 34
Anaitis, 149
anal intercourse, 41, 224; in primates,
    328; symbolism of, 257; *see also* ped-
    erasty; sodomy
anal interest, 88

anal masturbation, 215
anal rape, 216
analyst(s), as transferential father, 260;
    women as, 262, 293-294; *see also* psy-
    chotherapy; therapist
Anat, 149, 154
ancient world, adultery in, 147; gender
    role-changes in, 151-154; homosexu-
    ality and prostitution in, 146-148
Andaman Islanders, 13, 114, 116, 118
androgen, 38, 71; in castrated fowl, 37;
    in eunuchism, 48-49; gonadal pro-
    duction of, 52; libido and, 55; "or-
    ganizing" effect of, 39; sex object
    and, 57; sex-organ sensitivity and, 66;
    in women, 68
animals, ambisexuality in, 27-42; domi-
    nance–subordination roles in, 31-33;
    homosexuality in, 11, 41, 328
annelid worms, 30
Anolis, 34-35
antihomosexual legislation, 131
anxiety, as causal factor, 302-303;
    homosexual, 218-219, 223, 237, 263-
    264; pseudohomosexual, 220; *see also*
    fear
Apache Life-Way, An (Opler), 111
Aphrodite, 153
Arabs, homosexuality among, 147
arachnodactyly, 57
Aristophanes, 156
armed forces, homosexuality in, 21, 129,
    224
Arnim, Bettina von, 161
Artemis, 149
Astarte, 148, 154
As You Like It (Shakespeare), 201
Atargatis, 149
Attis, 154
attitudinal changes, 307
autosomes, 70